CO-AOF-692

THE
ECUMENICAL GIFT EXCHANGE

Margaret O'Gara

A Michael Glazier Book

THE LITURGICAL PRESS
Collegeville, Minnesota

BX
1785
.O33
1998

A Michael Glazier Book published by The Liturgical Press

Cover design by Greg Becker

© 1998 by The Order of St. Benedict, Inc., Collegeville, Minnesota. All rights reserved. No part of this book may be reproduced in any form or by any means, electronic or mechanical, including photocopying, recording, taping, or any retrieval system, without the written permission of The Liturgical Press, Collegeville, Minnesota 56321. Printed in the United States of America.

1   2   3   4   5   6   7   8

Library of Congress Cataloging-in-Publication Data

O'Gara, Margaret, 1947–
      The ecumenical gift exchange / Margaret O'Gara.
         p.   cm.
      "A Michael Glazier book."
      Includes bibliographical references and index.
      ISBN 0-8146-5893-8 (alk. paper)
         1. Ecumenical movement. 2. Catholic Church—Relations.
      3. Christian union—Catholic Church.   I. Title.
      BX1785.O33   1998
      280'.042—dc21
                                                                              97-34282
                                                                              CIP

My husband's family gave me my first experience of a large family gift exchange. With thanks for their many gifts of hospitality and loving companionship to me, I dedicate this book to them:

Kathleen McIntyre Vertin and the memory of Joseph M. Vertin, Jr.
Kathleen Vertin Sharkey and Emmett Sharkey
James Vertin
Thomas Vertin and Diane Nelson Vertin
Stephen Vertin and Margaret Smith Vertin
Mary Ann Vertin and Michael Conrad
John Vertin and Marilyn Rochat

and especially
Michael Vertin, whose greatest gift to me is himself.

CONTENTS

PREFACE

I came to know about the gift exchange when I married into a large family. At Christmas, each member of my husband's family would bring one gift to the family exchange and receive one in return. After the Advent season of repentance and hope, the gift exchange at Christmas gave us renewed appreciation for each other and deepened the ties of mutual love.

Ecumenism is a gift exchange as well. In ecumenical dialogue, each Christian communion brings one or many gifts to the dialogue table, and each receives riches from their dialogue partners as well. But in the ecumenical gift exchange, the gift-giving enriches all of the partners, since we do not lose our gifts by sharing them with others. In fact, the gift exchange of ecumenism means a reception of gifts for which we have been prepared by repentance and hope.

In its Dogmatic Constitution on the Church, *Lumen gentium,* the Second Vatican Council teaches that the catholicity of the Church results in a gift exchange. "In virtue of this catholicity each individual part of the Church contributes through its special gifts to the good of the other parts and of the whole Church," the Constitution says. "Thus through the common sharing of gifts and through the common effort to attain fullness in unity, the whole and each of the parts receive increase."[1] Pope John Paul II refers to this insight in his encyclical on commitment to ecumenism, *Ut unum sint.* "Dialogue is not simply an exchange of ideas," he writes. "In some way it is always an 'exchange of gifts.'"[2]

---

1. Vatican II, *Lumen gentium,* in *The Documents of Vatican II,* ed. Walter M. Abbott (New York: America Press, 1966) #13.
2. John Paul II, *Ut unum sint, Origins* 25 (1995–96) 49, 51–72.

Some people mistakenly think of ecumenical dialogue as a kind of melting pot which seeks the elimination of the distinctive gifts of the many churches. If applied to ecumenism, this could lead to a weakening of the distinctive traditions and emphases that each communion brings to the table of dialogue: it would be a loss of identity, not an enrichment. But in fact I have found that the gifts exchanged in ecumenical dialogue are more like a mosaic, where every piece is valuable and every piece is needed for the full picture of the one Church of Christ. The mosaic picture is damaged if any of the pieces is missing. Because of the divisions among Christians, explains Vatican II's Decree on Ecumenism, *Unitatis redintegratio,* "the Church herself finds it more difficult to express in actual life her full catholicity in all its aspects."[3]

At the same time, a church tradition's emphases that are exaggerated or distorted due to isolation are corrected and complemented in the emerging mosaic that results from ecumenical gift exchange. Vatican II teaches, "There can be no ecumenism worthy of the name without a change of heart,"[4] and John Paul II calls for "repentance" as the churches recognize their failings toward one another.[5] One of the gifts that Christian churches bring each other in dialogue is serious criticism, criticism that allows their weaknesses and sins to be acknowledged and overcome.[6] In this way I believe that the Holy Spirit is using the ecumenical dialogue today to bring about the renewal of the Church in our time so that it will be strengthened for its mission in the coming years.

This volume collects ten essays on topics related to ecumenical dialogue. Most of these essays were first presented to different audiences as talks about the unity of the Church, and so they have a certain topicality. I have revised some of them slightly by including a few later relevant developments, but I have left each essay substantially unchanged. This accounts for a certain repetition among a few of the essays, but it also allows each essay to be used independently for courses or discussion groups, since each essay has its own inner integrity. The footnotes are arranged to recognize the independence of each essay so that it can be used on its own. Most of the essays are more scholarly in style and a few less scholarly, but I have tried to choose readable pieces that would be accessible and interesting to a wide audience.

3. Vatican II, *Unitatis redintegratio,* in *The Documents of Vatican II,* ed. Walter M. Abbott (New York: America Press, 1966) #4.

4. Ibid., #7.

5. John Paul II, *Ut unum sint,* #15.

6. Vatican II, *Unitatis redintegratio,* #7.

The essays cover a variety of topics of importance today for ecumenism: infallibility, papal authority, feminism, dissent, the goal and nature of ecumenical dialogue, justification, Eucharist, interpretation of Vatican I and Vatican II, diversity, reception, and ecumenical formation. Because I think of ecumenism as a gift exchange, this theme weaves itself through all of the essays.

The main setting for the essays is my own involvement in ecumenical dialogue. For many years, I have been an appointed member of official bilateral commissions for dialogue: the Anglican-Roman Catholic Dialogue of Canada for eighteen years of very deep dialogue (1976–1993), along with my present rich involvements on the Disciples of Christ-Roman Catholic International Commission for Dialogue (since 1983) and the Lutheran-Roman Catholic International Commission for Unity (since 1995). Other experiences of dialogue were gained through the programs of the Institute for Ecumenical and Cultural Research in Collegeville, Minnesota; General Theological Seminary in New York City; the North American Academy of Ecumenists; and the U.S. Lutheran-Roman Catholic Coordinating Committee. It was from my colleagues in those many groups that I learned about the ecumenical gift exchange, and I give them my deep thanks.

I offer thanks as well to the faculty and students of Yale Divinity School, where my early theological studies first introduced me to the experience of the ecumenical gift exchange. Today this experience continues to be my living reality in the midst of my former professors, colleagues, and students at the Faculty of Theology in the University of St. Michael's College, and also of my colleagues and students from the other theological colleges in the Toronto School of Theology. I am grateful to all of them. I add a special thanks to Constance Price, a St. Michael's doctoral student in theology, whose reliability assisted me greatly in the final preparation of the manuscript for this book.

Before turning to the essays on the ecumenical gift exchange, I want to tell a story about families and ecumenism from the ecumenical setting of the Toronto School of Theology, a consortium of theological schools from the Roman Catholic, Anglican, and Protestant traditions. This is a story about something that happened in my class there a few years ago, and it illustrates something of ecumenism's meaning in a dramatic sort of way.

It was the end of the spring semester, and I had been teaching a course on christology. The class was divided into small discussion groups which met together with me to discuss the readings and lecture, and one group had gone especially well. Our discussion had been probing, and students had been able to discuss in real depth their understanding of who Christ is, their grasp of his saving work, his meaning to them in their own lives. They felt increasingly a sense of common bonds. It was the last class, and the students had turned to somewhat more personal discussion as we focused on pastoral questions for the proclamation of Christ. Two students, a man and a woman, found as we talked that their family roots several generations back both stemmed from Nova Scotia. One, a Roman Catholic man from Toronto, now was entering the Augustinian priory as a young friar. The other, an Anglican woman about the same age, was a candidate for ordination in the Anglican diocese of Nova Scotia. Two Christians, a Roman Catholic and an Anglican, facing a common future in ministry though in two different communions.

As they talked, the name of the woman's great-grandmother was mentioned. The man's great-grandmother had had the same name, rather an unusual name. Suddenly, the two began firing a series of questions at each other about names, marriages, families, children as the rest of us looked on in surprise, until at last one of them leaned across the seminar table and gave the other the kiss of peace.

Then the story came out. Long ago, it seems, two sisters had grown up in an Anglican family in Nova Scotia. But one had become a Roman Catholic and then married a Roman Catholic. And her Anglican family had been so upset with this decision that they had excluded her from the family and cut off all further contact with her. This was common in Nova Scotia at that time in both Anglican and Roman Catholic families—both sometimes followed the custom of this kind of exclusion if a family member left the communion or married someone from the other communion. So these two sisters, parted in life for conscience's sake, never saw each other again, and gradually their families lost all contact with each other except the knowledge that there was a missing branch of the family.

Well, those two sisters were the grandmothers of my two students. When we looked at them with new eyes, we could even see the family resemblance. Each student, raised in a fervent religious home, had been drawn by the love of Christ to seek ordination in the Church. And now, at last, the two branches of this divided family had found each other again through a course on Christ.

That summer there were two ordinations that had a special meaning. Each of my two students and their families attended the ordination of the other and shared in reading from the Scriptures. Each included a prayer that their ministries would be an instrument for the reconciliation, not only of their families, but for their whole church families, so that they could live again as sister churches. Each has made ecumenical work important in their ministry.

To reconcile the many families, the many traditions in the one Church of Christ: this is the work of ecumenism, and this is the work to which these two young students suddenly found themselves called. Their call came as they prepared for their vocation of evangelization: suddenly it changed and took on a whole new meaning in their lives, and in the lives of their families.

To nurture the changes, to exchange the gifts which the unity of the Church demands: this is their call now. It is the vocation of the whole Church of Christ at this time. I believe it is the work of the Holy Spirit among us.

ACKNOWLEDGMENTS

Seven of my articles from this book were published earlier in a slightly different form. I am grateful for permission to include the articles here.

"On the Road Toward Unity: The Present Dialogue Among the Churches." *Proceedings of the Catholic Theological Society of America* 48 (1993) 18–40.

"Listening to Forgotten Voices: The French Minority Bishops of Vatican I and Infallibility." *Theology Digest* 37 (1990) 1–13.

"Reception as Key: Unlocking ARCIC on Infallibility." *Toronto Journal of Theology* 3/1 (1987) 41–49.

"Understanding 'A Certain, Though Imperfect' Communion Between Anglicans and Roman Catholics." *Mid-Stream* 25/2 (April 1986) 190–91.

"Shifts Below the Surface of the Debate: Ecumenism, Dissent, and the Roman Catholic Church." *The Jurist* 56 (1996) 357–86.

"Ecumenism and Feminism in Dialogue on Authority." *Woman and Church*. Ed. Melanie May. Grand Rapids, Mich.: William B. Eerdmans Publishing Co. & New York: Friendship Press, 1991, 118–37.

"Formation for Transformation: The Ecumenical Directory Sets a Big Agenda." *Ecumenism* (#117, March 1995) 23–26. [*Ecumenism* is also published in French.]

1

On the Road toward Unity: The Present Dialogue among the Churches[1]

I first began thinking about ecumenical questions in earnest when I was twenty-two and found myself one of the few Roman Catholics among a very large number of Protestants in divinity school. I was the only Roman Catholic in the course on the Reformation. When it came time to study Martin Luther, the visiting Lutheran professor turned to me politely and asked if I would like to say a word in support of indulgences.

The Roman Catholic Church in his mind was still that of the sixteenth century, not the Roman Catholic Church that I knew, that had nurtured my love of liturgy and social justice, that had just four years earlier, in 1965, concluded its great council of reform and renewal. I determined to work to bridge the gap between his understanding and my own.

I have been asked in this talk to give a theological analysis of ecumenical dialogue today, gained in the years since I first made that determination in my Reformation class. I propose to discuss this dauntingly large topic in three steps: (1) a change of heart; (2) a change of mind; (3) cultivating new habits of the heart and the mind. I will not pretend to survey all of the literature relevant to ecumenical dialogue—that would be too large a task to accomplish in the time allotted me for this topic. Instead, as requested, I will give a theological analysis of dialogue today, sometimes using different official dialogues more familiar to many of you as examples to illustrate my analysis.

---

1. This paper was first presented as a plenary lecture to the Catholic Theological Society of America annual convention in June 1993; it was published in a slightly different form in *Proceedings of the Catholic Theological Society of America* 48 (1993) 18–40.

1. A Change of Heart

The question asked by my professor of Reformation studies began a deep restlessness in me, a restlessness that set me off on the journey toward the full union of the Church of Christ through a serious commitment to ecumenical dialogue. I know now that Christians who begin this journey are changed permanently; they face a long road ahead of them; but they know there is no going back any more.

Restlessness that changes us: the Second Vatican Council also shared this restlessness that leads to change. It called this change "a change of heart." "There can be no ecumenism worthy of the name without a change of heart," the Council taught.[2] I share with that Council the conviction that the discord and disunity among Christians "openly contradicts the will of Christ, provides a stumbling block to the world, and inflicts damage" on the proclamation of the Gospel.[3] After seventeen years as a member of the ecumenical consortium that constitutes the Toronto School of Theology and of bilateral and multilateral dialogues and consultations, it is easy for me to affirm the teaching of the 1964 Decree on Ecumenism, *Unitatis redintegratio*, that the divisions among Christians make it "more difficult" for the Church "to express" its catholicity,[4] and that "a change of heart" is required for these divisions to be overcome.

I was struck with the change in mood toward other Christian communions a few years ago when I was in England for an ecumenical dialogue meeting, and I made a visit to the tombs of two half-sisters, famous ones, buried in Westminster Abbey. They were, of course, the tombs of the two half-sister queens, children of Henry VIII, Mary and Elizabeth, whose lives were so enmeshed with the divisions in the Church in England. The inscription at the graves of Mary and Elizabeth encourages sober reflection: "Remember before God all those who divided at the Reformation by different convictions laid down their lives for Christ and conscience's sake."

We do remember them. And we do remember that their acts, on both sides, were done for Christ and conscience's sake. And Christians still have bonds of love and loyalty, on many sides, to those before us and the convictions that moved them, on many sides, so many centuries ago.

But today in the Roman Catholic Church, there is also a desire to be able to live as those sisters could not live, to live in full eucharistic com-

---

2. Vatican II, *Unitatis redintegratio,* in *The Documents of Vatican II,* ed. Walter M. Abbott (New York: America Press, 1966) #7.

3. Ibid., #1.

4. Ibid., #4.

munion with all our brothers and sisters in Christ, and to share fully together with them in the mission of the Church for a world that deeply
needs the united proclamation of the Good News of Christ. And with this
movement toward fuller unity, the Roman Catholic Church has joined
other churches in a spirit of repentance and of a new hope that we can
share our gifts with others and in turn be enriched by receiving gifts that
they offer to us. And, as John Paul II says frequently, this commitment to
ecumenism is irreversible.

These two spirits are linked together: repentance and the hope for reception of gifts. Since Vatican II we have focused on the reality of reception as a way to understand what ecumenism means. But before throwing
ourselves into each other's arms in a shared Eucharist, Jean-Marie Tillard
cautions, we must first be converted by each other.[5] Reception involves a
process of exchanging gifts among the churches, and to this gift exchange,
the Roman Catholic Church brings many rich offerings. But it needs as
well the readiness to receive from other churches what it lacks in its
poverty, for a full and fruitful proclamation of the Gospel. Part of the
change of heart means a willingness to be self-critical: to criticize first not
the mote in the other's eye, but the beam in our own.

Again and again in moments of ecumenical dialogue, I have shared
with my dialogue partners the experience of this kind of self-critical repentance that opens the way for the reception of new gifts. Frequently the
strengths that one partner has to offer, the other partner lacks and needs.
Where my Anglican partners have a rich understanding and practice of
the conciliarity of the Church, they need and are seeking the leadership in
teaching that can be provided in the Roman Catholic communion by the
bishop of Rome. Where my own Roman Catholic communion has emphasized the communal character of faith and decision-making, we need
to receive from my partners in the Disciples of Christ their effective emphasis on the personal appropriation of faith within the community of
baptized believers. Experiencing the link between repentance and reception is widespread in the ecumenical movement, reported also again and
again in other dialogues of which I am not a member. Where one communion is clear about the priority of grace, another is clear about the implications of the Gospel for the social order. Where one communion is
open to the opportunities provided by modern culture for proclaiming
the Gospel, another is clear about the centrality of our trinitarian foundations for any effective proclamation in any culture. After many years of

---

5. Jean-Marie Tillard, "One Church of God: The Church Broken in Pieces,"
One in Christ 17 (1981) 9.

dialogue with other communions, one member of my dialogue team put it this way: "The very process of the dialogue is an opening up, one to the other, of an agreement to help each other to be ready for the grace and unifying power of Jesus Christ. . . . We have to show ourselves, our churches to each other as we are—our gifts, for growth in understanding and mutual upbuilding in grace and love; our limitations and failures, for pardon and healing. It is a process in which the participants are called to a new faithfulness to the truth of Jesus Christ."[6]

"Called to a new faithfulness": understood in this way, we can easily see how the ecumenical movement is a reform movement in the Church which the Council recognized as a work of the Holy Spirit in our time.[7]

2. A Change of Mind

With the change of heart toward other Christians comes a change of mind. This change of mind clarifies the theoretical grounding for ecumenical dialogue. The Decree on Ecumenism, *Unitatis redintegratio,* called for a dialogue between churches conducted "on an equal footing."[8] How could it make such a request? Beneath this simple phrase stands the major ecclesiological shift in the Dogmatic Constitution on the Church, *Lumen gentium,* when, in the word *"subsistit,"*[9] the bishops of the Council recognized that the one Church of Christ extends "beyond the visible limits" of the Roman Catholic Church.[10] In *Unitatis redintegratio,* we see the implications of this shift in the recognition of the real though imperfect communion[11] that Roman Catholics already share with other baptized Christians.

---

6. Basil Meeking, "Review of the Dynamics and Issues in the Previous Five-Year Dialogue," *Mid-Stream* 23 (1984) 339.

7. Vatican II, *Unitatis redintegratio,* #4.

8. Vatican II, *Unitatis redintegratio,* #9; cf. George Tavard, "For a Theology of Dialogue," *One in Christ* 15 (1979) 14–15.

9. Vatican II, *Lumen gentium,* in *The Documents of Vatican II,* ed. Walter M. Abbott (New York: America Press, 1966) #8.

10. Johannes Willebrands, "Vatican II's Ecclesiology of Communion," *Origins* 17 (1987–88) 32.

11. The line from article 3 in *Unitatis redintegratio* is the following: *"Hi enim qui in Christum credunt et baptismum rite receperunt, in quadam cum Ecclesia catholica communione, etsi non perfecta, constituuntur"* (Vatican II, *Decretum de Oecumenismo* [Vatican City: Typis Polyglottis Vaticanis, 1964] #3). Harry McSorley has drawn my attention to the responses of the Secretariat for Promoting Christian Unity to proposed modifications of the text of article 3 from *Unitatis redintegratio* during the Second Vatican Council. In these responses, the

What does this mean for the understanding of ecumenical dialogue? Long ago, Edward Pusey answered this question quite simply: "I love the evangelicals because they love Our Lord," he wrote. Karl Rahner said it more precisely when he noted that ecumenical dialogue presupposes that Christians already share the reality of the common apostolic faith. But just as a reality may be only partially or even mistakenly expressed and takes time to be made explicit with accuracy, so also with the reality of Christian faith. Ecumenical dialogue, he explains, "is the attempt to render comprehensible to one's partner in the dialogue that that which is put to him in terms of concepts is merely a more correct, a fuller, and a more precisely defined expression of something which that partner has already grasped as his own faith through the power of the Spirit at the ultimate depths of his own human existence as justified, and which he has laid hold of as his own truth."[12] Hence ecumenical dialogue is founded on the presupposition that dialogue partners are already in real though imperfect communion. Our task is to seek full communion for the sake of the mission of the Church to proclaim the Gospel. Thus the Fifth World Conference on Faith and Order meeting in the summer of 1993 at Santiago de Compostela, Spain had as its theme a statement of what in fact was also its goal: "Towards *Koinonia* in Faith, Life, and Witness."

In exploring a change of mind, I notice that many Christians, both lay and ordained, have a rather hazy idea about what questions and issues did divide the churches in the past. Rahner notes the theological significance of this odd disjunction between the theological discussion and the perception of most people in the Church about Christian divisions. "What are the implications," he asks, "for a theological . . . sense of creed and Church with regard to their differences, if it is quite impossible to say that the majority of Christians formed in a particular church tradition know of the doctrinal differences dividing the churches or have made them their own?"[13]

Secretariat made it clear that the communion they intend to affirm is not only juridical but a real communion containing various elements of the spiritual and sacramental order; the Secretariat stresses that this is a *"vera communio, etsi non perfecta"* (*Schema Decreti de Oecumenismo MODI. . . Examinati: [Fascicle] I, Prooemium et Caput I* [Vatican City: Typis Polyglotttis Vaticanis, 1964] 20, 23, Responses to proposed amendments #5 and #8).

12. Karl Rahner, "Some Problems in Contemporary Ecumenism," *Theological Investigations,* trans. David Bourke (New York: Seabury, 1976) 14:251.

13. Ibid., 265–66.

I suspect many Christians have a reaction somewhat like that of the Canadian Anglican parishioner who was asked to give her response to a statement of agreement between Anglicans and Roman Catholics. She wrote, "I don't really know much about those old debates. But I am suspicious of ecumenism. Whatever those people were debating about in the sixteenth century, I'm sure they must have had a good point."

Love and loyalty to those in our churches who have gone before us—the certitude that they must have had a good point, whatever it was—is a persistent and not inappropriate reaction from many Christians when asked about ecumenism. Even if they have the nagging feeling that emerged in the 1983 *Faith and Ferment* study by the Institute for Ecumenical and Cultural Research in Collegeville, Minnesota—the feeling that there is something wrong about the division between the churches—they still don't want to lose the good points of their forebears, whatever they were.[14]

Theologians are in a different position, because we know what those old debates were about. But these reactions highlight our responsibility, as part of the change of mind, to explore those past debates and their present implications.

Sometimes when we return to an argument after the dust has settled, we are able to see it with new eyes, to notice the good points of others overlooked at the time of the argument, or to notice a few weaknesses that even we ourselves might have slipped into. Some people think that this kind of ecumenical discussion is a sort of spiritual horse-trading, a kind of holy bargain table where one church gives up part of its identity in return for the same from another. You know, a popular picture: we'll cut down the incense if they cut down the length of their sermons. Or, the theological version: we'll mention the necessity of the papacy less often if they'll let up on the semipelagianism of late medieval Catholicism. No: ecumenism, I have found, is not that kind of horse-trading, not a bargain table exchange. The search for deeper understanding tries to dig beneath debates and positions that once seemed irreconcilable and achieve a new level of understanding, where the insights of both positions are included and corrected in a larger vision.

Or again, some people think that ecumenical discussion is a kind of melting pot that seeks the elimination of the distinctive gifts of the many churches. Many Roman Catholics would rightly fear ecumenism if it meant reduction of Christian beliefs to the lowest common denominator,

---

14. Joan D. Chittister and Martin E. Marty, *Faith and Ferment: An Interdisciplinary Study of Christian Beliefs and Practices,* ed. Robert S. Bilheimer (Minneapolis: Augsburg Publishing House and Collegeville: The Liturgical Press, 1983).

losing those distinctive characteristics of Catholicism that manifest the intellectual richness and sense of mystery in our tradition. But I think ecumenical work is more aptly illustrated with the image of the mosaic, where the picture can be beautiful and whole only if the distinctive contribution of each piece is included. And notice that the mosaic is really a damaged picture if any piece is missing, and that the distorted emphasis presented by just one part of the picture is corrected when that part is set within its proper place in the whole. Instead of a melting pot, the emerging mosaic of a communion of communions presents us with a first glimpse of what the one Church of Christ will look like when its divisions are overcome.

The theoretical work undergirding ecumenism, then, is not horse-trading; it is not a melting pot. But then what does make up the change of mind that characterizes ecumenical convergence? I note three characteristics of ecumenism.

First, if we examine some agreed statements as examples of ecumenical dialogue, we see that they seek to recover the biblical and patristic understanding of issues that have caused division among Christians. Pope Paul VI and Archbishop Michael Ramsey, former archbishop of Canterbury, explicitly urged the newly formed Anglican-Roman Catholic International Commission to take this approach in 1966, when they inaugurated "a serious dialogue" between the two communions which is "founded on the Gospels and on the ancient common traditions."[15] Explaining their procedure in the "Preface" to *The Final Report,* the members of the Anglican-Roman Catholic International Commission (ARCIC) say that they "emphasized . . . avoidance of the emotive language of past polemics."[16] They hoped "to discover each other's faith as it is today and to appeal to history only for enlightenment, not as a way of perpetuating past controversy."[17] Pursuing together "that restatement of doctrine which new times and conditions are . . . regularly calling for," the Commission was able to claim substantial agreement on Eucharist, ministry and ordination, as well as a consensus or convergence on questions of authority.[18]

15. Paul VI and Michael Ramsey, "The Common Declaration by Pope Paul VI and the Archbishop of Canterbury [24 March 1966]," in Anglican-Roman Catholic International Commission [ARCIC], *The Final Report* (London: SPCK and Catholic Truth Society, 1982) 118.

16. Anglican-Roman Catholic International Commission [ARCIC], "Preface," *The Final Report* (London: SPCK and Catholic Truth Society, 1982) 2.

17. Ibid., #1–2.

18. Ibid., #2.

Ecumenical discussion on sacrificial interpretations of the Eucharist serves as a good example of the recovery of biblical and patristic understandings. In the sixteenth century, many continental and English Reformers were offended at the notion of the sacrifice of Christ repeated daily on church altars. Or, as one of my Protestant students wrote in an exam a few years ago, "Noncatholics felt that the sacrifice of Christ had been given once and that it was improper to have this occurring on a weekly basis."

Protestants popularly understood remembering as mental recall, and this allowed them to safeguard the once-for-all character of Christ's sacrifice; but it led them toward a static understanding of the Eucharist as only remembering a past event, and made it difficult for them to speak about the presence of Christ.

Roman Catholics, on the other hand, were scandalized at the suggestion that the Church is unable to enter into Christ's self-offering. But with their emphasis on the daily celebration of Christ's sacrifice in an unbloody way, they risked the suggestion that the priest controlled Christ and somehow contributed to that gift of salvation which Paul had taught was God's alone to give. Furthermore, by their often exclusive emphasis on the elements of bread and wine in discussion of the presence of Christ, Roman Catholics left themselves open to a materialist misunderstanding of the presence of Christ in the Eucharistic celebration.

But ecumenical discussion has allowed us to penetrate more deeply than these two meanings and to recapture a richer biblical meaning of memorial. The biblical sense of remembering is a dynamic one, in which an event of the past is recalled so that its benefits may be made effective in the present. As at Passover the Jewish community celebrates both God's mighty deliverance in the past and God's continuing deliverance in the present, so in a similar way at the Eucharist we celebrate this dynamic sense of God's work. Ecumenical statements on the Eucharist have recovered this biblical sense of remembering and have therefore broken past older disagreements based on more partial emphases. The *Baptism, Eucharist and Ministry* statement of the World Council of Churches, for example, explains, "The eucharist is the memorial of the crucified and risen Christ, i.e., the living and effective sign of his sacrifice, accomplished once and for all on the cross and still operative on behalf of all humankind."[19] Accomplished once for all *and* still operative: with these two emphases, the statement holds together both the Protestant and the Roman

---

19. World Council of Churches, "Eucharist," *Baptism, Eucharist and Ministry* (Geneva: World Council of Churches, 1982) #5.

Catholic concerns but has gone beyond them because it has recovered an original biblical sense of remembering. *The Final Report* of the Anglican-Roman Catholic International Commission does the same kind of biblical recovering when it emphasizes both that there is "no repetition or addition" to the once-for-all sacrifice of Christ,[20] but adds, "The eucharistic memorial is no mere calling to mind of a past event or of its significance, but the Church's effectual proclamation of God's mighty acts." In the Eucharistic prayer, it continues, "the Church continues to make a perpetual memorial of Christ's death, and his members, united with God and one another, give thanks for all his mercies, entreat the benefits of his passion on behalf of the whole Church, participate in these benefits and enter into the movement of his self-offering."[21] By recovering the dynamism of the biblical meaning of *anamnesis,* then, the statement has shown that all sides of the sixteenth-century debates were somewhat myopic in their vision of the Eucharist and has deepened all our understandings. Since these agreements were written, other developments in biblical studies show further promise as resources for ecumenical convergence on the Eucharist: reflections on how *anamnesis* may also make today's celebrants present to a past event, the centrality of the prayer of praise *(todah)* and its link to the peace-offering sacrifice, and the biblical importance of "prophetic remembrance" for the fresh recasting of the eucharistic narrative of praise.[22]

I have given just one example to illustrate the recovery of the biblical and patristic heritage in ecumenical work, but I could give others. The recovery of the biblical and patristic ecclesiology of communion stands behind the achievement of the entire work of the Anglican-Roman Catholic International Commission, as they make clear in their "Introduction" to *The Final Report*[23] and expand in *The Church as Communion.*[24] This ecclesiology of communion also undergirds the work of the Joint Commission

20. Anglican-Roman Catholic International Commission [ARCIC], "Eucharistic Doctrine," *The Final Report* (London: SPCK and Catholic Truth Society, 1982) #5.
21. Ibid., #5.
22. See David Power, *The Eucharistic Mystery: Revitalizing the Tradition* (New York: Crossroad, 1992) 42–65; cf. Gerard Austin, "Is an Ecumenical Understanding of Eucharist Possible Today?" *The Jurist* 48 (1988) 668–91.
23. Anglican-Roman Catholic International Commission [ARCIC], "Introduction," *The Final Report* (London: SPCK and Catholic Truth Society, 1982) #1–9.
24. Second Anglican-Roman Catholic International Commission, *The Church as Communion* (London: Church House Publishing & Catholic Truth Society, 1991).

for Theological Dialogue between the Roman Catholic Church and the Orthodox Church. For example, their statement on *The Mystery of the Church and of the Eucharist in the Light of the Mystery of the Holy Trinity* explains, ". . . because the one and only God is the communion of three persons, the one and only Church is a communion of many communities and the local church a communion of persons. The one and unique Church finds her identity in the *koinonia* of the churches. Unity and multiplicity appear so linked that one could not exist without the other."[25] Even two traditions as different as the Disciples of Christ and the Roman Catholic Church have found in the recovery of biblical and patristic ideas on Church a common way forward, as is clear in their statement, *The Church as Communion in Christ.*[26] It is not surprising that this work of recovering a common understanding of the Church as communion stands at the heart of both the statement by the 1991 Assembly of the World Council of Churches in Canberra[27] and the discussion paper for the 1993 Fifth World Conference on Faith and Order in Santiago de Compostela, Spain.[28]

A second aspect of the change of mind that characterizes ecumenical work is the recognition of the complementarity of traditions. In the past, our traditions were often understood as intractably contradictory, especially when they had developed separately from each other or in criticism of each other. But the fruit of ecumenical work is the repeated discovery that each tradition actually is enriched by another with a different emphasis.

The classical discovery of this complementarity is in the work on justification. The U.S. Lutheran-Roman Catholic Dialogue, for example, notes the different concerns of Lutherans and Roman Catholics which stand be-

---

25. Joint Commission for Theological Dialogue between the Roman Catholic Church and the Orthodox Church, "The Mystery of the Church and of the Eucharist in the Light of the Mystery of the Holy Trinity" [1982], *One in Christ* 19 (1983) 195.

26. Disciples of Christ-Roman Catholic International Commission for Dialogue, "The Church as Communion in Christ," *Mid-Stream* 33 (April 1994) 219–39.

27. Seventh Assembly of the World Council of Churches, "The Unity of the Church as Koinonia: Gift and Calling" [Canberra, 1991], in *Signs of the Spirit (Official Report. Seventh Assembly)*, ed. Michael Kinnamon (Geneva: World Council of Churches and Grand Rapids: William E. Eerdmans, 1991) 172–74.

28. "Towards *Koinonia* in Faith, Life, and Witness" [Discussion Paper], *Ecumenical Trends* 22 (1993) 81–104.

hind their different emphases on the character of justification, sinfulness and the justified, and the sufficiency of faith. Where Roman Catholic concerns focus on the process by which human beings are brought to new life and are "most easily expressed in . . . transformationist language," Lutheran concerns emphasize the situation of sinners standing before God hearing "at one and the same time" God's words of judgment and forgiveness, and so Lutherans have focused on "this discontinuous, paradoxical, and simultaneous double relation of God to the justified. . . ."[29] The recognition of complementarity in concerns allows the Lutheran-Roman Catholic Dialogue to reread the scriptural witness with fresh eyes, so that they conclude, "While righteousness/justification is the primary way the apostle [Paul] describes what God has done for us in Christ, it is complemented by other images which express aspects of God's activity in a nonforensic terminology that refers to personal and corporate transformation."[30] Their discovery of the complementarity and legitimacy of their different concerns on this topic at the heart of sixteenth-century divisions allows them today to agree together in affirming that "our entire hope of justification and salvation rests on Christ Jesus and on the gospel. . . ."[31] In a similar discussion on *Salvation and the Church,* Anglicans and Roman Catholics also describe salvation as both imputation and transformation, so that dialogue members can say together, "God's grace effects what he declares: his creative word imparts what it imputes. By pronouncing us righteous, God also makes us righteous. He imparts a righteousness which is his and becomes ours."[32]

I am especially struck with the complementarity that emerges in the discussions on authority. Frank discussion among dialogue partners often reveals a sense of appreciation for two great emphases among the churches. Some have a great sense of magisterium, of authority in teaching; others have a great appreciation for shared decision-making and the participation of the laity. Again and again, I have been in conversations where partners realized that the strength of one church was exactly the need of the other, and vice versa.

---

29. [U.S.] Lutheran-Roman Catholic Dialogue, "Justification by Faith: Common Statement," *Justification by Faith,* eds. H. George Anderson, T. Austin Murphy, Joseph A. Burgess (Minneapolis: Augsburg Publishing House, 1985) #96.

30. Ibid., #132.

31. Ibid., #4.

32. Second Anglican-Roman Catholic International Commission, *Salvation and the Church* (London: Church House Publishing and Catholic Truth Society, 1987) #15.

We see these recognitions reflected in agreed statements repeatedly. *The Final Report* of the Anglican-Roman Catholic International Commission discusses oversight in teaching using this complementary approach. On the one hand, it sees a role for oversight through conciliarity, the bishops speaking together, collaborating together and representing the local churches. On the other hand, it sees the importance of primacy, for leadership by one bishop who speaks in the name of all the bishops and "may . . . express their mind."[33] It seeks to restore the Anglican communion to full communion with the bishop of Rome, asserting that "a universal primacy will be needed in a reunited Church"[34] and is part of "God's design."[35] At the same time, it notes, though primacy and conciliarity are complementary, "it has often happened that one has been emphasized at the expense of the other, even to the point of serious imbalance."[36] It seeks the balance of the two, "with the responsible participation of the whole people of God."[37]

I think it was the recognition of alternative but legitimate complementary traditions that allowed *Baptism, Eucharist and Ministry* to make important breakthroughs in thought in areas which continue to be a source of division between churches. For example, the statement sees the forms of believer's baptism and infant baptism as alternative practices. "The differences between infant and believers' baptism become less sharp when it is recognized that both forms of baptism embody God's own initiative in Christ and express a response of faith made within the believing community."[38] If infant baptism emphasizes more God's own initiative and the community's faith, believer's baptism emphasizes more the explicit confession of the transformed person responding to God's grace. This statement invites the churches to regard these two practices as "equivalent alternatives" in their relationships with other churches.[39] In addition, it is

---

33. Anglican-Roman Catholic International Commission [ARCIC], "Authority in the Church I," *The Final Report* (London: SPCK and Catholic Truth Society, 1982) #20.

34. Anglican-Roman Catholic International Commission [ARCIC], "Authority in the Church II," *The Final Report* (London: SPCK and Catholic Truth Society, 1982) #9.

35. Ibid., #15; cf. ARCIC, "Authority in the Church I," *The Final Report*, #24b.

36. ARCIC, "Authority in the Church I," *The Final Report*, #22.

37. Ibid., #22.

38. World Council of Churches, "Baptism," *Baptism, Eucharist and Ministry* (Geneva: World Council of Churches, 1982) Commentary on #12.

39. Ibid.

able to see the weaknesses of each as well, and so help both kinds of churches see where they need reform through enrichment from the insights of the other.

I think that *Baptism, Eucharist, and Ministry* also uses this recognition of the complementarity of traditions in a way that has sometimes been overlooked when it discusses bishops. This multilateral statement stresses the importance of *episcope* and challenges nonepiscopal churches to consider whether the threefold pattern of ordained ministry as developed "does not have a powerful claim to be accepted by them."[40] It praises "the orderly transmission of the ordained ministry" as "a powerful expression of the continuity of the Church throughout history."[41] At the same time, the statement has some exhortations for churches that already have bishops. It notes that episcopal succession can be appreciated "as a sign, though not a guarantee, of the continuity and unity of the Church."[42] The succession of bishops, it argues, is just "one of the ways . . . in which the apostolic tradition of the Church was expressed"; other ways are, for example, "the transmission of the gospel and the life of the community."[43] And "churches which practice the succession through the episcopate," it notes, are recognizing "that a continuity in apostolic faith, worship and mission has been preserved in churches which have not retained the form of historic episcopate," though some may have preserved "the reality and function of the episcopal ministry" without the title "bishop."[44] But finally, in a challenge often overlooked by those of us congratulating ourselves on our episcopal succession or threefold division of ministry, the statement suggests flatly that the actual exercise of these structures is in need of "reform."[45]

The third aspect to the change of mind involved in ecumenical dialogue is the recognition of a new context for such dialogue. Ecumenism means more than a deepened understanding and resolution of issues from the past. It means also a sense of mission in facing the new issues and the new world in which Christianity finds itself today. Let me say something about this new context.

40. World Council of Churches, "Ministry," *Baptism, Eucharist and Ministry* (Geneva: World Council of Churches, 1982) #25.
41. Ibid., #35.
42. Ibid., #38.
43. Ibid., #36.
44. Ibid., #37.
45. Ibid., #24, #35.

Well, first, briefly but obviously, placing old debates in the broader context of the whole Church of Christ allows us a new perspective on those old
debates. For example, it is easier for Protestants and Roman Catholics to
overcome their debates about the presence of Christ in the Eucharist when
those debates are set in the broader context of the recovery of an adequate
pneumatology from the Orthodox churches, so that all can agree together,
in *Baptism, Eucharist and Ministry,* "The Spirit makes the crucified and
risen Christ really present to us in the eucharistic meal. . . ."[46] It is easier
to defuse some historic debates about the ordained ministry when these
debates are set in the broader context of the "calling of the whole people of
God" with its "diverse and complementary gifts."[47]

But there are other ways that the context has changed, and these ways
also play a role in the ecumenical change of mind. A second aspect of the
new context is a new collaboration in educational, liturgical, and justice
ministries. In many places, seminarians from many churches and others
preparing for pastoral ministry are being educated in the same classrooms. A few years ago at the Faculty of Theology at the University of St.
Michael's College, for example, I taught a course on creation, sin, grace,
and glory, a topic rife with issues that have caused Christian divisions; in
the course were students from all seven of the church colleges of the
Toronto School of Theology, representing a total of ten church traditions
among the students. Roman Catholics and Lutherans, Presbyterians and
Mennonites, United Church of Canada students and Anglicans, together
they studied the theology of creation, of original sin, of justification; their
shared experience and friendships made it easier for them to appreciate
and value the variety of emphases represented in the class. Multiply this
one course by all of the shared courses in systematic and moral theology,
in the study of Scripture and history, in pastoral care, religious education,
and traditions of worship, and it is easy to understand why some students
have a fresh perception of each other as they enter their future ministries.

While collaboration in theological education affects the studies of future ministers, collaboration in liturgical renewal has affected the entire
congregations of many Western churches. When my students visit each
other's churches, they often find the deep influence that their own liturgical tradition has had on the other, and vice versa. They may even find their
host congregation drawing from a common lectionary for the readings,

---

46. World Council of Churches, "Eucharist," *Baptism, Eucharist and Ministry*
(Geneva: World Council of Churches, 1982) #14.
47. World Council of Churches, "Ministry," *Baptism, Eucharist and Ministry,*
#5.

with the presider—who may be an ordained woman—joining a local discussion group weekly for prayer and collaborative homily preparation. They may also recognize some of the parishioners who are among the many interchurch families attending both my students' own parish and this one as well. Though my students may not feel at home in this congregation, they may at least find its prayer-forms familiar—though in Toronto they may be hearing these prayers in any one of over fifty languages. In the church bulletin of their host parish, they may read the same announcement they found in their own, inviting them to join one of the many interchurch coalitions working for justice. These Canadian task forces on refugee assistance, human rights in Latin America, hunger in Africa, peace in the Middle East, illegal alien sanctuary, food banks, the ecumenical decade in solidarity with women, racism and multiculturalism, and many other important questions of justice are cosponsored by a broad spectrum of Canadian churches. Their work is often assisted by the Canadian Council of Churches, in which the Roman Catholic Church is a full member. In short, this atmosphere of collaboration in theological education, liturgical renewal, and justice work contributes to a context that places ecumenical divisions in quite a new light.

My example is dramatized when we consider the third and fourth changes in context with deep importance for ecumenism. As to the third change, the twentieth century marks the emergence of what Karl Rahner calls the "World Church," a Church now genuinely multicultural and no longer simply the product of Semitic and Graeco-Roman conceptual traditions and European missionary outreach.[48] After two millennia of Christianity, one together and one divided, we move into the third millennium as genuinely World Church for perhaps really the first time.

In this new World Church, some of the older issues which caused Christians to divide look different. I do not mean that they look insignificant, but that they do not always seem a convincing basis for continuing the division among the churches when weighed in the balance against the urgency of unified Christian witness. The emergence of the World Church dramatizes the link between the unity of the Church and its catholicity, and so challenges us anew not to confuse differences among theological schools with doctrinal differences. As one of my students from the Philippines pointed out in the course on ecumenism a few years ago, debates about transubstantiation or consubstantiation and the disciplines

48. Karl Rahner, "Basic Theological Interpretation of the Second Vatican Council," *Theological Investigations*, trans. Edward Quinn (New York: Crossroad, 1981) 20:78.

governing eucharistic hospitality for noncatholics call more urgently for resolution in a place where Christians from many churches risked their lives together in the struggle for justice but could not share together the bread of life. *Baptism, Eucharist and Ministry* puts it concisely: "Insofar as Christians cannot unite in full fellowship around the same table to eat the same loaf and drink from the same cup, their missionary witness is weakened at both the individual and the corporate levels."[49]

In this new World Church, new issues emerge that overshadow those issues which initially caused divisions among Christians. For my Maryknoll missionary friend whose Christian commitment has taken him to announce the Gospel in Tanzania for the last thirty years, the questions are more basic. Which Christian theological understandings of evil and of the triune God are actually in conflict with native African religion, and which in fact are limited, inadequate conceptualizations which could be enriched by interaction with another thought pattern?[50] This question about the inculturation of the Gospel in Africa is not easy for Christians to answer. My students from China struggle with the distinction between Christianity and its Western forms, especially those imported to China from sixteenth-century European divisions. And one visiting Chinese colleague, newly converted to Christianity in the despair that followed Tianamen Square, probed the question: Is Christian faith compatible with ancient Chinese religious practices toward nature, or opposed to them? My missionary friend and African students ask: What about the African practice of levirate marriage, where a man takes as a second wife the widow of his brother at his brother's death? The Roman Catholic Church and other churches have taught against this; but in African society, with its sense of marriage into a family system that endures through death, Africans hear the Christian prohibition as recommendation of divorce.[51] How should Christians view this question?

On the other hand, many sexual and family practices urged by some North American Christians in the name of the Gospel look evil and inhuman to African Christians, my friend reports—practices such as abortion, or the isolation of the elderly in nursing homes. So for my friend and my students working in Africa, my students and colleague returning to China, ecumenism's change of mind means facing the demands of evan-

49. World Council of Churches, "Eucharist," *Baptism, Eucharist and Ministry,* #26.

50. Michael C. Kirwen, *The Missionary and the Diviner: Competing Theologies of Christian and African Religions* (Maryknoll, N.Y.: Orbis, 1988).

51. See Michael C. Kirwen, *African Widows* (Maryknoll, N.Y.: Orbis, 1979).

gelization today, in the World Church that is no longer identified with one culture but takes form in all cultures.

Ecumenists once saw doctrines, not morals, as the battle ground between the churches. Today they wonder if selective moral outrage contributes as well to the divisions between the churches—where some churches are outraged at abortion, for example, others are outraged at the refusal to ordain women: Each sees the other as unjust. But to doctrines and morals they add the third ingredient, culture, and they wonder: are we really divided by our faith and our morals, or is it rather our cultures that keep the churches apart? The Canadian Conference of Catholic Bishops took note of different legal traditions affecting Anglican-Roman Catholic dialogue: one that of English common law, another the Roman jurisprudence tradition behind Western Rite Catholic Canon Law;[52] these differences in cultural, legal style can make Anglicans and Roman Catholics suspicious of each other's structures of authority and treatment of dissenters, even when teaching precisely the same content on a doctrinal or moral question. Is the sometimes violent controversy today between the Russian Orthodox and Ukrainian Catholics in Ukraine based on their differing doctrinal assessments of the papacy? Or are these conflicts more linked to conflicting evaluations of each others' recent adaptation to a Marxist culture as Christians there emerge from a period of persecution and martyrdom? I wonder if a similar question should be asked about the turf-guarding and sheep-stealing between Roman Catholics and Pentecostals in Latin America today.

And women within Third World countries present us with a further question: when have earlier readings of the Bible by all of the churches been too colonial, when have they been too androcentric, and what would a correction of earlier misreadings mean today for all of the churches in their treatment of women? These questions bring us a long way from the debates my Reformation professor so politely posed for me twenty-nine years ago, but they too are part of the new context of ecumenism.

In the fourth and final change in this new context, the Church also faces the challenge of reevangelizing the West. In Toronto these days, Christians of different communions often feel more in common with each other than they once did when Orangemen parades drew big crowds onto city streets. Today they are driven to make common cause by the secular ideologies and secular presuppositions in politics, education, business, and

52. Canadian Conference of Catholic Bishops, "Response of the Canadian Conference of Catholic Bishops to the ARCIC-I *Final Report*," *Ecumenism* (Dec. 1987) 8.

the media used to attack or belittle a Christian faith vision. In facing such a world, Christians must reevaluate those divisions that leave us weakened before the task of evangelization. I think the churches are beginning to realize that they must make common cause together for the sake of the Gospel, and this can motivate them to complete work on the remaining problems that divide us.

I have been discussing the new context for ecumenism, in which I have included four points: new perspectives on old debates possible in the broadened setting of the whole Church of Christ; new collaborations in educational, liturgical, and justice ministries; new questions of faith and culture; and new challenges in reevangelization. Ecumenism means more than understanding the past; it also means facing new problems, for the present and future of evangelization, and shaping a Church that is equipped to carry out its mission.

3. Cultivating New Habits of Heart and Mind

Ultimately, the ecumenical mandate calls for more than simply a change of heart and a change of mind. The goal of ecumenical dialogue is the restoration of full, visible communion of the one Church of Christ for the sake of its mission. This will call for new decisions, changes in practice, reconciliation of communities and their ministries, the reform of structures of authority and accountability. Some of this has occurred already; some still lies ahead on the road. How will the Roman Catholic Church be prepared for the remainder of its journey toward this goal?

The Benedictine traditions of prayer and work I have shared during sabbatical years at the Institute for Ecumenical and Cultural Research in Collegeville, Minnesota, give us a clue to spiritual preparation for the future. They teach us that we must cultivate new habits of the heart, and of the mind, so that the changes so far achieved in dialogue can be deepened, tested, and finally brought to fruition. *The Rule of St. Benedict* knows that changes achieved in breakthrough moments need to be practiced regularly in order to become habits, take root, and flourish.[53] The Roman Catholic Church, too, needs to cultivate its new habits of the heart and of the mind in order to continue walking the road to the full unity of the Church.

Where these new habits are lacking, we can slide back into older, bad habits, older ways of doing things that fail to incorporate the important

---

53. *RB 1980: The Rule of St. Benedict in Latin and English with Notes*, ed. Timothy Fry, O.S.B. (Collegeville: The Liturgical Press, 1981).

advances dialogue has so far achieved. Bad habits cause slowdowns, detours, or total roadblocks on the journey. I would like to draw attention to a few examples where old bad habits still sometimes hold sway in the Roman Catholic Church, and to note the difficulty they cause for the dialogue with other churches. *Unitatis redintegratio* itself exhorts me to this task when it teaches that "the primary duty" of Roman Catholics doing ecumenical work "is to make an honest and careful appraisal of whatever needs to be renewed and achieved in the Catholic household itself, in order that its life may bear witness more loyally and luminously to the teachings and ordinances which have been handed down from Christ through the apostles."[54]

I'd like to say something, first, about the puzzling reception of recent ecumenical statements being offered by Vatican curial offices. An obvious example is the recent response of the Vatican to *The Final Report* of the Anglican-Roman Catholic International Commission. By coincidence, I was actually in Rome for an international bilateral meeting when this document was released there in December 1991, and I read my copy perched on the ledge of a pillar in St. Peter's Square in the warm December sunshine, sitting quite literally between the offices of the Pontifical Council for Promoting Christian Unity and the Congregation for the Doctrine of the Faith. It turned out that this location was symbolically revealing of the document itself, which we know resulted from a collaboration between these two offices.

The "Vatican Response" calls *The Final Report* "a significant milestone" in the "ecumenical movement as a whole"[55] and recognizes in it a significant number of agreements on the Eucharist, ministry, and authority. The "Vatican Response" emphasizes that such progress is an occasion for rejoicing and consolation, and it offers its reflection in the hope that its "reply will contribute to the continued dialogue."[56] Nevertheless, this "Vatican Response" is filled with negative evaluations and calls for further clarifications, some of them based on a misreading of *The Final Report* itself. At core many of its criticisms, especially on questions related to authority, come from an unflattering comparison of *The Final Report* with the traditions particular to the language and conceptual framework of Roman Catholic theology since the sixteenth-century divisions.

54. Vatican II, *Unitatis redintegratio,* #4.
55. "Vatican Response to *The Final Report* of the Anglican-Roman Catholic International Commission," *Origins* 21 (1991–92) 441.
56. Ibid., 447.

Such evaluations are somewhat puzzling to appointed members of this Commission, whose predecessors were instructed to pursue dialogue "founded on the Gospels and on the ancient common traditions."[57] Such theologians can become disheartened if they perceive a growing gap between their best theological efforts and the Vatican's understanding. In addition, if theological traditions distinctive to Roman Catholicism are to play a new role in the evaluation of ecumenical work, can these traditions be used in the spirit reported by the authors of *The Final Report,* who wished "to appeal to history only for enlightenment, not as a way of perpetuating past controversy"?[58] Commenting on this "Vatican Response," Francis Sullivan notes that "what the Vatican would require of an agreed dialogue statement is that it fully correspond to the language of official Catholic doctrine." The Vatican document, he points out, "seems to know no way to exclude . . . ambiguity except to use the precise formulas by which the Catholic Church is accustomed to express its faith."[59]

While this Vatican approach overlooks what some call "ecumenical methodology," it overlooks as well the commitment of the Roman Catholic tradition itself to reformulation of dogmatic teachings. Pope John XXIII distinguished between "the substance of the ancient doctrine of the deposit of faith" and "the way in which it is presented" at the opening of Vatican II,[60] and that Council followed his lead when it sought fresh statements on Church and Revelation, fresh perspectives on liturgy and the Church's relationship to the world. The Council acknowledged the "growth in the understanding of the realities and the words which have been handed down,"[61] an insight developed further by the Congregation for the Doctrine of the Faith in its teaching on the reformulation of dogmatic statements in *Mysterium ecclesiae.*[62] Ecumenical dialogue confronts the Roman Catholic Church with the opportunity—in fact, the mandate—to examine seriously and to contribute to a fresh, common formulation of the apostolic faith. While it surely must judge the adequacy of all new for-

57. See footnote #15.

58. See footnote #17.

59. Francis A. Sullivan, "The Vatican Response to ARCIC I," *Gregorianum* 73 (1992) 494.

60. John XXIII, "Opening Speech to the [Second Vatican] Council," in *The Documents of Vatican II,* ed. Walter M. Abbott (New York: America Press, 1966) 715.

61. Vatican II, *Dei verbum,* in *The Documents of Vatican II,* ed. Walter M. Abbott (New York: America Press, 1966) #8.

62. Congregation for the Doctrine of the Faith, *Mysterium ecclesiae, The Tablet* 227 (14 July 1973) 668.

mulations, it should recognize them as new wine for the testing; this means that the old wineskins may no longer be adequate to hold them.

Secondly, Roman Catholics are still tempted to the intellectual marginalization[63] of ecumenism, treating ecumenism as a special interest and those involved in the dialogue as a group with a peculiar bias. Sometimes interreligious dialogue is even used as an alternative to serious ecumenical dialogue among Christians; this fails to recognize the integrity and distinct contribution of each of these areas. Besides finding this marginalization a bit tiring, I also find it puzzling. While ecumenism demands expertise, it should not belong only to a small group of experts. Commitment to ecumenical dialogue is part of the identity of Roman Catholicism today: it is the birthright, or baptismal right, of my ministry students, of the many interchurch families, of all those directing RCIA classes or studying in them, of all who seek justice with other Christians in Christ's name, of all who celebrate Eucharist weekly in my multiracial, multilingual Toronto parish—it is for the whole Roman Catholic Church today. Further, it is implicated in every area of theology today, and I would think should be drawn on in teaching them all, divided any way you want—as tracts: sacraments, ecclesiology, Christian anthropology, also christology and trinitarian theology; or by fields: biblical studies, liturgy, systematics, pastoral care, history, canon law; or by functional specialties: research, dialectics, doctrines, systematics, communications—these are just examples, not a complete list, but consider how each area is impoverished without careful attention to theological views from other traditions and the insights drawn from ecumenical work in these areas. If theologians omit attention to ecumenism in our teaching and research, we will perpetuate old habits of thinking and fail to replace them with new habits of mind and heart.

A third area where old habits persist in the Roman Catholic Church is in the treatment of dissent. By "dissent" I mean disagreement from those teachings of the magisterium which are not exercises of infallibility. While dissent within the Roman Catholic Church may seem an internal housekeeping matter and of no concern to our ecumenical partners, I think that is quite wrong. Dissent and its treatment functions as a kind of litmus test of our beliefs, our priorities, and our practice in the area of authority. How we treat dissent and dissenters says a lot to other Christians about what full communion with the Roman Catholic Church would be like.

---

63. I first heard this term used to describe this problem in discussion with Jeffrey Gros, now on the staff of the Secretariat for Ecumenical and Interreligious Affairs of the [U.S.] National Conference of Catholic Bishops.

Ecumenical dialogue is full of discussion of the papacy, full of the hopes of Protestants, Anglicans, and Orthodox that, if renewed in accord with an ecclesiology of communion, the bishop of Rome might serve once again with a ministry of unity for the whole Church. *The Final Report* urges that he serve again with a primacy for the whole Church, explaining, "The primacy, rightly understood, implies that the bishop of Rome exercises his oversight in order to guard and promote the faithfulness of all the churches to Christ and one another."[64] It explains that primacy should help the churches "to listen to one another, to grow in love and unity, to strive together towards the fullness of Christian life and witness"; primacy should not "seek uniformity where diversity is legitimate, or centralize administration to the detriment of local churches."[65] One with primacy "exercises his ministry not in isolation but in collegial association with his brother bishops. His intervention in the affairs of a local church should not be made in such a way as to usurp the responsibility of its bishop."[66] It is heartrending to read these words of hope and then ponder the treatment of Raymond Hunthausen, former archbishop of Seattle, or more recently that of Bishop Isidore Borecky, Ukrainian Catholic eparch of Toronto. Lutherans report that they are open to receiving a petrine ministry for the Church if it were to be renewed on the principles of legitimate diversity, collegiality, and subsidiarity.[67] But these principles read like a checklist of what has been ignored in many recent cases of the treatment of dissent in the Roman Catholic Church. It is difficult to explain that Roman Catholics are committed to legitimate diversity, collegiality, and subsidiarity in the face of the treatment of an Agnes Mary Mansour, a Charles Curran, a Leonardo Boff. The Russian Orthodox theologian Paul Evdokimov expressed his readiness to accept a universal primacy that would exercise a "solicitude," a care for the "unity of faith, mission and life," but he warned that it must be based on an ecclesiology of communion in which the authority of each bishop in his local church is not undermined.[68] Is it not a time for Roman Catholics to be working hard for

64. ARCIC, "Authority in the Church I," *The Final Report*, #12.

65. Ibid., #21.

66. Ibid.

67. [U.S.] Lutheran-Roman Catholic Dialogue, "Differing Attitudes toward Papal Primacy: Common Statement," *Papal Primacy and the Universal Church*, eds. Paul Empie and T. Austin Murphy (Minneapolis: Augsburg Publishing House, 1974) #22–25.

68. Paul Evdokimov, "Can a Petrine Office Be Meaningful in the Church? A Russian Orthodox Reply," in Hans Küng, ed., *Papal Ministry in the Church*, *Concilium* vol. 64 (New York: Herder and Herder, 1971) 126.

the reform of the papacy according to the very principles we accepted in Vatican II so that it would again manifest such a "solicitude"? It seems to me that our treatment of dissent is one area where the Roman Catholic Church in its practice has not entirely made the shift to Vatican II's ecclesiology of communion or its recognition of the historicity of our understanding. While committed to these shifts in theory, sometimes in its practice towards dissent it slips back into old ways of doing things.

Of course, not all dissent from magisterial teaching has proved an advance in truth; but to neglect to leave space, on matters that are open to error, for the normal give-and-take, trial-and-error process that learning—even learning in the Church—must take means that learning will be stunted and the learners exhausted, sick, or losing heart. While many other Christians report that they would welcome the nonrelativizing leadership in truth that the bishop of Rome should provide, they are repeatedly scandalized by our tendency to regress to old habits in treating dissent. As one Anglican faculty expressed it after Curran's treatment, "The question as we perceive it now is whether or not the Anglican Communion should envision closer ecumenical relations with a church that seems officially determined to suppress public discussion, debate, dialogue, and even disagreement. . . ."[69] Breaking our bad habits here means a change of mind that takes hold in a change of practice by the bishop of Rome.

A fourth area where the Roman Catholic Church continues to use some bad habits of mind and heart is in our theological reflections on women. In particular, I want to highlight one argument being used more frequently lately against the ordination of women. The 1976 "Declaration on the Question of the Admission of Women to the Ministerial Priesthood," *Inter insigniores*, of the Congregation for the Doctrine of the Faith uses as its primary argument the practice of Jesus and the apostolic community in not including women among the twelve apostles or investing them with "the apostolic charge";[70] hence, it concludes, "the Church does not consider herself authorized to admit women to priestly ordination."[71] But in an argument it considers secondary, one from "fittingness," *Inter insigniores* argues from the maleness of Christ. Jesus Christ is a man, it argues,

69. General Theological Seminary Faculty to the Members of the Anglican-Roman Catholic International Commission, New York, 23 May 1986.

70. Congregation for the Doctrine of the Faith, "Declaration on the Question of the Admission of Women to the Ministerial Priesthood *[Inter insigniores]*," *Origins* 6 (1977–78) 520.

71. Ibid., 519.

and since he is a man then women cannot represent Jesus at the Eucharist because they cannot have the "natural resemblance" required for the presider of the Eucharist.[72] The supreme expression of the representation of Christ, the "Declaration" explains, is found in the "special form it assumes in the celebration of the eucharist," where the priest acts *in persona Christi* to the "point of being" the "very image" of Christ, bridegroom and head of the Church.[73] Hence only a man can take the role of Christ as a priest in presiding at the Eucharist.

This argument against the ordination of women from the maleness of Christ, though secondary in the "Declaration," has been playing an increasingly central role in several official Roman Catholic documents since the "Declaration" was written, notably in the 1986 letter of Cardinal Johannes Willebrands to the archbishop of Canterbury explaining why Roman Catholics opposed the decision of some Anglican provinces to ordain women;[74] in the 1988 meditation of Pope John Paul II "On the Dignity and Vocation of Women [*Mulieris dignitatem*]";[75] and in the 1992 proposed pastoral letter on women of the U.S. Roman Catholic bishops which they, prudently, failed to pass as a pastoral letter.[76] Hence the argument from the maleness of Christ, secondary in the 1976 "Declaration," is now becoming a primary vehicle to explain to Roman Catholics and to their ecumenical dialogue partners the reasons that we do not presently ordain women.

I regard the use of this argument as an unfortunate mistake in Roman Catholic theology. Its proponents often use it to uphold the distinction between the ordained and the laity, the distinction between men and women, or the fact that the presider of the Eucharist acts *in persona Christi*, all of which concerns I would share with them. But other means to uphold these points in Roman Catholic teaching would be more accurate than the argument from the maleness of Christ. In fact, arguing from Christ's maleness tends to call into question whether Roman Catholics accept the

72. Ibid., 522.

73. Ibid.

74. Johannes Willebrands to Robert Runcie, 17 June 1986, *Origins* 16 (1986–87) 160.

75. John Paul II, "On the Dignity and Vocation of Women [*Mulieris dignitatem*]," *Origins* 18 (1988–89) 279.

76. Ad Hoc Committee for a Pastoral Response to Women's Concerns of the National Conference of Catholic Bishops, "One in Christ Jesus" [fourth draft of proposed pastoral letter], *Origins* 22 (1992–93) 234; "One in Christ Jesus" [final form, released as Committee report], *Origins* 22 (1992–93) 502.

full implications of a central dogma of the faith we share with other Christians: that Christ, the Word of God, took on human nature, and hence, as redeemer of the world and head of the Church, represents all humanity, male and female, offering salvation to all by drawing them with him through his life, death, and resurrection. To suggest that women cannot represent Christ, who represented them, at precisely the high point of the celebration of his saving work, the Eucharist, is seen to undermine—albeit unintentionally—our soteriological teaching on Christ's saving work. It was precisely this dogma of Christian faith that the former archbishop of Canterbury, Robert Runcie, used in explaining to Pope John Paul II the reason some Anglican provinces felt themselves required, not merely permitted, to ordain women.[77] To counter that explanation with an argument from Christ's maleness is to enter the ecumenical dialogue with one of our worst arguments, rather than our best. The continuing use of this argument is, in my judgment, a bad theological habit we should break very soon.

If we left aside the argument from Christ's maleness, would we then be free to explore whether, and under what conditions, the Church could ever "consider" itself "authorized" to change its practice in not ordaining women?

On the one hand, it is encouraging to note that John Paul II does not use the argument from the maleness of Christ in his 1994 apostolic letter on the inadmissability of women to priestly ordination, *Ordinatio sacerdotalis*. While referring to earlier uses of the argument from Christ's maleness, John Paul II himself bases his own argument in this document against women's ordination on the conscious will and practice of Christ in choosing "the 12 men whom he made the foundation of his Church."[78] The Gospels and the Acts of the Apostles show that "this call was made in accordance with God's eternal plan: Christ chose those whom he willed . . . , and he did so in union with the Father, 'through the Holy Spirit' . . . , after having spent the night in prayer," explains John Paul II, and continues, "The Church has always acknowledged as a perennial norm her Lord's way of acting. . . ."[79] On the other hand, while avoiding the argument from Christ's maleness and using instead this argument from Christ's conscious will and practice, John Paul II declares "that the Church has no authority whatsoever to confer priestly ordination on

77. Robert Runcie to Johannes Willebrands, 18 Dec. 1985, *Origins* 16 (1986–87) 157.

78. John Paul II, *Ordinatio sacerdotalis, Origins* 24 (1994–95) 49, 51–52; see #2.

79. Ibid.

women and that this judgment is to be definitively held by all the Church's faithful."[80] In 1991 the Anglican-Roman Catholic Dialogue of Canada had proposed that "the issue of women's ordination be approached as a disputed question about the enculturation of the Gospel,"[81] but John Paul II wishes to underline that this issue is not "still open to debate."[82]

In 1995, the Congregation for the Doctrine of the Faith publicized its judgment that the teaching about women's exclusion from priestly ordination pertains to the deposit of faith and that it has been taught infallibly by the ordinary and universal magisterium.[83]

In recent years before the 1995 statement of the Congregation for the Doctrine of the Faith, several bishops had publicly questioned either the arguments or the irreversibility of the teaching against women's ordination. After *Ordinatio sacerdotalis,* many Roman Catholic theologians criticized the pope's argument from Christ's conscious will and practice. They also criticized the 1995 judgment by the Congregation for the Doctrine of the Faith that women's exclusion from priestly ordination has been taught infallibly by the ordinary and universal magisterium.[84]

These recent developments within the Roman Catholic Church also have a deep effect on ecumenical dialogue about the nature of ordained ministry, the role of theology, and the exercise of the primacy of the bishop of Rome.

80. Ibid., #4.

81. Anglican-Roman Catholic Dialogue of Canada, "Agreed Statement of the Anglican-Roman Catholic Dialogue of Canada on the Experience of the Ministries of Women in Canada," *Origins* 21 (1991–92) 616.

82. John Paul II, *Ordinatio sacerdotalis,* #4.

83. Congregation for the Doctrine of the Faith, "Reply to the *Dubium* Concerning the Teaching Contained in the Apostolic Letter *Ordinatio sacerdotalis,*" *Origins* 25 (1995–96) 401, 403.

84. In June 1996, the Catholic Theological Society of America [CTSA] received the first draft of a paper by an ad hoc committee appointed by the CTSA's executive board; the paper, entitled "Tradition and the Ordination of Women" (*Origins* 26 [1996–97] 90–94), raised questions about the arguments used by the Congregation for the Doctrine of the Faith in its 1995 "Reply to the *Dubium*" on the teaching about women's ordination. This committee paper was sent to all CTSA members for study and revision during 1996–97. On 5 June 1997, the board of the CTSA received the committee's revised paper and endorsed its conclusion. In addition, the members of the CTSA, assembled at their annual business meeting 6 June 1997 in Minneapolis, Minnesota, voted to endorse the conclusion of the paper "Tradition and the Ordination of Women" that "there are serious doubts regarding the nature of the authority of this teaching [namely, the teaching that the church's lack of authority to ordain women to the priesthood is

Fifth and finally, I want to say a word about reception, which Yves Congar recognized as an often-overlooked reality in the Church[85] and which *The Final Report* understands as "the final indication" that a teaching "has fulfilled the necessary conditions for it to be a true expression of the faith,"[86] the "ultimate indication that the Church's authoritative decision in a matter of faith has been truly preserved from error by the Holy Spirit."[87] Jean-Marie Tillard understands tradition as reception of the Gospel,[88] and indeed we could understand the whole history of the Church—including the present ecumenical discussion among Christians—as an ongoing reception in every age of the faith once delivered to the apostles. While the "Vatican Response" to *The Final Report* continues to misunderstand *The Final Report* on this topic and to distrust the idea of reception, I think recognition of reception in contemporary Roman Catholic theology gives us a fresh new opportunity for reconceptualizing some major issues central to Christian faith. Roman Catholic theology today is struggling to reconceptualize its understanding of the gift that Vatican I names "infallibility," and that Vatican II describes in a *relatio* as the assistance of the Holy Spirit by which "the Church . . . cannot completely fall away from the way of salvation."[89] Recognizing that reception is linked to what Vatican I names "infallibility," we can reconceptualize the delicate balance that is needed between teaching authority in the Church

---

a truth that has been infallibly taught and requires the definitive assent of the faithful] and its grounds in tradition. There is serious, widespread disagreement on this question not only among theologians, but also within the larger community of the church . . . . [I]t seems clear . . . that further study, discussion and prayer regarding this question by all the members of the church in accord with their particular gifts and vocations are necessary if the church is to be guided by the Spirit in remaining faithful to the authentic tradition of the Gospel in our day" (*Origins* 27 [1997–98] 75–76; for entire revised paper, see 76–79). Voting by secret ballot, with 248 members present, 216 voted yes, 22 voted no, and 10 abstained.

85. Yves Congar, "La 'réception' comme réalité ecclésiologique," *Revue des sciences philosophiques et théologiques* 56 (1972) 369–403.

86. Anglican-Roman Catholic International Commission [ARCIC], "Elucidation: Authority in the Church I," *The Final Report* (London: SPCK and Catholic Truth Society, 1982) #3.

87. ARCIC, "Authority in the Church II," *The Final Report*, #25.

88. Jean-Marie Tillard, "Tradition, Reception," *The Quadrilog: Tradition and the Future of Ecumenism, Essays in Honor of George H. Tavard*, ed. Kenneth Hagan (Collegeville: The Liturgical Press, 1994) 328–43.

89. *Schema Constitutionis de Ecclesia* (Vatican, 1964), *relatio* for n. 12(C) 45–46; cited by Harry McSorley, "Some Forgotten Truths about the Petrine

and the assent of the whole Church which is the final sign that such teaching is true. Overlooking reception is part of the old habit of thinking of the Church as "pyramidal," to use Congar's term,[90] rather than a communion of communions where the response of each local church is an indication important for discernment of the truth. In addition, if we include reception in our understanding of infallibility, we will be less worried about who first expresses a teaching; we will also be less uneasy with the diversity of cultural expressions of the Gospel, since inculturation is really the reception of the Gospel in every age in the variety of forms and expressions appropriate to the world Church. And we will recognize that reception also includes a new listening to those churches which Vatican II recognized are in real but imperfect communion with the Roman Catholic Church, churches in whom we recognize "the riches of Christ and virtuous works" with their "truly Christian endowments from our common heritage."[91] For the sake of our witness to the Gospel in the third millennium, we can no longer ignore their insights.

In this last section, I have been speaking of the need to cultivate new habits of mind and heart, so that the changes achieved so far through dialogue will take root and bear fruit in the achievement of the full, visible unity of the whole Church of Christ. I have given five examples where Roman Catholics should replace bad habits with good habits: responses to ecumenical statements, the marginalization of ecumenism, the reform of the papacy and its treatment of dissent, one theological argument used against women's ordination, and the nature of reception as the manifestation of infallibility's exercise. But you notice that this list includes some of the most important areas needing reform in Roman Catholic theology and practice today. This illustrates again my conviction that the ecumenical movement is actually a reform movement within the Church, calling it to a purified announcement of the Gospel for the sake of the world. Making its own contributions, Roman Catholic theology and practice is also being reformed by the ecumenical movement. You can see again why I find it easy to agree with Vatican II in concluding that the ecumenical movement is a work of the Holy Spirit in our day.[92]

Ministry," *Journal of Ecumenical Studies* 11 (1974) 225. The full text is the following: "The Church, in which Christ lives, having completed the work of salvation, and which is led by the Holy Spirit to the truth, cannot completely fall away from the way of salvation, and is therefore infallible in this sense."

90. Congar, "La 'réception' comme réalité ecclésiologique," 392.

91. *Unitatis redintegratio,* #4.

92. Ibid.

2

Purifying Memories and Exchanging Gifts: Recent Orientations of the Vatican toward Ecumenism[1]

I want to focus on two recent writings of Pope John Paul II on ecumenism: his encyclical on commitment to ecumenism, *Ut unum sint,* and his apostolic letter on the Eastern churches, *Orientale lumen.* My purpose is to provide a kind of updating on recent orientations of the Vatican to ecumenical dialogue. In addition, I will also include some reflection on another recent ecumenical document from the Vatican: the revised ecumenical directory which was published in 1993 by the Pontifical Council for Promoting Christian Unity. While these three documents are quite different in style and scope, together they indicate some directions that the Vatican is taking today in ecumenical dialogue with other Christians.

I would like to highlight certain key themes from these documents and then draw on examples from recent ecumenical dialogue work that provide illustration of these themes.

As an introduction, let me say that I first became committed to ecumenical dialogue during my theological studies when I was one of the very few Roman Catholics in a Protestant divinity school. There I discovered how little I really knew about Protestant churches, about the Reformation, about the convictions of present-day Lutherans, Presbyterians, Mennonites, Anglicans, and Christians of the other communions with a heritage from the Reformation. I knew even less about Orthodox Christians. But what I also discovered was how little they knew

---

1. This essay was first presented as a talk in December 1995 for the University of St. Thomas School of Theology at St. Mary's Seminary in Houston and the Continuing Education of Priests Committee of the Diocese of Galveston-Houston, Texas.

about me as a Roman Catholic. Once, during a class on the Reformation, I was asked politely if I wished to say a word in favor of indulgences. We were all together in the same classes, but when we began we hardly knew anything at all about each other.

John Paul II notes this situation in *Ut unum sint.* He acknowledges the doctrinal differences that divide the churches; but he adds that along with these doctrinal differences, we cannot underestimate "the burden of long-standing misgivings inherited from the past, and of mutual misunder-standings and prejudices." The situation is often made worse, he continues, by "complacency, indifference, and insufficient knowledge of one another."[2] At the end of *Orientale lumen,* he repeats this exhortation: "one important way to grow in mutual understanding and unity consists precisely in improving our knowledge of one another."[3]

My studies in theology made a permanent change in me; they made me restless to understand other churches and to help them to understand my own Roman Catholic communion. I was restless, and this restlessness re-ally set me off on the journey toward the full communion of the Church of Christ through commitment to ecumenical dialogue. As a Roman Catholic, I have been nurtured in this restlessness by my own church, which teaches that the ecumenical movement is the work of the Holy Spirit in our day. The Second Vatican Council taught that the discord and disunity among Christians "openly contradicts the will of Christ, provides a stumbling block to the world, and inflicts damage" on the proclamation of the Gospel.[4] After twenty-two years as a member of the ecumenical consortium that constitutes the Toronto School of Theology and of bilat-eral and multilateral dialogues, it is easy for me to affirm the teaching of the 1964 Decree on Ecumenism, *Unitatis redintegratio,* that the divisions among Christians make it "more difficult" for the Church "to express" its catholicity, and that "a change of heart" is required for these divisions to be overcome.[5] When Vatican II recognized that the one Church of Christ extends "beyond the visible limits" of the Roman Catholic Church, it took a step forward on the ecumenical journey that could not be reversed.[6] We see the implications of this step in the Council's recognition of the real

---

2. John Paul II, *Ut unum sint, Origins* 25 (1995) 49, 51–72; see #2.

3. John Paul II, *Orientale lumen, Origins* 25 (1995) 1, 3–13; see #24.

4. Vatican II, *Unitatis redintegratio,* in *The Documents of Vatican II,* ed. Walter M. Abbott (New York: America Press, 1966) #1.

5. Ibid., #4.

6. Johannes Willebrands, "Vatican II's Ecclesiology of Communion," *Origins* 17 (1987–88) 32.

though imperfect communion that Roman Catholics already share with other baptized Christians, and we hear it repeated again in the words of John Paul II when he emphasizes that the Roman Catholic Church's commitment to ecumenism is irreversible.

So I was nurtured in my restlessness by my own church, and it is not surprising that the encyclical *Ut unum sint* reflects this restlessness with the present division among the churches. Let me turn to my first theme from this encyclical, the purification of memories.

THE PURIFICATION OF MEMORIES

Christmas is a time of memories for most of us, and it reminds us of how powerful our memories can be. We think about family gatherings and familiar Christmas carols; we remember past Christmases, many happy, some sad perhaps with the shadow of illness, death, or family dissension. In my family, Christmas memories include the taste of a certain kind of nut bread always made for Christmas breakfast after 9 a.m. Mass on Christmas morning. In my husband Michael's huge family, there are memories of happy times all together eating spaghetti on Christmas Eve and then watching as the grandchildren dramatized the Christmas story for Michael's parents when his father was still alive, before we all got into the many cars needed to take the whole family to Eucharist at midnight. Memories have a powerful effect on our lives: they return to us again and again from the past and they shape our present attitudes and behavior.

John Paul II also is aware of the power of memory, and he believes that part of the ecumenical journey includes what he calls "the necessary purification of past memories."[7] He believes that Christians of different churches have not known each other well, and that we have misunderstandings and prejudices[8] about each other inherited from the past; they lead to misgivings in the present. I was talking about good memories of Christmas; but our churches also have some bad memories about each other. Sometimes these bad memories about the past are true, sometimes they are distorted—a kind of false-memory syndrome. But all of these bad memories, John Paul II believes, should not be ignored; they should be faced and purified.

For him, a first step toward this purification is repentance and conversion. "The sin of our separation is very serious," he writes in *Orientale*

7. John Paul II, *Ut unum sint*, #2.
8. Ibid.

lumen. "We feel the need to go beyond the degree of communion we have reached."[9] The pope calls for conversion; it is a conversion both personal and communal. It stems from a spirit of repentance. The pope urges us, in *Ut unum sint,* to change our "way of looking at things." This includes repentance for "exclusions which harm fraternal charity," for certain refusals to forgive, for a certain pride, for "unevangelical insistence on condemning 'the other side.'" Repentance is accompanied by the vision of new horizons, he says, as we discover ways that the Holy Spirit is at work in other churches, and learn of the holiness and Christian commitment present among members of those churches.[10]

In a sense, the entire ecumenical movement rests on the recognition of the need for repentance, a willingness to ask whether we have a beam in our own eye before we concern ourselves with the mote in the eye of the other. The pope returns repeatedly to this theme of repentance and conversion, linking it to a new perspective on the past. Roman Catholics, he explains, are called by the Spirit of God "to make a serious examination of conscience." This examination of conscience will lead the churches into a "dialogue of conversion," he says, which includes both repentance with its change of attitude, and intent to do the will of the Father. This is the way that the ecumenical dialogue will accomplish its goal. "Only the act of placing ourselves before God can offer a solid basis for that conversion of individual Christians and for that constant reform of the Church . . . which represent the preconditions for all ecumenical commitment."[11] He is concerned not only with personal sins, he explains, but also with sinful social structures "which have contributed and can still contribute to division and to the reinforcing of division."[12] In this repentance and conversion, common prayer with Christians from other churches has primacy of place in the ecumenical path to unity, he says. "If Christians, despite their divisions, can grow ever more united in common prayer around Christ, they will grow in the awareness of how little divides them in comparison to what unites them," he believes.[13]

The pope sees the common heritage of the holiness of the saints as a sign that can encourage us in the path to unity. He argues that all of our churches have martyrs who teach us that "thanks to the power given by

9. John Paul II, *Orientale lumen,* #17.
10. John Paul II, *Ut unum sint,* #15.
11. Ibid., #82.
12. Ibid., #34.
13. Ibid., #22.

the Spirit," obeying the will of the Father and overcoming obstacles are not beyond our reach.[14] But then, he asks, isn't this absolute attachment to Christ and the Father—so absolute "as to lead even to the shedding of blood"—"is not this same attachment at the heart of what I have called a 'dialogue of conversion?'"[15] But the Spirit poured out grace in an extraordinary way in the lives of all of the saints, he continues. "If . . . Communities are able truly to 'be converted' to the quest for full and visible communion, God will do for them what he did for their Saints. He will overcome the obstacles inherited from the past and will lead Communities along his paths to where he wills: to the visible *koinonia* which is both praise of his glory and service of his plan of salvation."[16]

When we have repented of our sins toward each other, then we are ready for a new look at the past. Inspired by a sincere desire for mutual forgiveness and reconciliation, the pope explains, the disciples of the Lord "are called to reexamine together their painful past and the hurt which that past regrettably continues to provoke even today."[17] In this reexamination, he explains, they are invited by the Gospel "to acknowledge with sincere and total objectivity the mistakes made and the contingent factors at work at the origins of their deplorable divisions. What is needed," he continues, "is a calm, clear-sighted and truthful vision of things, a vision enlivened by divine mercy and capable of freeing people's minds and of inspiring in everyone a renewed willingness, precisely with a view to proclaiming the Gospel to the men and women of every people and nation."[18] To illustrate his point, he even asks for forgiveness for the ways in which the papacy has contributed to the division among Christians. Roman Catholic conviction about the papacy "constitutes a difficulty for most other Christians," he acknowledges, "whose memory is marked by certain painful recollections. To the extent that we are responsible for these," he continues, "I join my Predecessor Paul VI in asking forgiveness."[19]

Why bother with the past, with old debates, when the Church of the present and the future is beckoning us forward and demands so much of our time and energy? If we ignore the past, we are like a person who had been abused or hurt in childhood trying to ignore and stifle the problems of that history, rather than facing it with loving help from others. John

14. Ibid., #83.
15. Ibid.
16. Ibid., #84.
17. Ibid., #2.
18. Ibid.
19. Ibid., #88.

Macquarrie comments, "Christians have been a long time growing into division, and we must expect that it will take them time to grow into unity."[20] To grow into the future, we must allow wounds from the past to be healed. John Paul II wants us to work directly on this healing.

The pope gives a number of examples where ecumenical dialogue is achieving real breakthroughs in the reexamination of the past with its sometimes painful memories. One important breakthrough is the set of agreements between Paul VI or John Paul II himself with the patriarchs of three Oriental Orthodox churches, agreements which declare a common faith in Jesus Christ, truly God and truly human. These Oriental Orthodox churches were once regarded as monophysite in their teaching, but in these recent agreements the patriarchs of these Oriental Orthodox churches are enabled to join with the bishop of Rome in witnessing to the same faith about Jesus Christ. After centuries of misunderstanding and division, today we Roman Catholics can recognize in the Coptic, Syrian, and Ethiopian Orthodox Churches a common confession of faith with us. John Paul II also signed a common christological declaration with the patriarch of the Assyrian Church of the East, with its distinctive historical background. John Paul II uses the words of the Magnificat in praise of God as he expresses his excitement about the agreements in this breakthrough,[21] the result of theological investigation and fraternal dialogue. He also thinks that "it is an encouragement for us," because, he explains, "it shows us that the path followed is the right one and that we can reasonably hope to discover together the solution to other disputed questions."[22]

Another area of breakthrough in the purification of memories is the plan for a common teaching on justification by Lutherans and Roman Catholics in 1998. In that year, which will follow the 450th anniversary, in 1997, of the Council of Trent's teaching on justification, Lutherans and Roman Catholics at the worldwide level are hoping to publish a joint declaration on justification. In that declaration, which is in its final stages of preparation, the two partners plan to state that Lutherans and Roman Catholics today share a consensus in basic truths of the doctrine of justification. While our two communions continue to maintain some different emphases in explaining our need for God's grace and its action in us, these differences are acceptable to each other. "Thus," a joint declaration would

---

20. John Macquarrie, *Christian Unity & Christian Diversity* (Philadelphia: The Westminster Press, 1975) 26.

21. John Paul II, *Ut unum sint*, #62.

22. Ibid., #63.

state, "the doctrinal condemnations of the 16th century, in so far as they relate to the doctrine of justification, appear in a new light: The teaching of the Lutheran churches presented in this Declaration does not fall under the condemnations from the Council of Trent. The condemnations in the Lutheran Confessions do not apply to the teaching of the Roman Catholic Church presented in this Declaration."[23] This joint declaration proposed by the Pontifical Council for Promoting Christian Unity and the Lutheran World Federation should have a major effect on relationships between the Roman Catholic and Lutheran communions and in fact among all of the churches of the West, since justification was such a central issue in the Reformation which began our divisions.

THE GIFT EXCHANGE

I have been talking about the first theme in John Paul II's recent teachings on ecumenism, and now let me turn to the second one, the theme of the gift exchange. Vatican II talked about the exchange of gifts among the churches, but for me the Advent/Christmas season is the source of my first experiences with a large family gift exchange. In my husband's large family, we could not all give each other a present at Christmas, so we set up a gift exchange in which each of us brought one gift to another family member and received one in return. The exchange of gifts in this way allowed each of us to participate; and we got to know each other better as well, too, since the gifts often highlighted some distinctive trait of the giver or receiver.

John Paul II also believes in a gift exchange, and he believes that ecumenism includes mutual enrichment among Christians. But these are special gifts because, while we give them to others, we continue to keep them ourselves. The gift exchange of ecumenical dialogue is the discovery that some of the differences among Christians that were once thought to be contradictory are now recognized as complementary. They are gifts we give each other. In his apostolic letter on the Eastern churches, *Orientale lumen,* the pope states this in an interesting way. "We have increasingly learned that it was not so much a historical episode or a mere question of pre-eminence that tore the fabric of unity as it was a progressive estrangement, so that the other's diversity was no longer perceived as a common treasure, but as incompatibility."[24] I think this is a very interesting idea: "so that the other's di-

---

23. Pontifical Council for Promoting Christian Unity and Lutheran World Federation, "Joint Declaration on the Doctrine of Justification: Final Proposal," #41.

25. Ibid., #17.

versity was no longer perceived as a common treasure, but as incompatibility." John Paul II wants us to recognize that some kinds of diversity are a richness, a common treasure, rather than a sign of incompatibility.

He emphasizes this especially when he speaks of those churches of the East which have a rich but different emphasis from the churches of the West. But these Eastern Christian emphases help show forth the unity in diversity that characterized the early councils[25] and should characterize our understanding of the Church today. "The Church should breathe with its two lungs," he says in *Orientale lumen,* as he has said often before. In fact, he believes that Christians should express their understanding of the Gospel "according to their own heritage of culture and thought"; and so he welcomes "the experience of the individual churches of the East" as "an authoritative example of successful inculturation."[26]

And so in this apostolic letter he opens the treasure chest of the East and describes lovingly many of the beautiful gifts he finds there for sharing with the whole Church. He describes the Eastern emphases on the mystery of the Trinity, our participation in trinitarian life understood as divinization, and the celebration of this communion in the Trinity through the mystical and ecstatic experience of the liturgical celebration. He describes also the importance of monasticism which in the East is presented "not . . . merely as a separate category of Christians . . . (but) as a symbolic synthesis of Christianity."[27] The monastic life highlights Eastern emphasis on apophatic theology which ends in adoring silence, "for the culmination of the knowledge and experience of God is his absolute transcendence."[28] John Paul II continues, "In the humble acceptance of the creature's limits before the infinite transcendence of a God who never ceases to reveal himself as God-Love, the Father of our Lord Jesus Christ in the joy of the Holy Spirit, I see expressed the attitude of prayer and the theological method which the East prefers and continues to offer all believers in Christ."[29] John Paul II wants the Latin Church to be converted so that it may respect and appreciate Eastern Christians, "the spiritual treasures they bear," and may show "concretely, far more than in the past, how much she esteems and admires the Christian East and how essential she considers its contribution to the full realization of the church's universality."[30]

26. Ibid., #7.
27. Ibid., #9.
28. Ibid., #16.
29. Ibid.
30. Ibid., #21.
31. Ibid., #22.

The pope believes that when we know the treasures of others' faith, we will have the "incentive for a new and more intimate meeting . . . which will be a true and sincere mutual exchange."[31] He believes that this is the work of the Holy Spirit.

Does the pope mean that our words or our convictions don't matter, that ecumenism means a kind of relativism? Not at all. He tells us in *Ut unum sint* that we must avoid "all forms of reductionism or facile 'agreement'" in our dialogue. But if we find that we have different doctrinal formulations, he continues, we must "determine whether the words involved say the same thing."[32] For example, he says, look at the recent agreements over christology between Roman Catholics and the Oriental Orthodox. Ecumenical dialogue, he explains, "makes surprising discoveries possible. Intolerant polemics and controversies have made incompatible assertions out of what was really the result of two different ways of looking at the same reality." So, he explains, "one of the advantages of ecumenism is that it helps Christian Communities to discover the unfathomable riches of the truth."[33] This is very different from relativism. Again, he explains in *Orientale lumen*, tradition is living memory, "not an unchanging repetition of formulas." "When the uses and customs belonging to each church are considered as absolutely unchangeable," he points out, "there is a sure risk of tradition losing that feature of a living reality which grows and develops, and which the Spirit guarantees precisely because it has something to say to the people of every age."[34] So he concludes in *Ut unum sint*, "authentic ecumenism is a gift at the service of truth."[35]

John Paul II has given us a great example of unity in diversity in his presentation of the Christian East, but we could look for other examples from Western ecumenical dialogue. One example is the one I have already mentioned, the plans to recognize that the different emphases in Lutheran and Roman Catholic teaching on justification do not contradict each other: they bring out different aspects of the richness of God's grace. Another example of this approach with which many of you may be familiar is the progress made on the Eucharist in ecumenical dialogue. In the Faith and Order work on Eucharist, for instance, two emphases are recognized but held together through discussion of *anamnesis*, memorial. In the sixteenth-century controversies, Protestants emphasized the once-for-all character of

32. John Paul II, *Ut unum sint*, #38.
33. Ibid.
34. John Paul II, *Orientale lumen*, #8.
35. John Paul II, *Ut unum sint*, #38.

Christ's sacrifice on the cross and Roman Catholics emphasized its continuing benefits for us today. The statement in *Baptism, Eucharist and Ministry* holds these emphases together when it writes that the Eucharist "is the living and effective sign of his [Christ's] sacrifice, accomplished once and for all on the cross and still operative on behalf of all humankind."[36] Hence this statement can speak of Christ's "unique" presence in the Eucharist, "the sacrament of his real presence" whose presence "does not depend on the faith of the individual. . . ."[37] The Anglican-Roman Catholic International Commission can speak in a similar way in *The Final Report*, when it says that there can be no repetition or addition to Christ's sacrifice on the cross, but that the Eucharist is the means "through which the atoning work of Christ on the cross is proclaimed and made effective in the life of the Church" so that the Church in the Eucharist even "participates in the benefits" of his passion and "enter[s] into the movement of his [Christ's] self-offering."[38] In these Eucharistic discussions, again there is the recognition that diverse emphases can enrich the Christian understanding and practice of the Eucharist. These different emphases are all gifts brought to the gift exchange that is the Church's ecumenical dialogue.

New Millennium's Resolutions

There is a third theme that this season reminds us of, and that is the theme of New Year's resolutions. Well, the pope also has some New Year's resolutions in his encyclical *Ut unum sint*, really New Millennium's resolutions. John Paul II is convinced that the coming of the third millennium since Christ's birth gives us an opportunity to overcome the scandalous divisions in the Church so that we can be strengthened for common evangelization in the modern world. "Christ cries out, but man [*sic*] finds it hard to hear his voice because we fail to speak with one accord," he says.[39] Again, he speaks of "the grave obstacle which the lack of unity represents for the proclamation of the Gospel."[40] So he has resolved to ask for help in reforming the papacy where such reform is needed.

36. World Council of Churches, "Eucharist," *Baptism, Eucharist and Ministry* (Geneva: World Council of Churches, 1982) #5.

37. Ibid., #13.

38. Anglican-Roman Catholic International Commission [ARCIC], "Eucharistic Doctrine," *The Final Report* (London: SPCK & Catholic Truth Society, 1982) #5.

39. John Paul II, *Orientale lumen*, #28.

40. John Paul II, *Ut unum sint*, #99.

We see that he has already asked for forgiveness in discussing the ways that Roman Catholic teaching about the papacy can be a difficulty for other churches, especially because their memory contains "painful recollections" about the papacy.[41] But John Paul II wants to go further than just to ask for forgiveness: he also wants to think about how the papacy could be improved.

The pope shares the Roman Catholic conviction that there is a ministry of unity that should be exercised in the midst of the Church, and that this ministry of unity has been preserved and continued by the bishop of Rome. He should keep watch like a sentinel so that through the bishops the true voice of Christ may be heard in all of the local churches,[42] and he must "ensure the communion of all the Churches."[43] In fact, John Paul II believes that one of his specific duties as bishop of Rome is "to encourage the effort of all who work for the cause of unity."[44]

He first asks for prayers for his own conversion so that he might be converted as Peter was converted,[45] and he emphasizes that the stories of Peter's weakness show how his ministry "derives altogether from grace."[46] But he also is happy that the question of the primacy of the bishop of Rome has become a topic of study in ecumenical dialogues; he notes that other churches are taking "a fresh look at this ministry of unity."[47] John Paul II is convinced, he says, that "whatever relates to the unity of all Christian communities clearly forms part of the concerns of the primacy."[48] He realizes that "Christ ardently desires the full and visible communion of all those Communities in which, by virtue of God's faithfulness, his Spirit dwells."[49] John Paul II believes himself to have "a particular responsibility" in this regard, especially in acknowledging the desires of other Christian churches for full communion and "in heeding the request made of me to find a way of exercising the primacy which, while in no way renouncing what is essential to its mission, is nonetheless open to a new situation."[50] He remembers that in the first millennium the

41. Ibid., #88.
42. Ibid., #94.
43. Ibid.
44. Ibid., #3.
45. Ibid., #4.
46. Ibid., #91.
47. Ibid., #89.
48. Ibid., #95.
49. Ibid.
50. Ibid.

Roman See acted as moderator by common consent among the churches, and he has suggested to former Ecumenical Patriarch Dimitrios I that pastors and theologians from their churches "may seek—together, of course—the forms in which this ministry may accomplish a service of love recognized by all concerned."[51]

This is a very radical and exciting suggestion, and John Paul II repeats it again as a request: "This is an immense task, which we cannot refuse and which I cannot carry out by myself." What a wonderful admission of the call and the burden of this ministry of unity! And he continues, "Could not the real but imperfect communion existing between us persuade Church leaders and their theologians to engage with me in a patient and fraternal dialogue on this subject, a dialogue in which, leaving useless controversies behind, we could listen to one another, keeping before us only the will of Christ for his Church and allowing ourselves to be deeply moved by his plea 'that they may all be one . . . so that the world may believe that you have sent me'(John 17:21)?"[52]

So the bishop of Rome in this encyclical is requesting forgiveness, praying for conversion, and then asking pastors and theologians from other churches to assist him in restructuring the papacy's exercise so that it will again be able to serve as a ministry of unity for the whole Church. This is quite an impressive approach.

John Paul II is correct in noting that ecumenical dialogue has already begun to discuss how the papal ministry could be exercised in new forms. The Lutheran-Roman Catholic Dialogue in the U.S., for example, notes the value of a petrine ministry that serves the unity of the Church, and Lutheran members argue that "papal primacy, renewed in the light of the gospel, need not be a barrier to reconciliation."[53] In fact, the Dialogue invites Lutherans to consider that such a renewed papal ministry would be possible, even desirable; Lutherans "increasingly recognize the need for a Ministry serving the unity of the Church Universal," members note,[54] one which "serves to promote or preserve the oneness of the Church by symbolizing unity, and by facilitating communication, mutual assistance or correction, and collaboration in the church's mission."[55] At the same time,

---

51. Ibid.

52. Ibid., #96.

53. [U.S.] Lutheran-Roman Catholic Dialogue, "Differing Attitudes Toward Papal Primacy: Common Statement," *Papal Primacy and the Universal Church*, eds. Paul C. Empie and T. Austin Murphy (Minneapolis: Augsburg Publishing House, 1974) #32.

54. Ibid., #28.

55. Ibid., #4.

Lutheran dialogue members also list what they see as "defects" in the papacy, including its present mode of operation—along with the operation of the Curia—and also the "close tie at the present time between primacy and infallibility."[56] The Dialogue members call for renewal of the papacy according to the Vatican II principles of legitimate diversity, collegiality, and subsidiarity.[57]

The Anglican-Roman Catholic International Commission is another dialogue that has examined the value of the papacy but called for its reform so that it can again minister to the whole Church. In *The Final Report*, the Anglican-Roman Catholic International Commission argues that a universal primacy should help the churches listen to each other, grow in love and unity, and seek the fullness of witness, not seeking uniformity where diversity is legitimate or centralizing administration to the detriment of the local churches. Well, this list gives us the impression that the writers have some examples in mind. Frequently today in ecumenical discussion I hear other Christians state that their disagreement with the papacy is not with the need for such a ministry, but with abuses in the actual way it is sometimes exercised. For example, the Anglican-Roman Catholic International Commission believes that primacy—leadership by one bishop—should always be kept in balance with conciliarity—oversight by the whole college of bishops. But "it has often happened that one has been emphasized at the expense of the other, even to the point of serious imbalance."[58] But the Commission believes that a ministry of unity is part of God's design for the Church, and it seeks a way forward so that the papacy could again serve Anglicans as well as Roman Catholics in this ministry.

So the New Millennium's resolutions of the pope have already been expressed as a hope by other churches through their dialogue commissions. Now the pope is asking for their collaboration to carry out his resolutions. This could be the start of an important step in the renewal of the papal ministry for our time.

56. [U.S.] Lutheran-Roman Catholic Dialogue, "Differing Attitudes Toward Papal Primacy: Reflections of the Lutheran Participants," *Papal Primacy and the Universal Church,* eds. Paul C. Empie and T. Austin Murphy (Minneapolis: Augsburg Publishing House, 1974) #38.

57. [U.S.] Lutheran-Roman Catholic Dialogue, "Differing Attitudes Toward Papal Primacy: Common Statement," *Papal Primacy and the Universal Church,* eds. Paul C. Empie and T. Austin Murphy (Minneapolis: Augsburg Publishing House, 1974) #22-25.

58. Anglican-Roman Catholic International Commission [ARCIC], "Authority in the Church I," *The Final Report* (London: SPCK & Catholic Truth Society, 1982) #22.

Reception

The last theme that I want to mention could be related to the Christmas season as well, if we wanted to focus on Epiphany. The Epiphany season is the time of reception; it is the time when the birth of Christ is really manifested, first to the Magi, then to the onlookers at the baptism of Jesus in the Jordan, then to the wedding guests at Cana. People begin to receive the meaning of Christ's coming, to take it in and reflect on its significance. Well, the ecumenical movement also needs to be received in the Church today, to be manifested and appropriated by the whole Church. John Paul II is quite committed to this reception by the whole Church; he notes in *Ut unum sint* that "commitment to ecumenical dialogue . . . is the duty of individual local or particular churches."[59] Dialogue is "an outright necessity," he emphasizes, "one of the Church's priorities."[60] Dialogue continues on many subjects, he explains, but "a new task lies before us: that of receiving the results already achieved."[61] This task includes a serious examination which must involve the entire Church in universal consent.

The reception of ecumenical work is a major focus of the "Directory for the Application of Principles and Norms on Ecumenism," published in 1993 by the Pontifical Council for Promoting Christian Unity. This Directory is a kind of guidebook for pastors and other ministers working in the local church, and it gives us some interesting insights on reception. It is blunt in its exhortations: "No Christian . . . should be satisfied" with the present real but imperfect forms of communion, it says. "They do not correspond to the will of Christ, and weaken his church in the exercise of its mission."[62] The Directory unfolds as a practical guide to remedying this situation.

The Directory understands ecumenism to be inherent in being a Roman Catholic today; it argues that "all the faithful are called upon to make a personal commitment toward promoting increasing communion with other Christians."[63] To enable this, the Directory states that ecumenical formation should be a basic component in all Christian formation, much as moral growth or a spirit of prayer are considered essentials for such formation.

59. John Paul II, *Ut unum sint,* #31.

60. Ibid.

61. Ibid., #80.

62. Pontifical Council for Promoting Christian Unity, "Directory for the Application of Principles and Norms in Ecumenism," [title printed as "1993 Directory for Ecumenism"] *Origins* 23 (1993–94) 129, 131–60; see #19.

63. Ibid., #55.

What are the instruments of ecumenical formation? The Directory thinks that all preaching, catechesis, liturgy, spirituality, and social action should be informed by knowledge of the Scriptures, the history of church divisions, the positions of other churches, and the results of contemporary ecumenical dialogue. Sometimes the Directory is quite specific in its directives. For example, Roman Catholics are to be taught the whole doctrine of the Catholic Church, it says, but, "respecting the hierarchy of truths and avoiding expressions and ways of presenting doctrine which would be an obstacle to dialogue." Catechists are told that when they speak of other churches, "it is important to present their teaching correctly and honestly."[64] And where should this ecumenical formation for all Roman Catholics be occurring? The Directory again casts a wide net in its vision of responsibility for formation, naming parishes, schools, church associations or movements, and families as places where ecumenical formation should occur. So, for example, parishes are told that one of their great tasks is "to educate" parishioners "in the ecumenical spirit," which "calls for care with the content and form of preaching, especially of the homily, and with catechesis."[65] Many Roman Catholic parishes all but ignore ecumenism today. But the Directory sees ecumenism as a central parish responsibility. It is also to be taught in schools, in group movements, and in university settings.

The Directory devotes special attention to the additional ecumenical formation needed by ordination candidates and other pastoral ministers. It believes that a seminarian should be "checking regularly his own language and capacity for dialogue so as to acquire an authentically ecumenical disposition."[66] The Directory is quite insistent on this viewpoint, explaining again, "Ecumenical openness is a constitutive dimension of the formation of future priests and deacons." In the curriculum of theological studies, the Directory wants an ecumenical approach used in all of the theological disciplines, and in addition it calls for a course focused specifically on ecumenism, offered early in the program of theological studies and "compulsory."[67] Lay and ordained religious pastoral workers also need an ecumenical formation parallel to that of ordination candidates, adapted to their level of studies. Finally, the Directory calls for the "continuous aggiornamento" in a "permanent formation" for ordained and nonordained pastoral ministers, even after their formal theological

---

64. Ibid., #61.
65. Ibid., #67.
66. Ibid., #70.
67. Ibid., #79.

studies have ended, because of the "continual evolution within the ecumenical movement."[68] In all of these recommendations for ecumenical formation, the Directory hopes to carry out the reception of the ecumenical movement throughout the whole Church.

In this reflection, I have highlighted four themes important in the recent Roman Catholic approach to ecumenism: purification of memories, the gift exchange, New Millennium's resolutions, and the reception of dialogue by the whole Church. I have used the two recent writings on ecumenism by John Paul II and the Directory for ecumenism to illustrate these themes, as well as examples from several bilateral and multilateral ecumenical dialogues. Together, they give us a good picture of the topic, and show clearly a part of the mission of the Roman Catholic Church in the immediate future. Let me close my reflections with the exhortation John Paul II himself offered in his prayer that the words spoken by East and West might soon be proclaimed in harmony: "May God shorten the time and distance. May Christ, the *Orientale lumen* [Light of the East], soon, very soon, grant us to discover that in fact, despite so many centuries of distance, we were very close, because together, perhaps without knowing it, we were walking toward the one Lord and thus toward one another."[69]

---

68. Ibid., #91.
69. John Paul II, *Orientale lumen,* #28.

3

LISTENING TO FORGOTTEN VOICES: THE FRENCH MINORITY BISHOPS OF VATICAN I AND INFALLIBILITY[1]

Karl Rahner says that the history of theology is a history of forgetting as well as remembering, of neglecting as well as assimilating.[2] Perhaps no group is so thoroughly forgotten, so thoroughly neglected, as the minority at a great council of the Church. Theology usually refers to the minority at a council to show how they were mistaken, one-sided, or even heretical in their views. Rarely is their thought studied for its own sake.

Into such oblivion fell the thought of the French minority bishops of the First Vatican Council, twenty-two bishops from France who opposed the definition of papal infallibility. This happened for at least two reasons. First, minority bishops—those bishops who opposed the definition of papal infallibility at the Council—were criticized or discounted for their opposition. Their dissent was not seen to have positive value in itself. Second, their thought was misunderstood and thus misrepresented. Biographers of minority bishops, embarrassed by minority opposition to papal infallibility, labeled the bishops "inopportunists." Critics of the bishops, such as August Hasler,[3] accused them of cowardice and dishonesty. Both traditions of interpretation represent an ideological presentation of the past.

1. This paper was first presented at a seminar of the Catholic Theological Society of America in June 1989. It was published in a slightly different form from this version in *Theology Digest* 37 (1990) 1–13.

2. Karl Rahner, "Current Problems in Christology," in *Theological Investigations,* trans. Cornelius Ernst (Baltimore: Helicon Press, 1961) 1:151.

3. August B. Hasler, *Pius IX. (1846–1878), Päpstliche Unfehlbarkeit und 1. Vatikanisches Konzil,* 2 vols. (Stuttgart: Anton Hiersemann, 1977).

In *Triumph in Defeat: Infallibility, Vatican I, and the French Minority Bishops,*[4] I seek to bring the French minority bishops out of oblivion and to understand why they opposed the definition of papal infallibility, why they accepted *Pastor aeternus,* and how they understood the doctrine of infallibility.

The French minority bishops were an important group within the Council's minority. With twenty-two members, they constituted the largest single group from one country within the seventy-three members of the Council's minority. Moreover, they worked as a group, holding regular meetings and discussions, developing a coherent unified view on the question of infallibility. Not all members of this group held exactly the same views on all topics. Not every member was equally outspoken. But taken as a whole, their thought forms a coherent pattern of ideas; hence it yields a somewhat fuller and more unified picture of minority arguments than has been obtained just by studying individual bishops or smaller groups. Finally, the French minority bishops' thought was shaped by their national tradition of gallicanism. In the Declaration of 1682, the French clergy had stated that in matters of faith the pope enjoyed the principal role but that his judgment was not irreformable unless it received the consent of the Church. The French minority inherited a moderate version of these views, and the troublesome phrase "and not from the consent of the Church" ["non autem ex consensu Ecclesiae"] was inserted into *Pastor aeternus* to counter the gallicanism suspected of some minority members. Thus the decree seemed to contradict the very theological tradition in which the French minority bishops had been formed. To understand *Pastor aeternus,* therefore, it is important to understand the thought of those it wished to criticize.

The study of the French minority bishops makes a contribution to several important areas of thought. It helps us to improve our understanding of Vatican I and the meaning of its decree on papal infallibility. We can also enrich the historical dossier on Vatican I, which is still incomplete. Further studies of the Council's history invite us to a "new 'reception' of the dogma of *Pastor aeternus,* a 'reception' under new conditions . . . ," notes Yves Congar.[5] Secondly, the study of the French minority bishops can also throw light on the contemporary discussion about the doctrine of infallibility and the whole issue of the exercise of au-

---

4. Margaret O'Gara, *Triumph in Defeat: Infallibility, Vatican I, and the French Minority Bishops* (Washington, D.C.: The Catholic University of America Press, 1988).

5. Yves Congar, "Bulletin d'ecclésiologie," *Revue des sciences philosophiques et théologiques* 60 (1976) 288.

thority in the Church, a discussion that is very important both for Roman Catholic theology and for the ecumenical dialogue among Christian communions. Finally, the study of the French minority bishops will help improve our understanding of the part dissent and disagreement play in the development of doctrine and in theological development.

THE COMMON CAUSE

Who were the French minority bishops? Most of the twenty-two from France who opposed the definition of papal infallibility throughout the Council had been given their seminary training in France, many attending Sulpician seminaries. They studied at a time when moderate gallicanism was a respectable theological opinion. In 1845 in his course on the Church at Saint-Sulpice in Paris, M. Philipin de Rivière pointed out the strengths and weaknesses of both the gallican and ultramontanist positions on papal infallibility.[6] He felt the question could be freely debated; he himself declined to take a position. This theological atmosphere shifted in 1852 when Pius IX placed the manual by Louis Bailly, widely used in France, on the Index; and in 1853 the encyclical *Inter multiplices* changed seminary training in France. But by then the twenty-two French minority bishops had completed their seminary studies. Now a manual used by many of them had been condemned, and rumor had it that a once theologically disputed question was being prepared for resolution by definition as a dogma of the faith.

These bishops went to the Council linked together in a network of relationships, many as friends, others as close colleagues, a good number as both. Some of the bishops could be classified as liberals, others as moderate gallicans; some were independent of both groups. But despite their many differences, the French minority bishops were bound together by a common cause: their fear that the Council would define the separate, personal, absolute infallibility of the pope. They formed their opposition to the definition of papal infallibility in an atmosphere of exaggerated personal devotion to the pope and alarming rumors about the Council's purpose. In this atmosphere, they came to believe that the Council was proposing for definition the separate, personal, absolute infallibility of the pope. Proceeding on this understanding, they argued against the proposed schema throughout the Council. While they did not wish to vote against *Pastor aeternus* in the presence of the pope, they were unable to vote in its favor, and so they left the Council without voting at all in the

6. O'Gara, *Triumph In Defeat*, 19–20.

final session of 18 July 1870. For the twenty-two minority bishops from France, the Council imposed a burden of "moral suffering," wrote Charles Colet, bishop of Luçon; but many could have echoed the words of Jean Bravard, bishop of Coutances and Avranches: "My conscience was stronger than my grief."[7]

With their gallican heritage, the French minority bishops emphasized the authority of the bishop as judge and the collegial nature of the episcopate judging in council. They were convinced that councils could speak infallibly, but they valued the tradition of unanimity at councils, and emphasized the need for careful study and discussion among the bishops before a judgment was made. They seemed to place a great emphasis on the corporate character of the Church and the communal nature of decision-making.

CASES AGAINST THE DEFINITION OF PAPAL INFALLIBILITY

Why did the French minority bishops oppose the definition of papal infallibility? The answer can be found in the cases the minority built against the proposed definition. Three questions synthesize the general concerns to which the French minority's many arguments responded: (1) Is the proposed teaching true? If yes, (2) Is the proposed teaching definable? If yes, (3) Should the proposed teaching be defined? These three questions can be used to illumine the structure or systematic framework which, though often implicit, stands behind the minority's arguments and shapes them into a coherent system of thought. Council members who answered each of these three questions affirmatively for the proposed teaching at Vatican I thereby placed themselves in the group supporting the proposed schema at that time, and made up the majority of the Council. On the other hand, opponents of the proposed teaching's definition answered *no* to at least one of these questions if posed explicitly. A *no* to the third question reveals only a mild opposition; a *no* to the second and third questions shows a stronger opposition; and a *no* to all three questions evidences the strongest opposition. We can begin to understand the three cases made by the French minority against the proposed schema, each with a number of arguments, when we understand them as answers to these three questions.

The French minority bishops, then, made three cases against the proposed definition of papal infallibility: a case against its timeliness, a case against its definability, and a case against its truth.

7. Jean Bravard, quoted in "Nouvelles et faits religieux du diocèse," *Revue catholique (Semaine religieuse) du diocèse de Coutances et Avranches* 3 (14 April 1870) 454.

In their first case, the French minority bishops argued that a definition of papal infallibility was not timely and that therefore papal infallibility should not be defined. A definition of papal infallibility would not serve the good of the Church, they argued; it would damage the unity of the Church and hence would produce a great wound in the Church. The French minority believed that definitions should be made only when they were necessary, and that freedom to hold a variety of theological opinions should be maintained where definition was not necessary. Hence, they argued, a definition is untimely because it is unnecessary: "why would . . . [the definition] of infallibility be timely now," asked Guillaume Meignan, bishop of Châlons, "when faithful, priests, and bishops all obey with so great unanimity the orders, even the desires of the sovereign pontiff?"[8] Definitions should be made only when a teaching is held as the clear consensus of the churches, they argued. In addition, they feared that a definition would hurt the chance for the reunion of the Roman Catholic Church with other churches. Speaking of his concerns for unity with Protestants, Anglicans, and Orthodox, Félix Dupanloup, bishop of Orléans, commented ironically, "A ditch separates us; we are going to turn it into an abyss." In an imaginary dialogue with an Orthodox Christian, he continued,

> Until now you have refused to recognize the simple primacy of jurisdiction of the Roman pontiff; we are going to oblige you, to begin with, to believe something entirely different, to accept something that until now Catholic doctors themselves have not acknowledged: we are going to erect into dogma a much more obscure doctrine—as far as you are concerned—in both Scripture and tradition, than the very dogma not yet believed in by you, namely, the personal infallibility of the pope, alone, "INDEPENDENTLY AND SEPARATELY FROM THE BISHOPS." It is under those conditions that we are proposing an understanding between us.[9]

The French minority bishops thought a definition of papal infallibility would be out of touch with the times. It was untimely because it ignored the modern spirit, argued François Rivet, bishop of Dijon.[10] In modern

---

8. Henri Boissonnot, *Le Cardinal Meignan* (Paris: Victor Lecoffre, 1899) 298–99.

9. Félix Dupanloup, *Observations sur la controverse soulevée relativement à la définition de l'infaillibilité au prochain concile* (Paris: Charles Douniol, 1869) 16. The phrase "INDEPENDENTLY AND SEPARATELY FROM THE BISHOPS" is quoted from Henry Edward Manning, archbishop of Westminster.

10. Joannes Dominicus Mansi, *Sacrorum conciliorum nova et amplissima collectio* (Graz: Akademische Druck u. Verlagsanstalt, 1961) 52:53C-D.

times, people resist legitimate authority and want some part in determining their own government, he pointed out. Georges Darboy, archbishop of Paris, also feared that a definition would be contrary to the modern spirit. On all those who would throw off as burdens the customs of the past, he argued, the definition would impose "a new and therefore heavy burden."[11] Those weak in faith would be overwhelmed, not healed; the definition will not heal a world that is sick, sick not from ignorance of truth but from flight from truth, he warned.

Some believe that, since the principle of authority is not respected in modern civil society, its exaltation in the Church will save the world, observed Dupanloup. But, he added, "To believe that by proclaiming the infallibility of the pope you are going to turn back the revolution is, in my opinion, one of those illusions despairing people sometimes hold, in human societies, on the eve of deadly crises."[12]

The French minority bishops also argued that a definition of papal infallibility was untimely because it might arouse hostility from civil governments and could lead to misunderstanding about Catholic teaching. Henri Maret, titular bishop of Sura and a professor of dogmatic theology at the Sorbonne, was convinced that most Roman Catholics would misunderstand the limits of papal infallibility: "This man [the pope] would become for the faithful a sort of *God-man*," he warned Council members. "Consequently could his *absolute* infallibility be kept within the bounds of matters of faith? By a very natural inclination would not Catholics tend to extend it to everything, at least to all moral, social concerns and, therefore, every political matter closely associated with them?"[13] But Jean Sola, bishop of Nice, told a German official cynically that such misunderstanding was precisely what proponents of the definition wanted as a support to the pope's authority: "They want the infallibility of the pope only to be able to add strength to the necessity of the temporal power."[14]

---

11. Mansi, *Sacrorum conciliorum nova et amplissima collectio,* col. 161B.

12. Dupanloup to Victor Dechamps, archbishop of Malines, 1 March 1870, *Collectio Lacensis: Acta et decreta sacrorum conciliorum recentiorum* (Freiburg im Breisgau: Herder, 1890) 7:1327D-1330B.

13. Henri Maret, *Mémoire* (25 March 1867), quoted in Jean-Rémy Palanque, *Catholiques libéraux et gallicans en France: Face au concile du Vatican, 1867–1870* (Aix-en-Provence: Éditions Ophrys, 1962) 67, n. 30; Henri Maret, *Du concile général et de la paix religieuse* (Paris: Henri Plon, 1869) 2:385-86.

14. Palanque, *Catholiques libéraux et gallicans en France: Face au concile du Vatican, 1867–1870,* 154, n. 84.

Dupanloup commented extensively on the dangers of misunderstanding to which a definition of papal infallibility would be subject. He was especially concerned about popular misunderstanding. What if a pope made an error in teaching when he was not speaking *ex cathedra?* "Doubtless here theologians will be able to distinguish the nuances and the fine points and to show that this is not exactly a definition," wrote Dupanloup, "but how will the multitude of those who are not theologians discern that the pope who is fallible even as pope in such and such an act is no longer fallible in this or that other act? How will they understand that he can be infallible and yet, by great pontifical acts [that are not *ex cathedra*], *foment heresy?* In the eyes of the public that will still be infallibility."[15]

In this first case against the definition of papal infallibility, the French minority bishops advanced a number of serious arguments to show that the proposed schema was untimely. While these arguments on the inopportuneness of the definition have sometimes been treated lightly, an examination of their content finds them substantive and pastorally sensitive.

The French minority bishops made a second case against the proposed schema, arguing that papal infallibility as proposed could not be defined. This case against the definability of the teaching again rested on a number of arguments.

A *de fide* definition cannot be made if it is not necessary, some argued, or if it is not clear and certain to the whole Church. Since the Church had succeeded in condemning heresy successfully for years without this teaching being defined, some argued, its definition certainly was not necessary. Furthermore, the teaching of papal infallibility was a theological opinion held by one theological school but disputed by others, they argued. In fact, in light of tradition, this teaching appeared as an innovation to some. "It is necessary to prove the devised and refined formula of the definition by arguments that are solid and exclude all doubt," argued Darboy.[16] But to meet this requirement, Darboy felt that a teaching must be clearly contained in the Scriptures and in the history of theology; it must be in accord with councils and pontifical acts, and held by all believers always, everywhere. But, Darboy concluded, the proposed schema does not meet these requirements.

French minority bishops gave many scriptural and historical examples that raised difficulties for them regarding the definability of the teaching on papal infallibility. They also criticized the formulation of the actual

---

15. Dupanloup, *Observations sur la controverse soulevée relativement à la définition de l'infaillibilité au prochain concile*, 41.

16. Mansi, *Sacrorum conciliorum nova et amplissima collectio*, col. 159A-B.

schema proposed, arguing that it was unclear and vague, or flawed. It speaks of the primacy but omits a discussion of the nature of the Church and its qualities, of the apostles and their primacy, of apostolic succession, and of the role of the bishops in governing and ruling the Church,[17] complained Jacques Ginoulhiac, bishop of Grenoble (who was made archbishop of Lyon during the Council). Dupanloup thought that a definition would have to decide among conflicting views of the theological schools about the conditions of infallibility, about what constitutes an exercise of infallibility, about when a particular pope was speaking as a private doctor and when as pope, about particular teachings by heretical popes. How would these conflicts be clarified, he wondered?[18] Others objected that the formulation of the proposed schema was unclear, or that it used scriptural and historical quotations out of their context or in support of false claims.

They complained, too, about irregularities in the Council's procedure. The poor acoustics and heat in the meeting hall made discussion so difficult that some feared the Council's validity was undermined. The great majority of Council participants, reported Colet at one point, could not hear the discussion. This seems to have been the experience of Paul Dupont des Loges, bishop of Metz, who read and reread the acts of the Council of Trent in the early days of the Vatican conciliar sessions, before acoustical repairs were made, because he could not hear the discussions.[19] More seriously, arbitrary decisions about the Council procedures kept minority viewpoints virtually unrepresented on the drafting deputation, and allowed closure of discussion and majority voting to settle a matter that French minority bishops felt could be defined only by virtual unanimity.

The emphasis on the need for consensus is at the heart of this second case against the proposed schema. Again and again, the French minority bishops repeat it: to define a dogma of the faith, the views of all the churches must be considered and a consensus must be reached. They linked this requirement with the authority of the bishop as judge in council: not only Peter but all of the apostles were responsible for guarding the deposit of faith, Ginoulhiac pointed out. The bishop represents his church, taught some. Others believed that a teaching could be infallibly defined only when the bishops together hold it. At the heart of this second

17. Mansi, *Sacrorum conciliorum nova et amplissima collectio*, col. 215B.

18. Dupanloup, *Observations sur la controverse soulevée relativement à la définition de l'infaillibilité au prochain concile*, 31–33.

19. Félix Klein, *L'évêque de Metz, vie de Mgr Dupont des Loges, 1804–1886* (Paris: Charles Poussielgue, 1899) 241.

case against the proposed schema we find an increasing emphasis on the ecclesial character of infallibility.

Some French minority bishops made a third case against the definition. They argued that papal infallibility as it was proposed in the conciliar schema was not true.

To some of the French minority bishops, the teaching on papal infallibility seemed in disagreement with the Church's tradition. Étienne Ramadié, bishop of Perpignan, maintained that Church tradition is silent on or even argues against the teaching on papal infallibility.[20] Infallibility of the pope is the most probable opinion, observed Guillaume Meignan, bishop of Châlons, but it was not a part of the ancient and universal faith.[21] And the medieval Church did not consider papal infallibility a *de fide* teaching. Citing numerous scriptural and historical quotations, Maret argues that the tradition teaches clearly that infallibility is found only in the accord of pope and bishops.[22] The common consent of the bishops is the absolute rule of faith in council, and even if a council cannot be called, wrote Maret. Many argued that to define papal infallibility as a dogma of the faith would be to make the opinion of one theological school into an article of faith. Colet reflected upon the French minority's view of the proposed schema when he later wrote: "In the presence of a definition demanded by one school, and of which the purpose was to establish, as an article of faith, a doctrine formulated in terms which gave it, in the eyes of a great number, the character of an innovation, it was almost impossible that the passions of the polemics not give rise, on both sides, to deplorable excesses."[23]

The French minority bishops also argued that the proposed schema was not true because, they claimed, it undermined the authority of the bishops and thereby changed the divinely established constitution of the Church. The bishops would become "echoes" instead of judges, wrote Dupanloup. "Now since what has always been a matter of faith," wrote Colet, "is that the sacred magisterium of the Church, made up of the pope and the bishops, assembled or dispersed, cannot err in matters of faith and morals and that the pope speaking in the name of the Church teaches the truth infallibly, it does not seem to me that one can logically conclude

---

20. Mansi, *Sacrorum conciliorum nova et amplissima collectio,* 52:1016D-1017B.

21. Guillaume-René Meignan, Written Remarks on the Schema, quoted in Boissonnot, *Le Cardinal Meignan,* 299.

22. Maret, *Du concile général et de la paix religieuse,* 1:129-540.

23. Charles Colet, "Souvenirs du concile du Vatican," 4 AI, 2, 2⁰, fol. Q, Archives de l'Archevêché de Paris.

that the pope is personally and separately infallible. On the contrary," he continued, "this doctrine seems a complete reversal of the preceding one."[24] Others emphasized that infallibility is found only in the accord of pope and bishops. Assistance in teaching and consequent preservation from error are promised to the body of the apostles as a group in Matthew 28:18-20, argued Rivet. Augustin David, bishop of Saint-Brieuc, was convinced that gallicanism remained a free theological opinion and, indeed, the older one. "The power of the supreme pontiff has its limits," he observed; to assert otherwise would be idolatrous. The great majority of believers throughout history held that "the infallible magisterium of the Church consists in this, namely, the supreme pontiff, the vicar of Christ, and all the bishops who adhere to him."[25] He urged Council members not to condemn this widely held viewpoint. And Maret wrote that infallibility is found in an absolutely certain fashion "only in the agreement and the concerted action of the pope with the bishops, the bishops with the pope. . . ."[26] Ginoulhiac reflected the deep concern about the role of the bishops that the French minority shared when he wrote to a correspondent, "Of course, one wouldn't dare go so far as to say that the pope is *everything*, that he is the *only* power in the Church, and that the agreement of the episcopate with the judgments of the Holy See is unimportant; but of necessity and in fact one would finally end up there. What kind of teaching body could teach only what only one doctor dictates? How would the bishops in council be judges of the faith, with a deliberative voice, when the voice, the vote of one individual suffices for everything?"[27]

Finally, some French minority bishops stressed that, when the pope taught infallibly, he acted in accord not only with the bishops, but also with the entire Church. The pope is infallible insofar as he is head and center of the Church's magisterium, taught Colet. Others emphasized the importance of the consensus of the churches in coming to a definition of the faith. A few even brought out the representative nature of the bishops, who witness to the faith of their churches. "It is the role of the bishops also to give witness to the vicar of Christ about their teaching,

24. Colet, "Souvenirs du concile du Vatican," fol. N, Archives de l'Archevêché de Paris.

25. Mansi, *Sacrorum conciliorum nova et amplissima collectio,* cols. 592C, 988B-C, 989D.

26. Maret, *Du concile général et de la paix religieuse,* 1:xx–xxi.

27. Jacques Ginoulhiac to unnamed correspondent, 23 April 1867, quoted in Fernand Mourret, *Le concile du Vatican d'après des documents inédits* (Paris: Bloud et Gay, 1919) 40.

just as about the faith of their sheep," Colet pointed out.[28] Both bishops and pope are bound by the faith of the whole Church, he noted. Ginoulhiac pointed to the corporate character of the witness provided by the bishops. He complained that the "unity of the episcopate" was being neglected, and admonished his hearers, "For not [just] one of the bishops but all the bishops have the right and duty to preserve the deposit of faith." Ginoulhaic also emphasized the importance of reception by the whole Church. A council is ecumenical, he wrote, only "insofar as it is recognized and accepted as ecumenical by the Church: not that this recognition communicates to the Council an authority that it would not have of itself; but the recognition declares and manifests the authority."[29] He distinguished between councils that are ecumenical in themselves, through adequate representation of the whole Church, and those that become ecumenical through their subsequent recognition by the whole Church. "So, in certain cases," he wrote, "the subsequent acceptance or approbation of the universal Church is an essential condition of the ecumenicity of a council, in other cases, it is only the seal."[30] And he noted that the definition of the Immaculate Conception was not made without request for it, the unanimous agreement of all of the bishops, the desires of the faithful, and agreement with the Church's tradition.

In this last case against the definition, some French minority bishops argued that papal infallibility as it was proposed in the schema was false. At the core of their arguments stands their conviction that infallibility has an ecclesial character. It was given first to the Church as a whole, and only expressions of the faith of the whole Church can be judged to be exercises of infallibility. The French minority bishops were not opposed to every concept of papal infallibility. Some envisioned that the pope could speak infallibly when he spoke in accord with the bishops, with Scripture and tradition, with the whole Church. But they did not find this nuanced view in the proposed schema. At the heart of their opposition stands their conviction that the exercise of infallibility in teaching must express the consensus of the churches, each local church with a bishop to witness and judge in union with the other bishops, together preserving the apostolic faith. They did not find their view in the schema. But their nuanced view of papal infallibility laid the foundation for their subsequent assent to *Pastor aeternus,* when they were able to satisfy themselves that the decree did not fundamentally contradict their earlier understanding of papal infallibility.

---

28. Mansi, *Sacrorum conciliorum nova et amplissima collectio,* col. 985A-B.
29. Ginoulhiac, *Le concile oecuménique* (Paris: C. Douniol, 1869) 64.
30. Ginoulhiac, *Le concile oecuménique,* 64.

"My friend, I bless God for calling me to himself before the definition," murmured Jean Devoucoux, bishop of Evreux, as he lay on his deathbed attended by Bravard in the spring of 1870 after months of opposing the definition at the Council.[31] But Bravard and his fellow bishops in the minority found themselves facing the very situation that Devoucoux had been glad to avoid: after all of their arguments against it, the Council had nevertheless passed a definition of papal infallibility. What should they do?

CASES FOR THE RECEPTION OF *PASTOR AETERNUS*

The French minority bishops all accepted *Pastor aeternus*. They made two cases in its favor. As with their cases against the proposed schema, so with their cases in favor of *Pastor aeternus*, a systematic framework can be discerned behind the thought of their arguments. Again the concerns that shape this systematic framework can be expressed by the responses to a set of questions: (1) Does the formal authority of *Pastor aeternus* require its reception? (2) Does the material authority of *Pastor aeternus* require its reception? Every French minority bishop found that he was able to answer *yes* to at least one of these questions.

After the decree on papal infallibility had been passed at the Council, with the vote of 533–2, the French minority bishops felt obligated to accept it. Although seventy bishops had left the council session early due to disagreement with the schema, the French minority bishops found the majority vote decisive enough that they accepted the formal authority of the decree. Many had pledged themselves to accept the Council's decisions before they left their dioceses; now they began to keep this pledge.

Many spoke of their obedience, as when David wrote, "As I am, in my diocese, the first in rank, so I wish also to be the first in obedience."[32] And Rivet wrote to his clergy, "Now, our very dear brothers, on this much disputed question on the infallibility of the Roman pontiff in the exercise of his supreme magisterium, the Church, gathered in the Vatican ecumenical Council, has made a pronouncement in such a way that doubt is no longer possible in this matter and that the minds most opposed to it have

31. Bravard reports Devoucoux's deathbed words in a speech quoted in *Revue catholique (Semaine religieuse) du diocèse de Coutances et Avranches* 3 (9 June 1870) 588–89. Devoucoux met with the French minority as an active minority participant during the Council until his health forced him to leave Rome in the spring of 1870; he died in his diocese on 2 May 1870.

32. Augustin David to Pius IX, 25 October 1870, quoted in Palanque, *Catholiques libéraux et gallicans en France: Face au concile du Vatican, 1867–1870,* 178.

only to bow their heads and to submit."[33] Although moderate gallican convictions had been a cause for their opposition to a definition, the French minority bishops now felt obligated by those same moderate gallican convictions to accept the decree of the Council. Even though seventy minority bishops had absented themselves from the final vote, most of the French minority bishops believed that the witness of the 533 bishops who had voted *placet* constituted a sufficient authority to make the Council's decisions binding upon them.

Some distinguished between their obligations during a council and after its close. Jean Callot, bishop of Oran, wrote, "The often painful duty of discussing and of judging has given place to the easier and the sweeter duty of accepting and submitting."[34] Ginoulhiac, though, used the distinction in another way in a conversation shortly before the final vote on the schema. "We [bishops] are judges of the faith and Christians," he explained. "If we cannot subscribe to the definition as judges, we will submit as Christians when the Holy Father has approved the constitution. But naturally those who will be forced to say *non placet* at the public session will lack vigor in defending, as Christians, a definition whose terms they could not approve as judges."[35]

Did the French minority bishops have inner hesitations about the ecumenicity of the First Vatican Council that they did not express? These comments of a correspondent about Charles Place, bishop of Marseille, suggest that Place at least had more questions than he expressed:

> Until now he does not admit that the Vatican meeting is a council nor that the dogma is a dogma, but he does not wish, either, to say the contrary because, he says, the value of unity is so great that it demands many sacrifices; he thinks that the future alone will reveal God's judgments; if, a hundred years from now, when all the passions have died down, the Church recognizes the Vatican Council and teaches the dogma, it is because both are matters of faith; if, on the contrary, the opposite happens, it will be God who will take upon himself to make known the truth.[36]

33. François Rivet, "Lettre circulaire au clergé (22 August 1870)," quoted in Gustave Chevallier, *Mgr Rivet, évêque de Dijon* (Dijon: L'Union Typographique, 1902) 189–90.

34. Mansi, *Sacrorum conciliorum nova et amplissima collectio,* 53:1045C.

35. Ginoulhiac, quoted in "Copie des procès-verbaux rédigés par Mgr Colet des séances tenues par les évêques de la minorité," 4 AI, 2, 3⁰, fol. 70, Archives de l'Archevêché de Paris.

36. Madam Marie de Forbin d'Oppède to Lady Charlotte Blennerhassett 26 December 1870, quoted in August Hasler, *Pius IX. (1846–1878), Päpstliche*

But most French minority bishops concluded simply that the teaching merited their acceptance. Félix de Las Cases, bishop of the French colony of Constantine in Africa, emphasizes in his last testament that he and the other minority bishops really opposed the proposed schema. He hopes this opposition will not be forgotten: first, because "one was in danger of not being absolutely historically exact," he wrote, and secondly, because ". . . one was adding nothing to that incomparable triumph of the Catholic faith after the Vatican Council, which the minority bishops left, without exception, docilely submissive to the definition, after having loyally, courageously, respectfully opposed it as long as it had not become an article of faith, as long as their conscience urged them on to the duty of defending what they believed to be the true doctrine of the Church."[37]

Some French minority bishops made a case for the material authority of *Pastor aeternus*. Gradually, guardedly, with careful explanations, they came to agree that the content of *Pastor aeternus* could be interpreted in a way acceptable to their understanding. "The minority has triumphed in its defeat," wrote Maret after the Council,[38] because he came to believe that minority bishops had managed to prevent the Council from defining the separate, personal, absolute infallibility of the pope. "God did not allow it," he wrote in personal notes to himself.[39]

Arguments for the material authority of *Pastor aeternus* by the French minority bishops were guarded. Rather than finding *Pastor aeternus* compelling, they found it acceptable when interpreted in certain ways. They struggled to find such interpretations, and for the most part their struggle was given impetus by their *a priori* assumption of the decree's formal authority.

Several French minority bishops argued for the material authority of *Pastor aeternus* by finding an interpretation that was acceptable to them. Rather than adopting the somewhat ultramontanist interpretation, which would come to dominate the manuals, these bishops adopted instead an

---

Unfehlbarkeit und 1. Vatikanisches Konzil (Stuttgart: Anton Hiersemann, 1977) 2:473, n. 31.

37. Mansi, *Sacrorum conciliorum nova et amplissima collectio*, 53:1042C-1043A.

38. Maret, in personal notes written to himself, cited by Georges Bazin, *Vie de Mgr Maret, évêque de Sura, archevêque de Lépante, primicier de l'insigne chapitre de Saint-Denys, doyen et professeur de la Faculté de Theologie en Sorbonne* (Paris: Berche et Tralin, 1891) 3:218.

39. Maret, cited by Bazin, *Vie de Mgr Maret, évêque de Sura, archevêque de Lépante, primicier de l'insigne chapitre de Saint-Denys, doyen et professeur de la Faculté de Théologie en Sorbonne*, 3:218.

understanding of *Pastor aeternus* that gave strict attention to the wording of the decree and that located papal infallibility within the context of ecclesial infallibility. They were aided in their efforts by the moderate interpretations of the German bishops, the Swiss bishops, and Joseph Fessler, Council secretary. Aimé Guilbert, bishop of Gap, cited the Swiss bishops' pastoral letter to show the limits of papal infallibility, noting that the pope "is infallible only and exclusively when, in his role as supreme teacher, he makes, with regard to faith and morals, a decision which must be accepted and considered obligatory by all the faithful. His infallibility is then that of the teaching Church itself. His infallibility has no other scope and is essentially identical to that of the teaching Church: for the pope is never nor cannot ever be separated from the episcopate, no more than the head can be separated from the members of a living body."[40] The pope teaches infallibly only when he teaches as head of the Church, said Meignan in his diocese after the Council. He does not create new doctrines. Dupanloup located papal infallibility within the context of ecclesial infallibility, and he emphasized that its purpose is to serve the unity of the episcopate and hence of the Church.

Some French minority bishops also argued that *Pastor aeternus* had, after all, not defined the separate, personal, absolute infallibility of the pope, and hence that their opposition had borne some fruit. Léon Thomas, bishop of La Rochelle, believed that the decree had succeeded in breaking through the debates of the schools. Darboy told one man, "I wasn't opposed to it as a theologian, for it is not false, but as a man, because it is inept."[41] French minority bishops emphasized that *Pastor aeternus* had simply clarified the truth, it had not added a new doctrine to the faith. Maret even came to believe that *Pastor aeternus* clarified an essential condition of papal infallibility: "the assistance and the preceding or concomitant assent of the episcopate" are clarified in the decree, he wrote, "not as the cause but as a condition of pontifical infallibility."[42] In another place he wrote, "The consent of the Church which seems to be left out here can be only the subsequent consent, which is not necessary, when there is a

---

40. Aimé Guilbert, *La divine synthèse ou l'exposé au double point de vue apologétique et pratique de la religion révélée*, 2d ed. (Gap: J. C. Richaud, 1875) 2:274.

41. Georges Darboy, archbishop of Paris, quoted by Hyacinthe Loyson in Palanque, *Catholiques libéraux et gallicans en France: Face au concile du Vatican, 1867–1870*, 182.

42. Maret in personal notes to himself, quoted in Bazin, *Vie de Mgr Maret, évêque de Sura, archevêque de Lépante, primicier de l'insigne chapitre de Saint-Denys, doyen et professeur de la Faculté de Théologie en Sorbonne*, 3:219.

preceding and concomitant consent."[43] With this understanding of it, Maret felt that he could give his adherence to *Pastor aeternus* in good conscience. "One can conscientiously and sincerely accept the decree of 18 July, if this does not include the doctrine of *absolute, separate, personal* pontifical infallibility," he had written.[44] He came to conclude that the decree had excluded this absolute, separate, personal infallibility of the pope and so it could be accepted with this understanding.

With their way of understanding *Pastor aeternus*, the French minority bishops found convincing arguments for the material authority of the decree. They were able to find interpretations acceptable to their own thinking and thus they were able gradually to justify to themselves the adherence to a decision they had vigorously opposed. In these interpretations, they were not simply fooling themselves. The decree passed on 18 July 1870, notes Roger Aubert, was "decidedly more nuanced than the primitive text and gave fundamental satisfaction to the legitimate demands of the great majority of the bishops."[45] This was the minority's "triumph in defeat."

Maret's conviction that the minority bishops had triumphed in defeat has a deeper meaning today, in light of Congar's call for a new reception of Vatican I's teaching on papal infallibility. Over one hundred years have passed since the Council met, and Roman Catholics are interpreting it with new eyes. The French minority bishops can provide us with a valuable interpretive perspective. Of course, their authentic interpretation "implies a further broadening of the spectrum of acceptable interpretations of infallibility," John T. Ford points out.[46] But beyond that, their insight about the ecclesial character of infallibility can provide us with an important lens through which to reinterpret the teaching itself. Today, the interpretive work of the French minority seems not only legitimate but prophetic.

What can these bishops teach us today? Basically, the French minority saw that infallibility has an ecclesial character. They saw that discernment of the truth takes part in community, and hence they were uneasy with

43. Maret, Personal Notes, quoted in Hasler, *Pius IX. (1846–1878), Päpstliche Unfehlbarkeit und 1. Vatikanisches Konzil*, 2:479, n. 30.

44. Maret, in personal notes written to himself, quoted in Bazin, *Vie de Mgr Maret, évêque de Sura, archevêque de Lépante, primicier de l'insigne chapitre de Saint-Denys, doyen et professeur de la Faculté de Théologie en Sorbonne*, 3:218.

45. Roger Aubert, "Documents concernant le tiers parti au concile du Vatican," in *Abhandlungen über Theologie und Kirche*, Festschrift für Karl Adam (Düsseldorf: Patmos-Verlag, 1952) 255.

46. John T. Ford, "Infallibility: A Review of Recent Studies," *Theological Studies* 40 (1979) 298.

any accounts of papal infallibility that seemed to take the pope out of the Church or to isolate his judgment from that of the bishops. This basic emphasis on the ecclesial character of infallibility led the French minority to three conclusions: that infallibility's purpose is the good of the Church, that the Church is the subject of infallibility, and that evidence provides the basis on which to judge whether infallibility has been exercised.

If infallibility's purpose is the good of the Church, the French minority bishops thought that its proclamation should be good news. Presentations of infallibility that furthered divisions among Christians, or that deepened the growing isolation of the Church from modern insights, did not seem to them to be serving the Church's good. They foresaw as well many of the misunderstandings that have accompanied the teaching on papal infallibility, and they foresaw also that such misunderstandings would lead to an expansion of the exercise of papal primacy in ways unhealthy for the Church. These are problems in theory and practice that still face the Roman Catholic Church today. The French minority impress us now in the accuracy with which they read the signs of the times.

Because the French minority thought of the Church as the subject of infallibility, they were motivated to take very seriously the witness of the whole Church in Scripture and the tradition's history. Although their method of interpretation tended to be static in style, their commitment to a consideration of all of the evidence ensured that less from the Church's past would be lost from memory. Because they believed that each bishop should be a judge, not an echo, they also retained a strong emphasis on the collegial way that infallibility should be exercised. Many pointed out that a bishop testified to the faith of his local church, and that the assistance of the Holy Spirit for the discernment of the faith was given to the successors of the apostles as a group. Behind these emphases lay an ecclesiology of communion that is instructive for us today. Vatican II recovered an ecclesiology of communion, but its full implications still need to be developed and implemented within the Roman Catholic Church and in ecumenical dialogue among the churches.

The French minority believed that evidence provides a basis on which to judge whether infallibility has been exercised. Consensus of the churches, or reception by the whole Church, or moral unanimity of the bishops after free and lengthy discussion: these were signs that indicated to them an exercise of infallibility. They emphasized that knowledge, even divinely assisted knowledge, had to include the step of judgment as to whether or not a teaching was in fact an exercise of infallibility. Behind these insights, I think, lay a discursive epistemology that recognized—if dimly—that human knowing, even the knowing of what is part of the deposit of faith, involves a judgment of the human mind that grasps the evidence as sufficient. This cognitional understanding is closely tied to their emphasis on infallibility's ecclesial character. Because they took knowing to include judgment, they maintained the possibility of error in judgment. They saw that even popes had made such errors, and they concluded that God's assistance to the Church made use of the human mind in a self-correcting communal setting, where one's error in judgment could be corrected by another's true insight. They did not think human knowing was like a vision—it was not inspiration, but rather the result of laborious effort. It was this knowing that God assisted as God had promised, not by eliminating it and replacing it with a vision but rather by being present to the human minds of a self-correcting community, where one's error in judgment could be corrected by another's true insight, and only the common teaching of a doctrine by the whole Church was adequate evidence that the Church was speaking by the Holy Spirit in an exercise of infallibility. The French minority bishops remind us of the importance of an accurate epistemology, one that avoids intuitive cognitional theories, as a foundation for the work of transposing the concept of infallibility from a "classicist" form into "historical-mindedness."[47]

The French minority bishops illustrate the complexity of the definition of papal infallibility. Hasler failed to understand the minority because he thought the definition had a clear, univocal meaning. But this definition, like all conciliar definitions, was not that simple. Listening to minority voices helps us to see the range of legitimate interpretations that *Pastor aeternus* received, and to understand more fully the way in which interpretation of any conciliar teaching is a part of its reception by the Church. In fact, many of the French minority's interpretations today seem to point us forward in the modern task of reinterpreting the meaning of infallibility. Perhaps this illustrates quite simply the central conviction of the French minority bishops: it is to the whole Church that God's assistance has been promised. Theologians whose views are ignored or rejected during their lives might yet be shown to have contributed to the Church's teaching of the truth. The breadth of the Church extends backward and forward through time, and outward to include even those whom we call "minorities." The French minority bishops would be glad that we remember this breadth.

---

47. See Bernard Lonergan, "The Transition from a Classicist World-View to Historical-Mindedness," in *A Second Collection: Papers by Bernard J. F. Lonergan, S.J.* (London: Darton, Longman & Todd, 1974) 1–9.

4

RECONCEPTUALIZING INFALLIBILITY IN ECUMENICAL DIALOGUE: EPISTEMOLOGY, ECCLESIOLOGY, AND THE ISSUE OF RECEPTION[1]

I suppose that I began my preparation for this Jesuit congress last December after a Rome meeting of an international bilateral dialogue. There I made a short pilgrimage through the rain to visit for the first time the Gesu Church and the tomb of Ignatius Loyola. While kneeling before his tomb, with its impressive gold and silver decoration and statue of Ignatius, I noticed the group of statues to the right of the tomb. Looking more closely, I saw that they depict the figures of True Religion Overcoming Heresy, with Heresy presented as the Protestant Reformation. When I compared the attitude of these statues to the reality many centuries later of the attitude of this International Congress of Jesuit Ecumenists, I recognized a shift in approach!

I share with you a commitment to this shift in approach, which I have learned with Vatican II to call conversion or a change in heart. "There can be no ecumenism worthy of the name without a change of heart," I learned from the Decree on Ecumenism, *Unitatis redintegratio*.[2] But Vatican II was convinced that a change of heart would lead to a deepened understanding of other traditions and of our own tradition as well, an essential component in our work toward the full unity of the Church of Christ. It taught that study, prayer, common witness, and

---

1. This talk was first presented in a slightly different form as a lecture to the International Congress of Jesuit Ecumenists, meeting at Boston College in July 1994.

2. Vatican II, *Unitatis redintegratio,* in *The Documents of Vatican II,* ed. Walter M. Abbott (New York: America Press, 1966) #7.

dialogue together with Christians of other traditions conducted "on an equal footing"[3] were the means by which such a deepened understanding would be fostered. The new ecumenical Directory repeats this conviction, urging ecumenical formation for all Roman Catholics and a "continuous aggiornamento of the ordained ministers and pastoral workers, in view of the continual evolution within the ecumenical movement."[4]

I was asked to give an overview on some aspect of the future direction in ecumenical discussion. In this presentation I want to focus on the deepened understanding of infallibility that is emerging through ecumenical dialogue and the place that the idea of reception holds within this deepened understanding. I believe that Roman Catholics are reconceptualizing the issue of infallibility, equipped for this reconceptualizing by internal shifts within Roman Catholic theology itself and impelled to such reconceptualizing by dialogue with our ecumenical partners. In my first section I will focus on the way the theology of infallibility is deepening through this ecumenical dialogue and highlight what it looks like in the crucible of ecumenical dialogue. I will use two familiar bilateral dialogues to illustrate my picture, the Anglican-Roman Catholic International Commission and the U.S. Lutheran-Roman Catholic Dialogue. Then in my second section I will highlight an issue that continues to be disputed in discussions of infallibility, the issue of reception, and propose a way forward past disputes that surround it.

1. An Emerging Ecumenical Understanding of Infallibility

Ecumenical dialogue partners disagree about many issues, but they continue to agree on at least one thing: claims about infallibility, especially papal infallibility, remain a stumbling block for progress toward reunion of the Church. The Anglican-Roman Catholic International Commission called claims for papal infallibility an area of "grave difficulty" for Anglicans,[5] while the U.S. Lutheran-Roman Catholic Dialogue called the dogma of papal infallibility "both theologically and emotionally the most

---

3. Ibid., #9.

4. Pontifical Council for Promoting Christian Unity, "Directory for the Application of Principles and Norms on Ecumenism," [title printed as "1993 Directory for Ecumenism"] *Origins* 23 (1993–94) 129, 131–44; see #91.

5. Anglican-Roman Catholic International Commission [ARCIC], "Authority in the Church I," *The Final Report* (London: SPCK & Catholic Truth Society, 1982) #24.

divisive of all the issues separating the Roman Catholic communion from the churches of the Reformation."[6]

But to Roman Catholics engaged in ecumenical dialogue with Christians from other traditions, the need to rethink claims about infallibility had been clear for a while. Most of them would have agreed with the concise but pensive observation offered by Roman Catholic members of the U.S. Lutheran-Roman Catholic Dialogue: "The concept of infallibility is by no means free from difficulty."[7] Particularly in the crucible of bilateral dialogues, Roman Catholics find themselves challenged by their ecumenical partners to find new ways of expressing the meaning of the concept of infallibility. The results give hope that a deeper grasp of the reality behind this concept is being forged, a grasp that will improve the understanding which Roman Catholics themselves have of their own belief in this area.

I want to examine two general trends in the treatment of infallibility by the two bilaterals, which are among the few bilateral groups that have addressed the subject of infallibility directly through official statements.

1.1. Infallibility Reinterpreted within the Shift in Epistemology from a Classicist Mentality to Historical-Mindedness

The first trend in a reinterpretation of infallibility is part of the shift from a classicist mentality to historical-mindedness. Bernard Lonergan describes two worldviews, the classicist mentality and historical-mindedness, which he understands as "two different apprehensions" of humankind. In the first, he explains, "One can apprehend man [sic] abstractly through a definition that applies *omni et soli* and through properties verifiable in every man"; this approach focuses on humankind as such in its unchanging aspects. "On the other hand," he continues, "one can apprehend mankind as a concrete aggregate developing over time, where the locus of development and, so to speak, the synthetic bond is the emergence, expansion, differentiation, dialectic of meaning and of meaningful performance. On this view intentionality, meaning, is a constitutive component of human living; moreover, this component is not fixed, static, immutable, but shifting, developing,

---

6. [U.S.] Lutheran-Roman Catholic Dialogue, "Teaching Authority and Infallibility in the Church: Lutheran Reflections," *Teaching Authority and Infallibility in the Church,* eds. Paul Empie, T. Austin Murphy, and Joseph Burgess (Minneapolis: Augsburg Publishing House, 1980) #4.

7. [U.S.] Lutheran-Roman Catholic Dialogue, "Teaching Authority and Infallibility in the Church: Roman Catholic Reflections," *Teaching Authority and Infallibility in the Church,* eds. Paul Empie, T. Austin Murphy, and Joseph Burgess (Minneapolis: Augsburg Publishing House, 1980) #4.

going astray, capable of redemption. . . ."[8] Lonergan argues, of course, that the modern period is characterized by its shift from a classicist mentality to historical-mindedness. What does this mean for infallibility?

On first sight the idea of "infallibility" seems firmly entrenched in classicist mentality. It seems naïve, pompous, or uninformed for a person or group to lay claim to any kind of guaranteed freedom from error. At a more basic level, the notion of infallibility seems tied to an older world view that was static and that saw our knowledge of truth as eternal, unchanging, the same at all times and places for all people. The claim that a person or group could ever speak infallibly seems a denial of the historicity of knowledge; even more offensive to modern ears is the teaching of Vatican I that certain definitions are irreformable.

What would infallibility look like if it were reinterpreted within a framework of historical-mindedness? The two bilateral dialogues being examined begin to do this by focusing less on the word "infallibility" and instead focusing on its underlying meaning. The U.S. Lutheran-Roman Catholic Dialogue statement on "Teaching Authority and Infallibility in the Church" is instructive, for example, in the wide net of issues that it relates to papal infallibility: "the authority of the gospel, the indefectibility of the Church, the infallibility of its belief and teaching, and the assurance or certainty which Christian believers have always associated with their faith."[9] This dialogue links infallibility to the general issue of the faithful transmission and authoritative interpretation of the gospel. "Whatever one may think about the appropriateness of the term 'infallible,'" the writers note, "it points to the unavoidable issue of the faithful transmission of the gospel and its authoritative interpretation, guided by the Spirit."[10]

The statement continues by focusing, not on the word "infallibility," but on the problem of faithful transmission. Such transmission is possible because of the guidance of the Spirit in later developments, the statement argues. It explains belief in "indefectibility" as the "trust that the Holy Spirit guides the Church in transmitting the Christian message to new generations in fidelity to the gospel."[11] Such guidance is necessary because "the

---

8. Bernard Lonergan, "The Transition from a Classicist World-View to Historical-Mindedness," *A Second Collection* (Philadelphia: Westminster Press, 1974) 5–6.

9. [U.S.] Lutheran-Roman Catholic Dialogue, "Teaching Authority and Infallibility in the Church: Common Statement," *Teaching Authority and Infallibility in the Church*, eds. Paul Empie, T. Austin Murphy, and Joseph Burgess (Minneapolis: Augsburg Publishing House, 1980) #1.

10. Ibid., #23.

11. Ibid., #28.

historical-cultural context of the Christian faith . . . at times demands re-formulation of the Church's teaching."[12] On the one hand, the statement notes, "human language remains inadequate to the transcendent mystery of God and to the fulness of the paschal mystery of Jesus Christ." Yet on the other hand, "with respect to the truth and certainty of the message, Christians trust that through their Scriptures, their creeds, their conciliar definitions and their confessional writings, they are led by the Holy Spirit to the truth of the gospel and to an authentic life of faith."[13] Hence, if Lutherans and Roman Catholics have differences with regard to infallibility, the statement continues, both traditions do "share the certainty of Christian hope that the Church, established by Christ and led by his Spirit, will always remain in the truth fulfilling its mission to humanity for the sake of the gospel."[14] This is a striking convergence.

At the end of their statement, the Lutheran and Roman Catholic writers return to the theme of the historicity of human language, noting the impermanence and historically conditioned character of language structure. Because of this historicity, statements can only be interpreted correctly when the context of their formulation is taken into account. And, though members were unable to agree completely about infallibility, they note, "Because the questions and concerns of our period differ from those of the nineteenth century, it becomes necessary to reinterpret or reformulate the concept of infallibility so that its valid theological insights may become more persuasive."[15] They follow their own advice in interpreting *Pastor aeternus,* emphasizing the conditions to which a pope acting infallibly is subject. Roman Catholic members, in a separate section, continue this historically sensitive interpretation of Vatican I, emphasizing its strict interpretation and suggesting that Vatican II and *Mysterium ecclesiae* have begun a reinterpretation of the reality that is partially expressed in the concept of infallibility.[16]

The U.S. Lutheran-Roman Catholic Dialogue statement thus provides a good example of a fruitful approach to infallibility that restates its meaning within historical-mindedness. It raises the issues of faithful transmission

12. Ibid., #27.
13. Ibid., #26.
14. Ibid., #28.
15. Ibid., #49.
16. [U.S.] Lutheran-Roman Catholic Dialogue, "Teaching Authority and Infallibility in the Church: Roman Catholic Reflections," *Teaching Authority and Infallibility in the Church,* eds. Paul Empie, T. Austin Murphy, and Joseph Burgess (Minneapolis: Augsburg Publishing House, 1980) #14–20.

and authoritative interpretation of the Gospel and it understands that such transmission and interpretation will always demand reformulation and reconceptualization. Hence, the reason for introducing a concept like infallibility is revealed: it is related to faithful transmission of the Gospel throughout history, a kind of inculturation of the Gospel in every age and place. In addition, the concept is radically disconnected from any static worldview by the emphasis on the historicity of all human language. Such historicity is used to show first the continual need for new formulations, to which the issue of infallibility is closely tied, and then the need even for a new interpretation of the reality to which the concept of infallibility points. The members of this bilateral group believe that "the convergences . . . outlined provide both the context and the beginning of a reinterpretation of infallibility."[17]

How does the Anglican-Roman Catholic International Commission interpret infallibility with historical-mindedness? The Anglican-Roman Catholic statement also treats infallibility by pointing to the reasons for such a concept. First, it notes, reformulation of the Gospel is sometimes necessary. "All generations and cultures must be helped to understand that the good news of salvation is also for them," the statement notes. "It is not enough for the Church simply to repeat the original apostolic words. It has also prophetically to translate them in order that the hearers in their situation may understand and respond to them."[18] The second reason relates infallibility to defense of the Gospel. "In times of crisis or when fundamental matters of faith are in question," the writers explain, "the Church can make judgements consonant with Scripture, which are authoritative," judgments which "do not add to the truth but, although not exhaustive, . . . clarify the Church's understanding of it."[19]

Having established these two reasons for the concept of infallibility—translation and defense—the members of the Anglican-Roman Catholic International Commission are ready to treat infallibility in more detail. Under a section labeled "infallibility," they first describe the indefectibility of the Church: "The Church is confident that the Holy Spirit will effectually enable it to fulfill its mission so that it will neither lose its essential character nor fail to reach its goal."[20] But then members go on to affirm

---

17. [U.S.] Lutheran-Roman Catholic Dialogue, "Teaching Authority and Infallibility in the Church: Common Statement," #50.

18. Anglican-Roman Catholic International Commission, "Authority in the Church I," #15.

19. Ibid., #19.

20. Anglican-Roman Catholic International Commission [ARCIC], "Authority

that "a special ministerial gift of discerning the truth and of teaching" can be bestowed on one person at crucial times "to enable him to speak authoritatively in the name of the Church in order to preserve the people of God in the truth";[21] such a teaching could, like some conciliar teachings, become a part of the Church's "permanent witness," both clarifying the truth and strengthening the Church's confidence for proclamation.[22] "Through both these agencies [council and universal primate] the Church can make a decisive judgement in matters of faith, and so exclude error," the members state clearly.[23] Such judgments function not to add to the content of revelation, points out the statement, but rather to recall, emphasize, expound, expose, draw out implications, show contemporary applications. The statement again emphasizes the crisis context for such judgments, noting that "situations may occur where serious divisions of opinion on crucial issues of pastoral urgency call for a more definitive judgement."[24] At the same time, it also emphasizes that reception, "assent of the faithful," is "the ultimate indication" that an authoritative teaching on a matter of faith "has been truly preserved from error by the Holy Spirit," who will bring members of the Church "to receive the definition as true and to assimilate it if what has been declared genuinely expounds the revelation."[25]

Like the first statement, this second statement also provides a fruitful rethinking of infallibility within historical-mindedness. Because the Gospel must be translated within new cultures and defended at crisis moments, the Church is given concrete ministries which are enabled to do this work of translation and defense. This statement reflects less on the inadequacy of human language to express the Gospel and more on the positive possibilities and needs for reformulation. Again it reflects a significant convergence.

1.2. Infallibility Reinterpreted within the Shift from a Pyramidal Ecclesiology to an Ecclesiology of Communion

I have been discussing the reinterpretation of infallibility within the first shift, the shift from a classicist mentality to historical-mindedness;

---

in the Church II, *The Final Report* (London: SPCK and Catholic Truth Society, 1982) #23.

21. Ibid., #23.
22. Ibid., #24.
23. Ibid., #26.
24. Ibid., #27.
25. Ibid., #25.

this is a shift in epistemology. But I believe that the documents also show the influence of a second shift, a shift in ecclesiology; this is the shift from a pyramidal ecclesiology to an ecclesiology of communion. It was Yves Congar who spoke of the shift away from "pyramidal ecclesiology" to an ecclesiology of communion,[26] and this shift has been widely discussed in Roman Catholic theology. A pyramidal understanding of the Roman Catholic Church emphasized the unity of the Church, but it sometimes confused unity with uniformity. Local churches were seen as pieces of a big pie which was the universal Church, and there was an increasing centralization in government and personal devotion around the person of the bishop of Rome. Jean-Marie Tillard writes, "The Catholic Church was in practice seen not as a communion of local Christian communities, each of them keeping its own traditions and its own ways of living faithfully the common faith, but as an *[sic]* unique and huge diocese governed by an unique and real chief and bishop, the bishop of Rome helped by the offices of his curia." Pyramidal ecclesiology "transformed the Roman Catholic community into a monolithic Church," he concludes.[27] But Vatican II marks the shift from this ecclesiology into the recovery of another ecclesiology from biblical and patristic sources, i.e., an ecclesiology of communion. Vatican II emphasized the local church, the collegiality of bishops, and the mission of the whole Church. The recovery of an ecclesiology of communion is shared explicitly in the work of the 1993 Fifth World Conference on Faith and Order on the Church as communion in faith, life, and witness.[28]

What does infallibility look like when reinterpreted within an ecclesiology of communion? Again, at first glance, such a task looks fairly daunting: infallibility may appear like an inherently pyramidal concept, with one authority or a group of authorities speaking from the top of the pyramid. More deeply, it suggests a sharp division of labor between a teaching Church and a learning Church.

How do the two bilateral statements tackle the reinterpretation of infallibility within an ecclesiology of communion?

26. Yves Congar, "La 'réception' comme réalité ecclésiologique," *Revue des sciences philosophiques et théologiques* 56 (1972) 392–93.

27. Jean-Marie Tillard, "The Roman Catholic Church: Growing towards Unity," *One in Christ* 14 (1978) 221–22.

28. See the discussion paper of the Fifth World Conference on Faith and Order, "Towards *Koinonia* in Faith, Life and Witness," *Ecumenical Trends* 22 (1993) 81–104; and the message of the conference, "On the Way to Fuller *Koinonia*," *One in Christ* 29 (1993) 329–32.

The U.S. Lutheran-Roman Catholic Dialogue distinguishes carefully between papal primacy and papal infallibility. In their considerations of papal primacy, Lutheran members are able to affirm that "papal primacy, renewed in the light of the gospel, need not be a barrier to reconciliation."[29] In fact, Dialogue members invite Lutherans to consider that such a renewed papal ministry would be not just legitimate but even possible and desirable. Lutherans "increasingly recognize the need for a Ministry serving the unity of the Church Universal," members note,[30] one which "serves to promote or preserve the oneness of the Church by symbolizing unity, and by facilitating communication, mutual assistance or correction, and collaboration in the church's mission."[31] At the same time, Lutheran dialogue members also list what they call "defects" in the papacy, which include "the present mode of operation of the papacy and the Roman curia" as well as the "close tie at the present time between primacy and infallibility," leading to "consequences in Roman Catholicism" that will need "thorough investigation in . . . future discussions."[32] The statement calls for renewal of the papacy according to the Vatican II principles of legitimate diversity, collegiality, and subsidiarity.[33]

But how is this discussion of a petrine ministry within an ecclesiology of communion related to infallibility? After looking at the way that the Gospel was proclaimed with authority in the Church and emphasizing the need for its reformulation, the Lutheran-Roman Catholic Dialogue then concludes to the necessity "for the Church to develop structures concerned with the task of reformulation."[34] Members note that traditional organs for continuing the process of interpretation, such as ecumenical councils, were "largely lost to the Lutheran churches" during the Reformation; today Lutheran churches are "increasingly sensitive to the

29. [U.S.] Lutheran-Roman Catholic Dialogue, "Differing Attitudes toward Papal Primacy: Common Statement," *Papal Primacy and the Universal Church,* eds. Paul Empie and T. Austin Murphy (Minneapolis: Augsburg Publishing House, 1974) #32.

30. Ibid., #28.

31. Ibid., #4.

32. [U.S.] Lutheran-Roman Catholic Dialogue, "Differing Attitudes toward Papal Primacy: Reflections of the Lutheran Participants," *Papal Primacy and the Universal Church,* eds. Paul Empie and T. Austin Murphy (Minneapolis: Augsburg Publishing House, 1974) #38.

33. [U.S.] Lutheran-Roman Catholic Dialogue, "Differing Attitudes toward Papal Primacy: Common Statement," #22–25.

34. [U.S.]Lutheran-Roman Catholic Dialogue, "Teaching Authority and Infallibility in the Church: Common Statement," #27.

shortcomings of their structures for teaching and mission in a worldwide ministry."[35] While Lutherans believe that Catholics have "overconfidently identified the locus of the work of the Spirit with a particular person or office,"[36] nevertheless their sense of the worldwide nature of the Church's communion leads Lutheran members to comment that "many Lutherans are reawakening to the importance of an ecumenical or universal teaching Ministry within the Church."[37] For their part, Roman Catholics "recognize that all members of the people of God share in principle the responsibility for teaching and formulating doctrine"; the bishop of Rome himself "acts in dependence on the faith of the Church."[38] In their convergences, the members agree both that there may appropriately be a ministry of unity in the universal Church, with responsibility for the oversight of the Church's proclamation and, where necessary, the reformulation of doctrine faithful to the Scriptures, and that harmony between the teachings of ministers and acceptance by the faithful "constitutes a sign" of the teaching's fidelity.[39] The Spirit-filled community "plays an authenticating role in the reception of Scripture and the gospel," they agree.[40]

In short, by locating the issues of infallibility and teaching authority within an ecclesiology of communion, the U.S. Lutheran-Roman Catholic Dialogue is able to offer criticisms about historic abuses of authority while also envisioning a teaching ministry that would serve worldwide communion with leadership but without domination or sacralization.

The Anglican-Roman Catholic International Commission statement also envisions infallibility's exercise within an ecclesiology of communion. It sees the Church as the communion that is "a sign that God's purpose in Christ is being realized in the world by grace" and "an instrument for the accomplishment of this purpose."[41] It envisions primacy and conciliarity as the two complementary elements by which oversight fosters commun-

---

35. Ibid., #39.

36. Ibid., #42.

37. [U.S.] Lutheran-Roman Catholic Dialogue, "Teaching Authority and Infallibility in the Church: Lutheran Reflections," *Teaching Authority and Infallibility in the Church,* eds. Paul Empie and T. Austin Murphy (Minneapolis: Augsburg Publishing House, 1974) #18.

38. [U.S.] Lutheran-Roman Catholic Dialogue, "Teaching Authority and Infallibility in the Church: Common Statement," #47.

39. Ibid., #41.

40. Ibid., #12.

41. Anglican-Roman Catholic International Commission [ARCIC], "Introduction," *The Final Report* (London: SPCK and Catholic Truth Society, 1982) #7.

ion; but, the statement adds frankly, "it has often happened that one has been emphasized at the expense of the other, even to the point of serious imbalance."[42] We get the idea that the writers have some examples in mind, and this is confirmed with their lengthy correction on what primacy ought to mean: primacy should help the churches listen to each other, grow in love and unity, and seek the fullness of witness. Primacy "does not seek uniformity where diversity is legitimate, or centralize administration to the detriment of local churches."[43] While "neither theory nor practice . . . has ever fully realized these ideals," the statement observes, "yet the primacy, rightly understood, implies that the bishop of Rome exercises his oversight in order to guard and promote the faithfulness of all the churches to Christ and one another."[44]

Infallibility exercised by a primate for the universal Church, or by a council of bishops, is set, then, within this vision of oversight that fosters communion. While bishops and the bishop of Rome give authoritative expression to insights about the Gospel, "The community, for its part, must respond to and assess the insights and teaching of the ordained ministers." The statement sees this as a "continuing process of discernment and response, in which the faith is expressed and the Gospel is pastorally applied, the Holy Spirit declares the authority of the Lord Jesus Christ, and the faithful may live freely under the discipline of the Gospel."[45] The statement is clear that "maintenance in the truth requires that at certain moments the Church can in a matter of essential doctrine make a decisive judgement which becomes part of its permanent witness."[46] But, as with all other insights, so also a teaching proposed as essential doctrine involves the whole Church in "active reflection upon the definition."[47] Reception of a definition "does not create truth"; rather, it is "the final indication that such a decision has fulfilled the necessary conditions for it to be a true expression of the faith."[48] Again, the statement says carefully, "although it is not through reception by the people of God that a definition first acquires authority, the assent of the faithful is the ultimate indication

42. ARCIC, "Authority in the Church I," #22.

43. Ibid., #21.

44. Ibid., #12.

45. Ibid., #6.

46. ARCIC, "Authority in the Church II," #24.

47. Ibid., #25.

48. Anglican-Roman Catholic International Commission [ARCIC], "Authority in the Church I: Elucidation (1981)," *The Final Report* (London: SPCK and Catholic Truth Society, 1982) #3.

that the Church's authoritative decision in a matter of faith has been truly preserved from error by the Holy Spirit."[49]

With its careful balance between authoritative teaching and reception by the whole Church, the statement underlines its commitment to an ecclesiology of communion. Infallibility within this interpretation is linked to reception because the whole Church is involved in the process of discerning authoritative teachings, including those on matters of essential doctrine.

In this first section, I have been illustrating the way that infallibility is being reconceptualized within ecumenical dialogue. Two shifts—the shift to historical-mindedness and the shift to an ecclesiology of communion—provide the framework within which two bilateral statements rethink the central issue of infallibility. But while much of this reconceptualization has passed by many readers without comment, the issue of reception has continued to find objections. It is on this issue of reception that I now want to focus.

2. THE ISSUE OF RECEPTION
WITHIN THE REINTERPRETATION OF INFALLIBILITY

Reception plays an important role within infallibility's reconceptualization; it is affirmed in both of the bilateral statements we have been examining. But the Vatican has shown itself hesitant regarding affirmations of reception when linked with infallibility. To see illustrations of this hesitation, we need only look at the two Vatican responses to the Anglican-Roman Catholic International Commission's *The Final Report*. In 1982, the Congregation for the Doctrine of the Faith complains that the Commission's statement "makes reception by the faithful a factor which must contribute . . . to the recognition of the authority and value of the definition as a genuine expression of the faith."[50] But this contradicts Vatican I, the Congregation believes, which teaches in *Pastor aeternus* that the divine redeemer "willed his church to be endowed (with infallibility) in defining doctrine concerning faith and morals"; it also contradicts Vatican II, which gives the task of authentic interpretation to the living teaching office of the Church.[51]

49. ARCIC, "Authority in the Church II," #25.

50. Congregation for the Doctrine of the Faith, "Observations on the ARCIC *Final Report*," *Origins* 11 (1981–82) 755–56.

51. Ibid., 756.

In 1991, a Vatican response to *The Final Report* was issued which again registers hesitations about the statement's perspective on reception when linked with infallibility. By coincidence, I was actually in Rome for another international bilateral meeting when this document was released there in December, and I read my copy perched on the ledge of a pillar in St. Peter's Square in the warm December sunshine, sitting quite literally between the offices of the Pontifical Council for Promoting Christian Unity and the Congregation for the Doctrine of the Faith. It turned out that this location was symbolically revealing of the document itself, which we know resulted from a collaboration between these two offices. This Vatican response acknowledges that the Anglican-Roman Catholic statement does not believe reception creates truth nor legitimizes a particular decision to define the faith.[52] Nevertheless, it continues, the statement "sees the 'assent of the faithful' as required for the recognition that a doctrinal decision of the pope or of an ecumenical council is immune from error." But, the Vatican response continues, "for the Catholic Church, the certain knowledge of any defined truth is not guaranteed by the reception of the faithful that such is in conformity with Scripture and tradition, but by the authoritative definition itself on the part of the authentic teachers."[53]

Now what should we think about these hesitations, which in 1991 had still not gone away after almost ten years of widespread discussion of the Anglican-Roman Catholic International Commission's statement? A first reaction I had was frustration: the Vatican has misunderstood the Commission's statement, I observed. The Vatican charges the statement with claiming that assent of the faithful guarantees certain knowledge of defined truth, whereas the statement actually says that the assent of the faithful "is the ultimate indication that the Church's authoritative decision in a matter of faith has been truly preserved from error by the Holy Spirit."[54] My second reaction is echoed by Francis Sullivan when he comments that the Vatican response "seems to know no way to exclude . . . ambiguity except to use the precise formulas by which the Catholic Church is accustomed to express its faith."[55] But below these first two reactions, there are deeper questions. *Why* did the Vatican again misunderstand the statement in its viewpoint on reception? *Why* did it seek only the same familiar formulas in evaluating an ecumenical agreement? How are

---

52. "Vatican Responds to ARCIC I *Final Report,*" *Origins* 21 (1991–92) 444.
53. Ibid.
54. ARCIC, "Authority in the Church II," #25.
55. Francis A. Sullivan, "The Vatican Response to ARCIC I," *Gregorianum* 73 (1992) 494.

we to judge its hesitations? Let me attempt to answer these questions in three steps.

First, is infallibility worth reconceptualizing? Some might say no because they see infallibility inherently tied to world views that must be rejected. But I would argue that belief in infallibility is an important conviction within Roman Catholicism and an important contribution we make to ecumenical dialogue. Vatican II in a *relatio* describes the gift named "infallibility" by Vatican I as the assistance of the Holy Spirit by which "the Church . . . cannot completely fall away from the way of salvation."[56] The conviction of such assistance from God to the Church seems intrinsic to Christian faith, a kind of doxological praise of God's faithfulness and saving purpose. Furthermore, this conviction would seem to stand at the heart of the Roman Catholic insight that the Church needs a living, proclaiming magisterium at its center in every age. Such a conviction is worth reconceptualizing if it has become unclear to Roman Catholics or to other Christians.

Second, are the shifts in epistemology and ecclesiology discussed above legitimate frameworks within which to reconceptualize infallibility? Again, I would say yes. The shift to historical-mindedness reflects widely used work of such Roman Catholic theologians as Karl Rahner and Bernard Lonergan. John XXIII distinguished between doctrine and the way it is presented at the start of Vatican II,[57] and Vatican II itself began to shift toward historical-mindedness, teaching that "there is a growth in the understanding" in the Church "of the realities and the words which have been handed down."[58] It affirmed the historicity of understanding and embraced some practical implications of this insight by endorsing historical-critical tools for the study of Scripture. This shift to historical-mindedness is confirmed more thoroughly in the 1973 teaching *Mysterium ecclesiae* of the Congregation for the Doctrine of the Faith in its teaching on the reformulation of dogmatic statements.[59] The shift to an ecclesiology of communion also reflects the work of many Roman Catholic theologians, such as Yves Congar and Jean-Marie Tillard. Vatican

56. *Schema Constitutionis de Ecclesia* (Vatican, 1964), *relatio* for n. 12(C), 45–46.

57. John XXIII, "Opening Speech to the [Second Vatican] Council," in *The Documents of Vatican II*, ed. Walter M. Abbott (New York: America Press, 1966) 715.

58. Vatican II, *Dei verbum*, in *The Documents of Vatican II*, ed. Walter M. Abbott (New York: America Press, 1966) #8.

59. Congregation for the Doctrine of the Faith, *Mysterium ecclesiae*, *The Tablet* 227 (14 July 1973) 668.

II also made this shift to an ecclesiology of communion, recovering the biblical and patristic heritage by emphasizing the local church in its celebration of the Eucharist as the locus of Church, and seeing the communion within the triune God shared with those in the Church, binding them into one. The local church was given many gifts and charisms for the sake of its mission, and among them is a ministry of leadership to assist the local church to remain in the faith of the apostles and in communion with other local churches. So Vatican II emphasized the collegiality of bishops, each bringing the views of his church to the college of bishops, and located the bishop of Rome within the college of bishops as center and servant of communion.[60] Both shifts in thought, then, are deep in contemporary Roman Catholic theology and have been affirmed by Vatican II.

Third, is reception a necessary aspect of the reinterpretation of infallibility within these two shifts in thought? Again, I would say yes.

Once the shift to historical-mindedness is made, we can see that the Church is not only a teacher but also a learner. Frederick Crowe notes that these two activities are each processes in which the whole Church must engage. And learning is something which takes time. Learning, points out Crowe, means "asking questions . . . forming an idea of a possible answer; indeed forming several ideas of different possible answers; weighing the pros and cons of the several alternative ideas; finally, coming to a judgment, and being able to say: 'I've learned something.'" Crowe gives some examples to make his point, noting that Peter went through a process of learning to understand his Christian freedom from the Mosaic Law, and that the early Church went through another process of learning before it could teach that Christ was *homoousios* [one in being] with the Father.[61]

Now the recognition of the reality of learning in the Church is linked with the shift to historical-mindedness. Truth is grasped through a process of inquiry which takes time; the transposition of the meaning of the Gospel from one culture to another, from one epoch to another, all this takes time, time for inquiry, weighing the evidence, balancing the pros and cons, reaching a preliminary judgment, testing it, coming finally to be able to say: we've got it. The reality of infallibility, then, includes this process within time, a process which Roman Catholics believe is ultimately guided by the Holy Spirit. The recognition that such guidance

---

60. Vatican II, *Lumen gentium*, in *The Documents of Vatican II*, ed. Walter M. Abbott (New York: America Press, 1966) 14–96.

61. Frederick Crowe, "The Church as Learner: Two Crises, One 'Kairos,'" *Appropriating the Lonergan Idea*, ed. Michael Vertin (Washington, D.C.: The Catholic University of America Press, 1988) 370–84.

takes place within and over time seems, if anything, basis for giving greater glory to the God whose respect for human dignity and freedom within the work of salvation is sure.

Reception also seems intrinsic to an ecclesiology of communion. Its recognition takes cognizance of the delicate balance between authoritative teaching and the discernment by the whole Church which characterizes the history of the Church. In fact, Tillard understands all of tradition as the reception of the Gospel, the faith once delivered to the apostles but received anew in each generation.[62] Recognizing reception as a sign of the exercise of that infallibility given by God to the whole Church can make us less worried about who first expresses a teaching within the community and more concerned with the truth of the teaching. It also should make us less uneasy with the diversity of cultural expressions of the Gospel, since inculturation is really the reception of the Gospel in every age in the variety of forms and expressions appropriate to what Rahner called the "World Church."[63] In fact, the ecumenical movement itself is a form of reception in which the divided communions within the one Church of Christ seek to receive gifts from each other in order to restore full visible unity. Recognition that reception is linked with infallibility seems again to deepen our basis for giving greater glory to God who celebrates the multiplicity of ages and cultures in the Church so much more fully than we have managed to do.

I believe that the Vatican hesitations about reception's link to infallibility come from incompleteness or inconsistency sometimes characterizing its epistemology and ecclesiology. While committed in principle to the shift to historical-mindedness and the shift to an ecclesiology of communion, the Vatican at times does not see the full implications of these shifts. Old perspectives die hard, and in the area of reception, it seems, the Vatican responses continue to emerge more from pre-Vatican II perspectives on infallibility that emphasize unchanging knowledge of truth and centralized exercise of authority. This leads these responses to misunderstand new perspectives or simply to ask for the repetition of old formulations. Here, I respectfully suggest, the Vatican could draw more thoroughly from the work of reconceptualization occurring in ecumeni-

---

62. Jean-Marie Tillard, "Tradition, Reception," in *The Quadrilog: Tradition and the Future of Ecumenism, Essays in Honor of George H. Tavard*, ed. Kenneth Hagen (Collegeville: The Liturgical Press, 1994) 328–43.

63. Karl Rahner, "Basic Theological Interpretation of the Second Vatican Council," *Theological Investigations*, trans. Edward Quinn (New York: Crossroad, 1981) 20:78.

cal bilaterals and among Roman Catholic theologians than it sometimes has.

I would also suggest that you—Jesuits committed to ecumenical work—could assist in a special way in the reconceptualization of infallibility, with its attendant recognition of reception. Many of the themes I have discussed are especially dear to Jesuit life. Jesuits emphasize the process of growth when learning about the Gospel, as well as the freedom and the dignity of the learner. Your educational and preaching apostolates have made you concerned with the translation and defense of the Gospel. You emphasize as well the reality of discernment of the meaning of the Gospel for our day. Your commitment to the papacy emphasizes the importance of an effective apologetic for our times. In some ways infallibility is an aspect of inculturation, and your commitment to worldwide mission echoes that emphasis on inculturation. All of these Jesuit concerns are in fact part of the discussion of reception. Helping others to see the faithfulness in those concerns would also make a contribution to the ecumenical movement's discussion of infallibility and, with it, reception.

5

RECEPTION AS KEY:
UNLOCKING ARCIC ON INFALLIBILITY[1]

One of Eugene Fairweather's many important contributions to ecumenical dialogue was his work on *The Final Report*[2] of the Anglican-Roman Catholic International Commission (ARCIC). The meaning and depth of that contribution have become evident to me in the courses on Anglican-Roman Catholic dialogue which he and I taught together in the Toronto School of Theology and in meetings over many years as colleagues on the Anglican-Roman Catholic Dialogue of Canada. Again and again he has guided students and colleagues to deeper appreciation of *The Final Report's* meaning and of the theology that stands behind it. In gratitude for our time together in the classroom and on the Dialogue, I would like to show how ARCIC's understanding of reception contributes to breaking an impasse in ecumenical discussions of infallibility.

Reception is a major theme in ARCIC's discussion of infallibility. I believe that use of this theme allowed the writers of *The Final Report* to break through various disagreements and resolve them. Reception serves as a key to unlock puzzling sections of the statement; it provides a part of the framework within which the infallibility section as a whole should be read. While discussion of reception has been common among Roman Catholic theologians for the last two decades, the ARCIC statement represents a new step in

1. This essay was first published in a slightly different form in *Toronto Journal of Theology* 3/1 (1987) 41–49, as part of a collection of articles in that issue honoring Rev. Eugene Fairweather, former professor of theology in the Faculty of Divinity in Trinity College, Toronto and an Anglican member of the Anglican-Roman Catholic International Commission during its writing of *The Final Report*.

2. Anglican-Roman Catholic International Commission [ARCIC], *The Final Report* (London: SPCK & Catholic Truth Society, 1982).

its use by a group which includes officially appointed Roman Catholic theologians who concur in seeing reception as the final sign or manifestation that a particular teaching has been an exercise of infallibility.

What is ARCIC's understanding of reception? Is such an understanding acceptable to Roman Catholic theology? Will ARCIC's understanding of reception allow a genuine inclusion of both Anglican and Roman Catholic traditions at a deepened level that respects the insights of each and goes beyond them in a larger vision? These are the three questions I wish to address here.

ARCIC's Understanding of Reception

ARCIC's discussion of reception is set within *The Final Report's* wider picture of conciliarity and primacy as complementary modes of the exercise of authority within the Church.[3] This approach is emphasized a final time in the *Report's* last paragraph, which evokes the complementarity of "both a multiple, dispersed authority, with which all God's people are actively involved, and also a universal primate. . . ."[4]

In its first statement on authority, ARCIC introduces reception within a discussion of normative conciliar decisions. When councils reach decisions on controversial questions affecting the whole Church, criteria for their evaluation become especially important.[5] "A substantial part in the process of reception is played by the subject matter of the definitions and by the response of the faithful. This process is often gradual, as the decisions come to be seen in perspective through the Spirit's continuing guidance of the whole Church."[6] Recognition by the see of Rome and by other principal sees was one of the factors which contributed to the recognition of conciliar decisions, ARCIC notes.[7]

In its "Elucidations," ARCIC responds to questions about its understanding of reception. "By 'reception' we mean the fact that the people of God acknowledge such a decision or statement because they recognize in it the

3. Anglican-Roman Catholic International Commission [ARCIC], "Authority in the Church I," *The Final Report* (London: SPCK & Catholic Truth Society, 1982) #22.

4. Anglican-Roman Catholic International Commission [ARCIC], "Authority in the Church II," *The Final Report* (London: SPCK & Catholic Truth Society, 1982) #33.

5. ARCIC, "Authority in the Church I," #16.

6. Ibid.

7. Ibid., #17.

apostolic faith. They accept it because they discern a harmony between what is proposed to them and the *sensus fidelium* of the whole Church," ARCIC writes.[8] Reception neither creates truth nor legitimizes the decision reached; rather, "it is the final indication that such a decision has fulfilled the necessary conditions for it to be a true expression of the faith."[9] The whole Church is involved in this acceptance, ARCIC believes, "in a continuous process of discernment and response."[10] In this view on reception, ARCIC wishes to avoid two extremes. "On the one hand it rejects the view that a definition has no authority until it is accepted by the whole Church or even derives its authority solely from that acceptance. Equally, the Commission denies that a council is so evidently self-sufficient that its definitions owe nothing to reception."[11]

The centrality of the concept of reception for ARCIC becomes clear when we look at its treatment of infallibility. On the one hand, ARCIC underlines the importance of authoritative teaching. The Church at certain times "can in a matter of essential doctrine make a decisive judgement which becomes part of its permanent witness," ARCIC believes; and it envisions that either council or primate might articulate such a decision.[12] But, on the other hand, the entire Church must assess such a decision; that assessment clarifies the decision's significance. "Moreover," ARCIC continues, "although it is not through reception by the people of God that a definition first acquires authority, the assent of the faithful is the ultimate indication that the Church's authoritative decision in a matter of faith has been truly preserved from error by the Holy Spirit."[13] Reception finally is the work of the Holy Spirit, maintaining the Church in truth. It is the Spirit who "will bring its members to receive the definition as true and to assimilate it if what has been declared genuinely expounds the revelation."[14] I think that ARCIC understands reception as a part of the exercise of infallibility that functions, if you will, within the "order of knowing." It is the epistemological side of doctrine, as it were, just as the process of discerning the canon was the epistemological side of inspiration. Reception

---

8. Anglican-Roman Catholic International Commission [ARCIC], "Authority in the Church I: Elucidation," *The Final Report* (London: SPCK & Catholic Truth Society, 1982) #3.

9. Ibid.

10. Ibid.

11. Ibid.

12. ARCIC, "Authority in the Church II," #24.

13. Ibid., #25.

14. Ibid.

is a sign or manifestation that a teaching is true; it is the means by which we discover what truth the Holy Spirit is helping the Church to understand more deeply. Reception is not an enlarged voting booth: it is the Spirit crying "Abba" within us. We hear this in many voices that have become one. In this sense, ARCIC is simply stating in phenomenological terms what we have tended to describe only metaphysically when discussing authentic teaching.

RECEPTION AND ROMAN CATHOLIC THEOLOGY

How does Roman Catholic theology regard such an approach? At first glance, some might conclude that ARCIC's understanding of reception is opposed to Roman Catholic thought. The Congregation for the Doctrine of the Faith suggests this in its preliminary response of 1982. ARCIC, says the Congregation, makes "reception by the faithful a factor which must contribute, under the heading of an 'ultimate' or 'final indication,' to the recognition of the authority and value of the definition as a genuine expression of the faith."[15] But such an understanding, argues the Congregation, is opposed by *Pastor aeternus* of Vatican I, which notes that Christ wished his Church to be endowed with infallibility in defining; by *Lumen gentium,* which attributes this infallibility to bishops assembled in council; and by *Dei verbum,* which teaches that the task of authentically interpreting the Word of God is entrusted exclusively to the teaching office of the Church.

In its 1991 response to *The Final Report,* the Vatican continues to raise questions about ARCIC's view of reception. ARCIC makes clear that reception "'does not create truth nor legitimize the decision,'" the authors of the response note with approval; but, they add, "it would seem that elsewhere *The Final Report* sees 'the assent of the faithful' as required for the recognition that a doctrinal decision of the pope or of an ecumenical council is immune from error. . . ."[16] The response continues, "For the Catholic Church, the certain knowledge of any defined truth is not guaranteed by the reception of the faithful that such is in conformity with Scripture and tradition, but by the authoritative definition itself on the part of the authentic teachers."[17]

---

15. Sacred Congregation for the Doctrine of the Faith, "Observations on *The Final Report* of ARCIC," *The Tablet* 236 (15 May 1982) 495, # B.III.5.

16. "Vatican Responds to ARCIC I *Final Report,*" *Origins* 21 (1991) 444.

17. Ibid.

But this Vatican response seems to overlook ARCIC's careful clarification on this point. "Authority in the Church II" writes that "it is not through reception by the people of God that a definition first acquires authority"; it then adds that "the assent of the faithful is the ultimate indication that the Church's authoritative decision in a matter of faith has been truly preserved from error by the Holy Spirit."[18] The Vatican sees a claim that reception is a guarantee, but ARCIC actually claims that reception is "the ultimate indication" of a teaching's preservation from error.

If we look at the wider Roman Catholic theological community, we find that reception has been increasingly used over the last thirty years to understand the Church's process of discerning the Gospel. Older views were convinced that Vatican I's *Pastor aeternus* excluded reception from Catholic thought by its clause that "such definitions of the Roman pontiff are irreformable of themselves, and not from the consent *[consensus]* of the Church," a clause in which the pope's unique ministry is emphasized.[19] But Roman Catholic theologians today agree that this clause was inserted to avoid making the binding character of papal teaching dependent on a subsequent juridically verifiable ratification by the churches. Discernment and proclamation of the real consensus of the Church about its faith is not excluded, but intended.[20]

More broadly, however, reception is today understood to be a part of an ecclesiology of communion which is the preferred vision of the Church among Roman Catholic theologians. Yves Congar, in his watershed discussion of reception, underlines the importance of reception within a

18. ARCIC, "Authority in the Church II," #25.

19. Translation of *Pastor aeternus* is mine in Margaret O'Gara, *Triumph in Defeat: Infallibility, Vatican I, and the French Minority Bishops* (Washington, D.C.: The Catholic University of America Press, 1988) 269; the Latin from *Pastor aeternus* is "*Romani Pontificis definitiones ex sese, non autem ex consensu Ecclesiae irreformabiles esse.*"

20. See, for example, Avery Dulles, "Papal Authority in Roman Catholicism," *A Pope for All Christians? An Inquiry into the Role of Peter in the Modern Church* (New York: Paulist Press, 1976) 62; John T. Ford, "Infallibility," *The New Dictionary of Theology*, 519; Heinrich Fries and Johann Finsterhölzl, "Infallibility," *Sacramentum Mundi* 3:135; Roger Aubert, *Vatican I* (Paris: Éditions de l'Orante, 1964) 235; Georges Dejaifve, *Pape et évêques au premier concile du Vatican* (Brussels: Desclée de Brouwer, 1961) 130; Gustave Thils, *L'infaillibilité pontificale: Source—conditions—limites* (Gembloux: J. Duculot, 1968) 250; cf. the *relatio* of Vincent Gasser at Vatican I, in Vincent Gasser, *The Gift of Infallibility: The Official Relatio on Infallibility of Bishop Vincent Gasser at Vatican Council I*, trans. James T. O'Connor (Boston: Daughters of St. Paul, 1986) 42–55.

sound ecclesiology.[21] For him, it is the whole Church which is the subject of the gift of the Gospel's truth. Hence the response of the whole Church is important in assessing the truthfulness of a teaching. The ancient councils, believing that the whole Church could not err, took unanimity in teaching as the necessary sign of the presence of the Holy Spirit, and Congar reminds us that reception is tied to a theology of local church, to an enlivened pneumatology, to a vision of the Church as a communion of churches, and to a theology of tradition that sees its dynamic present character.[22] In a profound way, reception points to the conciliarity of the Church, to the link between two or three gathered and Christ's presence.

Congar contrasts an ecclesiology of the pyramid, where power and truth come from the top down, with an ecclesiology of communion, where the gifts of the Holy Spirit are given to each, with charisms to accomplish his or her unique mission within the body.[23] If one thinks in terms of the first, pyramidal model, one will think also of a society under a visible head, and one may then attribute to the head the sole importance in reception. Roman Catholics have often interpreted Vatican I in this way, as though the pope not only represented the whole Church but also replaced it. More tragically, they have often allowed a practice of papal authority that enacted such an understanding. In such a pyramidal ecclesiology, reception would be unimportant, obedience the only response to magisterial teaching, and the Congregation for the Doctrine of the Faith correct in its criticisms. But scholars of Vatican I insist increasingly that Vatican I itself was not monolithically pyramidal in its viewpoint. Jean-Marie Tillard, for example, argues, "Vatican I refuses to turn the episcopate into a body of functionaries or delegates of the pope, an army of shadows carrying out as doubles what in fact the supreme head would more fittingly do by himself. The Council does not consider (in fact it refuses to do so) the 'primacy' of the Bishop of Rome as an omnipresent 'power' enveloping all episcopal activities. The pope's jurisdiction cannot be an obstacle to that of each individual bishop. And unanimously the 'Fathers (of the Council) reject the idea that the Roman Pontiff would intervene in their diocese *ordinarie*. . . .'"[24]

21. Yves Congar, "La 'réception' comme réalité ecclésiologique," *Revue des sciences philosophiques et théologiques* 56 (1972) 369–403.

22. Ibid., 392.

23. Ibid., 392–93.

24. Jean-Marie Tillard, "The Horizon of the 'Primacy' of the Bishop of Rome," *One in Christ* 12 (1976) 12–13.

I do not want to be guilty of what Georg Denzler calls the high-wire acrobatics of completely denying the intentions of the fathers of Vatican I in my interpretation of their words.[25] But I believe that in the new reception of Vatican I for which Congar has called,[26] Roman Catholics are finding the second model of which Congar speaks, an ecclesiology of communion, echoed at least in the modifications written into the text by the minority council members. In such an ecclesiology of communion, reception takes central place. Discernment, not obedience, is the central category for the Church's responsibility.

But let us not strain too hard to find the remaining elements of an ecclesiology of communion in the thought of Vatican I. While minority voices managed to keep a vestige of this vision in the document, surely much of its overall vision and impact was pyramidal in style. But *Mysterium ecclesiae* reminded Roman Catholics that the particular worldview of a dogmatic teaching is not the teaching's message.[27] Roman Catholics are no more bound by what is pyramidal about Vatican I's worldview of authority than they are obligated to adopt a classicist understanding of truth as represented by the choice of the term "irreformable" in the definition. Instead, they are free through a critical recovery to find out with what gift of the Gospel Vatican I has equipped them for contribution to the ecumenical discussion. What important aspects of Vatican I must the whole Church of Christ not forget, keeping them as part of its living tradition if it is to deepen its fidelity to the Gospel?

I find two things which seem central to Vatican I's teaching on infallibility. The first is an affirmation of God's fidelity to the Church as a place where the Gospel will be preserved, even at times of crisis or deep disagreement. It seems to me that Vatican I makes an almost speculative, hypothetical affirmation: if it should happen that the Gospel be threatened by human error, God will ensure its preservation, for the sake of the salvation of humankind. A sense of this is captured in the statement on infallibility by the Anglican-Roman Catholic Dialogue of Canada: "The Church as a whole can be said to be infallible in the analogical sense that,

---

25. Georg Denzler, "The Discussion about Bernard Hasler's Publications on the First Vatican Council," *Who Has the Say in the Church?* eds. Jürgen Moltmann and Hans Küng, *Concilium*, Vol. 148 (Edinburgh & New York: T & T Clark Ltd. & Seabury Press, 1981).

26. Yves Congar, "Bulletin d'ecclésiologie," *Revue des sciences philosophiques et théologiques* 60 (1976) 288.

27. Sacred Congregation for the Doctrine of the Faith, *Mysterium ecclesiae, The Tablet* 227 (14 July 1973) 668–69.

by God's grace, it will never deceive or err so gravely concerning the truths of the Gospel that the message of salvation is lost to humankind. . . . It is simply to assert that the Church can be confident in the sufficiency of the Holy Spirit, who will safeguard the faith and enable the Church to fulfill its mission."[28] Though other Christian churches make such an affirmation, perhaps I could say that Vatican I has a preoccupation with crisis, and wishes to emphasize God's fidelity in such situations.

To this first preoccupation, it adds a second. Vatican I always envisions God's fidelity taking form, shape, concrete particularity. Its own specific concerns led it to emphasize the role of the bishop of Rome as an instrument in the exercise of infallibility, a role which it understood to parallel that of the college of bishops. Perhaps we could summarize this second preoccupation as an emphasis on the concrete form which infallibility's exercise must take, and a presumption in favor of the bishop of Rome, in addition to the whole college of bishops, as likely candidates for such exercise. Jerome Theisen wishes to speak of the "reliability" of the bishop of Rome, and I think this term catches my meaning here. "The doctrine of papal infallibility signifies a confidence in the acts of the pope," Theisen writes. "His communication can be deficient and even erroneous. But in the main he communicates the Christian tradition in a trustworthy and dependable fashion."[29] Or again, Dulles summarizes this core concern of Vatican I in this way: ". . . the celebrated definition of papal infallibility really commits one to very little. . . It is hardly more than an emphatic assertion that the pope's primacy, as defined in the first three chapters of *Pastor aeternus,* extends also to his teaching power. He is not only the first pastor but also the first teacher in the Church. In view of his special responsibility for the unity of the whole Church in the faith of the apostles, it is antecedently credible that in him the infallibility of the whole Church may come to expression."[30] Vatican I's central interest, it seems, was the identification of one concrete instrument by which the Church's infallibility, under certain conditions, might be exercised.

RECEPTION AND ECUMENICAL DISCUSSION

Let us return now to the thought of ARCIC on reception. By making reception a central category, ARCIC is able to show the complexity of the exer-

28. Anglican-Roman Catholic Dialogue of Canada, "Agreed Statement on Infallibility," *Journal of Ecumenical Studies* 19 (1982) 86, #2.

29. Jerome Theisen, "Models of Papal Ministry and Reliability," *American Benedictine Review* 27 (1976) 281.

30. Dulles, *A Pope for All Christians?* 64.

cise of infallibility within the Church. In *The Final Report,* a delicate balance is maintained between the role of authoritative statements by a council or a universal primate on the one hand, and the responsibility of the whole Church for preserving the Gospel on the other hand. On the one hand, ARCIC states, "Maintenance in the truth requires that at certain moments the Church can in a matter of essential doctrine make a decisive judgement which becomes part of its permanent witness."[31] ARCIC cites as an example the decisions of councils, and later adds that a universal primate as well "can make a decisive judgement in matters of faith, and so exclude error."[32] At the same time, ARCIC maintains, the "active reflection upon the definition in its turn clarifies its significance."[33] The assent of the faithful is the ultimate indication that the decision has been preserved from error by the Holy Spirit. In this balance I believe that the two concerns of Vatican I are preserved but integrated into a larger picture in which an ecclesiology of communion sees a role for the many charisms within the Church.

It is clear that ARCIC does not wish to downgrade the importance of the college of bishops or of a universal primate. "Although responsibility for preserving the Church from fundamental error belongs to the whole Church," it comments, "it may be exercised on its behalf by a universal primate."[34] It is also clear that ARCIC does not want its emphasis on reception to leave only the authority of individual judgment. "It would be incorrect to suggest that in controversies of faith no conciliar or papal definition possesses a right to attentive sympathy and acceptance until it has been examined by every individual Christian and subjected to the scrutiny of his private judgement."[35]

At the same time, by its use of the more ample ecclesiology of communion, ARCIC does wish to correct the onesidedness of Vatican I's concerns. Hence, it emphasizes, "The Church's teaching authority is a service to which the faithful look for guidance especially in times of uncertainty; but the assurance of the truthfulness of its teaching rests ultimately rather upon its fidelity to the Gospel than upon the character or office of the person by whom it is expressed. The Church's teaching is proclaimed because it is true; it is not true simply because it has been proclaimed."[36] Reception

31. ARCIC, "Teaching Authority in the Church II," #24.
32. Ibid., #26.
33. Ibid., #25.
34. Ibid., #28.
35. Ibid., #31.
36. Ibid., #27.

by the whole Church is needed as a final indication that a definition has been a genuine expounding of revelation.[37] Later in the text, ARCIC notes that "Anglicans do not accept the guaranteed possession of such a gift of divine assistance in judgement necessarily attached to the office of the bishop of Rome by virtue of which his formal decisions can be known to be wholly assured before their reception by the faithful."[38] But, in light of the understanding of reception which they have just helped to elaborate, Roman Catholic signers could well have added, "and neither do we." With its understanding of reception, ARCIC can maintain the authoritative role of a universal primate without necessitating the *a priori* certitude that his formal decisions will always in fact be exercises of the Church's infallibility.

In their response to *The Final Report*, the Canadian Conference of Catholic Bishops comment, "By keeping a balance between authoritative teaching and its reception, the *Report* is able to reach a significant degree of agreement on infallibility."[39]

Perhaps the insight of Tillard on the *sensus fidelium* can help us to understand ARCIC here. Tillard sees the *sensus fidelium* as the instinct of discernment present in the body of the faithful. He does not wish to be naïve about this capacity: for him, there are healthy tensions between a simple faith and an educated faith, and between the faithful and the magisterium of bishops. The magisterium lives in symbiosis with the simple faithful and often sides with them against an educated theological analysis. Tillard understands that the truth of the Gospel is finally discerned in a living way by the interaction, the complementarity of these forces, ensuring "the progress of the people of God in truth."[40] For him the magisterium has a special role in this process; it offers a service of discernment, to guide the Church as it makes the truth incarnate.[41]

It is just such a notion of the magisterium which ARCIC seems intent to maintain, granting the uniqueness of the role of council or universal primate but insisting that these only act for, and are evaluated by, the whole Church. "We can now together affirm that the Church needs both a multiple, dispersed authority, with which all God's people are actively involved, and also a universal primate as servant and focus of visible unity

---

37. Ibid., #25.

38. Ibid., #31.

39. Canadian Conference of Catholic Bishops, "Response of the Canadian Conference of Catholic Bishops to the ARCIC-I *Final Report*," *Ecumenism* 88 (December 1987) 17.

40. Jean-Marie Tillard, "*Sensus fidelium*," *One in Christ* 11 (1975) 27.

41. Ibid., 28.

in truth and love," it concludes.[42] In my judgment, ARCIC's delicate handling of the interplay between reception by the whole Church and oversight in teaching allows Roman Catholics to find in *The Final Report* their own faith as well as a means by which the catholicity that they share with others can be recognized.

As Roman Catholics and Anglicans continue to work and pray for the day when such recognition comes to be formally confirmed by both communions, we should express our gratitude to Eugene Fairweather for helping to lay the foundations for that day.

---

42. ARCIC, "Teaching Authority in the Church II," #33.

6

UNDERSTANDING "A CERTAIN, THOUGH IMPERFECT" COMMUNION BETWEEN ANGLICANS AND ROMAN CATHOLICS[1]

The Decree on Ecumenism of Vatican II, *Unitatis redintegratio,* states that those who believe in Christ and have been baptized are brought into "a certain, though imperfect, communion" with the Roman Catholic Church.[2] Furthermore, it notes that among Western churches which were separated from the Roman See, "the Anglican Communion occupies a special place."[3] The specialness of this place has been further confirmed by the commitment of these two communions to the achievement of full unity through a series of stages begun with the Malta Report of 1968[4] and continued in the publication of *The Final Report* of 1982, the work of the Anglican-Roman Catholic International Commission on Eucharist, ministry, and authority in the Church.[5] The commitment to achievement of this unity has been confirmed by the continuation of appointments to the Anglican-Roman Catholic International Commission and by the joint renewed dedication to the goal made on the occasion of the pastoral visit

1. This paper was first written to help the Anglican-Roman Catholic Dialogue of Canada respond to the request of the Anglican-Roman Catholic International Commission for background papers on the nature of communion. It was printed in a slightly different form in *Mid-Stream* 25 (1986) 190–99.

2. Vatican II, *Unitatis redintegratio,* in *The Documents of Vatican II,* ed. Walter M. Abbott (New York: America Press, 1966) #3.

3. Ibid., #13.

4. Anglican-Roman Catholic Joint Preparatory Commission, "The Malta Report," appendix to Anglican-Roman Catholic International Commission, *The Final Report* (London: SPCK & Catholic Truth Society, 1982) 108–16.

5. Anglican-Roman Catholic International Commission [ARCIC], *The Final Report* (London: SPCK & Catholic Truth Society, 1982) 1–100.

of the bishop of Rome to the archbishop of Canterbury in England in 1982. Since that time, the mutual commitment to work for full visible unity has been repeated, most recently on the occasion of the Rome visit by the archbishop of Canterbury with the bishop of Rome in December 1996.

The *acta* of Vatican II manifested that council's intention to refer to a communion that is real, even though imperfect. Nevertheless, the ecclesiology of imperfect communion is a theme which has not been fully explored. What is the concrete meaning of this important theme, which forms an underlying concept in the whole of *Unitatis redintegratio?*[6] In particular, what does it mean for these two communions with their special and deepening relationship? In this paper, I intend—in response to the request of ARCIC—to explore some answers to these questions.

Imperfect Communion and Full Communion

With Jean-Marie Tillard, I understand the Church of Christ to be one but divided, visible but broken into pieces by the sins of those whom God has made brothers and sisters but who refuse to be fully brothers and sisters to each other.[7] Despite this division within the one Church, those baptized share "the most fundamental and radical bond of communion possible; the Spirit of God has marked them all with the seal of belonging to Christ. . . . And this seal—as the theology of the baptismal character shows—is so strong that nothing, not even schism, can blot it out."[8] In the baptismal "yes" to the saving plan of God, Christians are already in communion. But there is a second "yes," a more noetic "yes," which involves the understanding of what is implied in the first "yes." Necessary to faith, it means some particular understanding of the meaning of the kerygma. "The split inside the *unica Ecclesia* has its origin in the passage from the first 'yes' to the second 'yes.' Though all are agreed about the first 'yes,' Christian communities differ about the second."[9] In fact, Tillard concludes, this is the absurdity of the situation. "While all Christians together, in an irrevocable decision, pronounce their 'yes' to the plan of God which saves them by making them brothers and sisters

---

6. Yves Congar, *Diversity and Communion,* trans. John Bowden (Mystic, Connecticut: Twenty-Third Publications, 1984) 131.

7. Jean-Marie Tillard, "One Church of God: The Church Broken in Pieces," *One In Christ* 17 (1981) 2–9.

8. Ibid., 5.

9. Ibid., 10–11.

of Christ and of one another, when they come to the doctrinal implications of this 'yes' they can no longer agree."[10]

This gives us some preliminary idea of a meaning, then, for real but imperfect communion. But what would communion perfected be like? What is the nature of the unity we seek?

If we share with Vatican II and *The Final Report* an ecclesiology of communion, then we understand the Church united to be a communion of eucharistic communities. This means that the oneness of its unity is intimately related to its catholicity, a universality "which emerges from and integrates diversity, not a universality which imposes uniformity and suppresses diversity."[11] The reunited one Church of Christ would not mean, then, a collapse of the different communions with their unique theological traditions, liturgical forms, governing structures, and spiritual riches. It would mean a communion of communions. All of these diverse gifts would be preserved in a Church reunited. All are part of the catholicity of the Church.

When I say this, I do not mean that the many communions in the one Church would be unrelated to each other. On the contrary, they would be involved in relations of mutuality, of interdependence, in which they would allow themselves to be converted by each other.[12] Like a healthy interpersonal relationship which includes both autonomy and mutuality, so the one Church would be graced at once with the richness of diversity and the bond of unity.

REASONS FOR DIFFERENT EXPRESSIONS OF THE ONE FAITH

But why are there different expressions of the one faith such that different expressions of it occur in the one Church?

One important reason underlined by Yves Congar is the variety of authentic apostolic traditions. It is very important to recognize that some of the differences between East and West are "not just the result of Catholicity and a variety of spiritual gifts, but go back to apostolic origins," he notes.[13] And *Unitatis redintegratio* remarks that "the heritage handed down by the apostles was received in different forms and ways, so that from the very beginnings of the Church it has had a varied development

10. Ibid., 11.
11. Jean-Marie Tillard, "The Church Is a Communion," *One in Christ* 17 (1981) 123.
12. Tillard, "One Church of God: The Church Broken in Pieces," 9.
13. Congar, *Diversity and Communion,* 19.

in various places, thanks to a similar variety of natural gifts and conditions of life."[14]

Another reason for the different expressions of the one faith is that no expression of the reality of Christian faith is exhaustive. Congar comments, "The transcendence of Reality has to be translated into history. . . . Since no expression is ever totally adequate to what it expresses or its final outcome, a number of expressions are possible and even desirable."[15] Closely related to this reason is a third: faith is received by a variety of peoples with different histories, cultures, and problems. "Christianity is subject to geography and history. The individual or collective subjects who live it out make it their own. Inevitably they express it in different ways."[16] Modern theology is especially aware of this historicity of our understanding, and uses this insight with fruitfulness in interpreting critically the meaning of the Scriptures and of earlier conciliar teaching.

The ecumenical task is possible because different expressions of the one faith are possible, indeed necessary.

"All the dogmatics which have multiplied in this way are focussed on the fullness of God's communication of himself in revelation and the covenant. None of them can express it adequately. The faithful live by it without ever exhausting it. . . . Between these expressions and the fulness of the gift there always remains the margin which we have recognized between every element or form of the historical life of the Church and eschatology. It is in this margin that the enterprise of ecumenism is inscribed."[17]

DIVERSITIES WITHIN COMMUNION

I have been examining the foundational reasons which explain the existence of the many expressions of the faith, many expressions in theology, liturgy, governing structure, and spirituality. But this examination is relevant for our consideration of the nature of the full communion that would retain its catholicity.

Full communion, for example, allows the presence of different rites, understanding a rite as "the multiple and coherent expression of the faith" of a community which "includes above all the liturgy, steeped in dogmatic truth, the images, the style of monastic life, the disposition of the churches,

---

14. Vatican II, *Unitatis redintegratio*, #14.
15. Congar, *Diversity and Communion*, 40.
16. Ibid., 40–41.
17. Ibid., 170.

the presiding genius in the ordering of church life."[18] When Congar discusses the relationship between East and West, he wishes to speak of it as "complementary." This means more than seeing the same reality in two different ways, he insists.[19] It means rather "that there are two constructions of the mystery, each of which is coherent and complete—although each is unsatisfactory on some point—and which cannot be superimposed."[20] An inadequate but real vision of the possibility of keeping such complementary rites in full communion is provided by the communion of both Latin and Eastern rites with the bishop of Rome. Of course, we know all of the injustice and abuse which the Eastern rites have suffered in this relationship, and so it poses many problems as an example of communion. Still, it is suggestive, because it allows us to "recognize the legitimate existence of two theological and even dogmatic traditions in the profession of the same faith."[21]

Lukas Vischer makes another suggestion which can help us imagine how our diverse governing traditions could be fruitfully appropriated in a united Church of the future. He finds in Christian traditions four insights about governing: personal leadership by those with oversight, collegial consultation among them, congregational reception, and the prophetic voices raised up within the churches at unexpected places.[22] All of these sorts of governing structures "respond to impulses which are deeply rooted in the Gospel," he points out.[23] All "have proved their special worth at crucial moments in history."[24] He concludes that "the Church needs to be capable of different emphases at different times and in different contexts"; we need all four insights about governing structure in a reunited Church.[25] If we look closely, we see that ARCIC seems to agree. Vischer's argument is even easier to see today when we are aware of the historicity of the forms of governing. He writes: "In recent times we have come to realize clearly the extent to which the forms and manners of decision-making in all the Church have been the fruit of historical development. This even applies to the ancient Church. However strongly people may insist that

18. Ibid., 83.
19. Ibid., 75.
20. Ibid., 76.
21. Ibid., 1.
22. Lukas Vischer, "Visible Unity: Realistic Goal or Mirage?" *One in Christ* 18 (1982) 26–29.
23. Ibid., 26.
24. Ibid., 27.
25. Ibid.

certain structures of leadership were established by God, hardly anyone is any longer prepared to deny that these structures were developed in different ways in different historical contexts."[26]

Congar underlines this point as well: "Roman Catholics need to progress in recognizing the historicity of the papacy and the hierarchical structures of their church."[27] When we recognize the historicity of governing structures in the Church, we can be more open to the Gospel values embodied in governing traditions other than our own.

Finally, within full communion in the Church, there are theological schools. When I speak of "schools," I do not mean, of course, academic institutions. Nor do I mean merely schools of thought, of ideas. I think rather of "schools" in an embodied sense that includes not only a theology but also its expression in liturgy, in characteristic governing forms, and in spirituality and a way of life. By a "theological school," then, I mean not just ideas but an embodied particular form of the Christian life, with its characteristic emphasis, its genius. Perhaps this way of understanding the theological school is much like the idea of "types" suggested by Cardinal Jan Willebrands. Full communion of the many traditions, he suggests, might also be envisioned to include the many types which have developed within the Church. Within a type he sees a characteristic canonical discipline, characteristic liturgical expression, and a tradition of spirituality and devotion.[28]

The theological schools, explains Karl Rahner, "express the variety of ways, legitimate and historically conditioned, in which finite men [sic] in the Church can make revelation their own."[29] He continues, "To wish to belong to no school would be the part of a proud and stupid man [sic] who imagines that here and now he can possess eternal truth outside historical time. To cling to a system as if it fully expressed the faith of the Church would be to deny the historicity of truth."[30]

Theological schools, understood as different embodied ways to live the Christian life, have always existed in the one Church. Within each of our communions now, there are many such schools. Even within one rite,

---

26. Ibid., 23.

27. Congar, *Diversity and Communion*, 171.

28. Cardinal Jan Willebrands, "Cardinal Willebrands' Address in Cambridge, England, January 18, 1970," *Documents on Anglican/Roman Catholic Relations* (Washington, D.C.: United States Catholic Conference, 1972) 1:32–41.

29. Karl Rahner & Herbert Vorgrimler, "Schools of Theology," *Theological Dictionary*, 427.

30. Ibid., 428.

there are many theological schools. A glance at most Latin rite Catholic faculties of theology today confirms this easily. Another glance at the range of pieties and spiritualities within popular worship in the Latin rite confirms the breadth of the differences. With healthy tension and sometimes frustration, but without breaking communion, the many schools of theology coexist in the Church.

RECONCEPTUALIZING
THE ANGLICAN-ROMAN CATHOLIC RELATIONSHIP

I have been discussing the many reasons for diversity in the expression of faith, and the many forms which such diversity has taken or might take within the communion that is the Church. But how does this relate to our attempt to understand the relationship between the Roman Catholic and the Anglican communions today?

In searching for the next stage toward full communion, our dialogues have been making a mistake, I think. We have believed the next stage would be accomplished only by taking a deliberate large step. Of course, this is not to deny that the arrival at a new stage in our relationship would need eventually to be formally confirmed. But in fact something else is required first: it is a reconceptualization of our relationship. Looking for the next step to take, we may have failed to notice the small steps that we have already taken toward each other, so that gradually we have reached a new stage almost without noticing it. What is needed is to open our eyes in order to see the way in which we are relating to each other, to reconceptualize the character of our two communions.

It is hardly accurate to think of these two communions in terms of the differences suggested by the complementarity of different rites, making such different constructions of the mystery as do East and West. We are too close in thought for that, and in fact *The Final Report* shows us growing in our common understanding on even long-disputed topics, such as Eucharist and ministry. Similarly, we have too much in common to understand ourselves as deeply opposed in our governing structures. Both are committed to episcopal leadership. Yet our theologians found it possible in *The Final Report* to insist on the importance of all four of the aspects of governing that Vischer highlights.

What then is the way that our two communions are beginning more and more to relate to each other? I think it is as two "schools of theology."

I see this with my students training for ministry. Increasingly, they relate to each other's traditions with respect and affection, with puzzlement or even suspicion, but as different schools of thought. By this I do not mean that they ignore the present disciplines of our division; in general, there is very little practice of intercommunion among Anglican and Roman Catholic students, and there is certainly a feeling of separate homes. Anglican and Roman Catholic students do not know each other very well, and they recognize fully that for the moment their two communities are not in full communion. Still, they come and go among each other intellectually as among two theological schools.

My Eastern Catholic students, my Latin Catholic students, and my Anglican students take together the courses on Christ, on the Trinity, even those on human nature, the Fall, and grace. Frequently the Eastern Catholics identify with certain of the theologians we study; the Anglicans and Latin Catholics together identify with others. Other times, Anglican and Latin Catholic students trade arguments while the Eastern Catholic students look on in puzzlement. Sharing in common these core courses, both Eastern Catholic and Anglican students also take separate courses in their own liturgical and theological traditions for study of the sacraments and, often, the Church. With a core of commonly held doctrines, the three groups of students yet receive them differently and maintain their own liturgical and ecclesial traditions and celebrations. The three groups do not celebrate the Eucharist together: Anglicans and Latin Catholics, because they are not in full communion; Eastern Catholics and Latin Catholics, because, though in full communion, they are in different rites. They are, as it were, three schools; two are in full communion.

To suggest that the Anglican and Roman Catholic communions are theological schools, or perhaps sets of schools, may sound as though it says too little about their structural separateness as communions. But again Congar can help us push this idea further. He notes that, besides the objectivity of the hierarchy of truths—some less central and some more central—there is also the actual hierarchy which we give to the truths of the faith. There is "a *de facto* hierarchy arising from the way in which a particular truth is understood and lived out by a group, a school . . . a given period, which is succeeded by another, or even a church and its particular setting."[31] Is it possible to see the differences among our communions as those among different schools of theology, each enshrining a slightly different constellation of the truths of the faith, each embodied through its attendant structural forms and particular genius? It is in this embodied sense that I mean schools of theology: an embodied way of life with its correlated governing forms, thought patterns, liturgical expres-

---

31. Congar, *Diversity and Communion*, 129.

sion, and spirituality. Normally, we notice that each of our communions contains many such schools. But can we also think of each communion, overall, as a "school" in this sense?

Congar suggests another idea: to understand the different confessional traditions as each "a development in response to a particular charism."[32] The Lutheran tradition, for example, would be understood to have a charism to "make clear the message of salvation by pure grace, of Christian liberty in the faith, of the sovereignty of the Word of God, and finally of a theology of the cross."[33] Such a school in a reunited Church would be recognized as a school with this charism and would keep its own organizational structure, though in communion with other traditions.[34]

The language of different "charisms" is interesting because today many Roman Catholic religious communities use it to describe their distinctive missions in the one Church. My Roman Catholic students from their many religious communities speak easily and noncompetitively (for the most part!) about the charism of their order. If we adopted such language to speak of the charism particular to the Anglican communion as a theological school, what would that charism be?

Surely the charism of the Anglican communion would be to witness to the collegial character of the exercise of authority. Is this not at the heart of where our theological discussion still is passionate, unfinished, and raises the sense of absolute identity issues for Anglican partners in dialogue? Among my Anglican and Roman Catholic students, their anger and passion against each other focuses on the misuse of episcopal authority, including the authority of the bishop of Rome. Anglicans and Roman Catholics are fighting over a very narrow set of issues; in fact, they are like two siblings with the same set of values, each expressing this dearly held set of values in slightly different ways. It is for love of the very same values—the right use of episcopal authority—that we struggle with each other in a family feud.[35] In this struggle, while we have just managed, in *The Final Report,* to achieve a germinal understanding of "the desired ecclesiology," we have not yet fully achieved in our communions "the desired praxis."[36] In the absence of such praxis, Anglicans appropriately seek

32. Ibid., 148.
33. Ibid.
34. Ibid.
35. Jean-Marie Tillard, "Schismatics in Communion," paper presented at General Theological Seminary, New York, 6 October 1983.
36. Jean-Marie Tillard, "The Roman Catholic Church: Growing Towards Unity," *One in Christ* 14 (1978) 220–29.

"assurance that acknowledgement of the universal primacy of the bishop of Rome would not involve the suppression of theological, liturgical and other traditions which they value or the imposition of wholly alien traditions."[37] It is their charism in the Church of Christ to insist on such assurance.

Schools of Theology and the Reform of the Church

But such assurance about the right exercise of authority should be part of the life of the whole Church. Ecumenical dialogue reforms each of our communions by eliminating the elements in them that distort, narrow, or exaggerate the emphases which have shaped us in our isolation from each other. The key to the reform of the Roman Catholic communion at the present time is the reform of its exercise of authority. Alone, it has been unable to accomplish this fully; only in dialogue with other embodied schools of theology is it gradually finding the understanding to correct its distortions.

In one communion the limitations of one theological school are corrected by "at least a potential openness to the complementary aspect."[38] In fact, it is their openness to mutual correction that preserves these different groups from misleading or false distortions. Because they have this openness to each other for the correction of their limitations, at least in principle, they can be schools of thought in one Church. In other words, it is the openness to correction by the others that is characteristic of a school within the one Church.

But our two communions, Roman Catholic and Anglican, increasingly relate in this way to each other. Aware of its own limitations, each recognizes its inability to reform itself without the insight of the other. This is a new development after our centuries of mutual hostility and self-assurance. We in fact wish increasingly to be converted by the other. "Those involved in the ecumenical movement have by virtue of that a *votum unitatis, votum catholicitatis* [desire for unity, desire for catholicity], which gives to their present belief a dynamic dimension in which their intention of plenitude is fulfilled," reflects Congar.[39]

Is not the growing *votum unitatis* with its accompanying openness to correction by the other a significant fact on which we should reflect more deeply? If our two communions were to be moving slowly into a new re-

---

37. Anglican-Roman Catholic International Commission, "Authority in the Church II," *The Final Report* (London: SPCK & Catholic Truth Society, 1982) #22.
38. Congar, 151, elaborating the thought of Johann Adam Mühler.
39. Congar, 133.

lationship with each other, would their movement not be characterized by this desire? Slowly, the desire for unity may have transformed our two communions into two theological schools in some of the ways they relate to each other. We may have moved into this new stage of unity and failed to recognize it. This is my suspicion.

Of course, this movement is not complete. Many in each communion continue to define themselves over against the other; many are convinced that the other has nothing to teach them; many still tend to confuse their particular theology, liturgy, governing form, and spirituality with the common confession of the apostolic faith. But my point here is to note the ecclesiological significance of the readiness for self-correction from the other which is growing steadily within each of our communions. Does this not give us some phenomenology of what a movement from imperfect to more full communion might look like?

If I am correct, then our two communions are coming slowly to share communion in the reality, the *res* of salvation without sharing full communion in the *sacramentum* instituted to bring about this reality. If this is true, does it not help us to envision a time when the appropriate authorities of each side would confirm for us the age-old conviction of the Church: that different theological schools are yet in communion in the one Church and must therefore one day share the one bread and the one cup which are the sacrament of this communion?

7

ECUMENISM, DISSENT, AND THE ROMAN CATHOLIC CHURCH: SHIFTS BELOW THE SURFACE OF THE DEBATE[1]

The understanding and treatment of dissent within the Church is an important though often overlooked topic in ecclesiology and in ecumenical dialogue.

In this article I want to address the topic of dissent in the Roman Catholic Church and its ecumenical implications. This topic is controversial, filled with land mines. But the commitment of Ladislas Örsy to probe difficult areas in ecclesiology and in ecumenical dialogue has encouraged me to study this one further.

DISSENT AS A LITMUS TEST

A few years ago one of my young, earnest divinity students asked me, "Why are theologians talking about dissent so much recently? Isn't Christian life focused on assent?" Answering this question took me into a long discussion with my student, but his question helps us focus on one reason that dissent should be a topic of our study.

While confession, not dissent, is at the core of Christian life, dissent and its treatment in Christian communions functions as a kind of litmus test. First, it serves as a litmus test to discover what a church community regards

1. This paper was first presented as a lecture at a conference on Authority, Dissent, and Models of Church Unity sponsored by the Graymoor Centre in Garrison, New York, in November 1987. It was revised and published in an issue of *The Jurist* serving as a *festschrift* for Ladislas Örsy (professor of canon law at The Catholic University of America, Washington, D.C.) as "Shifts below the Surface of the Debate: Ecumenism, Dissent, and the Roman Catholic Church," *The Jurist* 56 (1996) 357–86. It is republished here in a slightly revised version.

as more important, what less important, and how authority in the community functions to reach and implement decisions. Secondly, it serves as a litmus test as well by manifesting the actual, operational—though perhaps implicit—ecclesiological model with which a Christian communion functions, rather than only the theoretical, articulated self-understanding. Both of these are important areas of concern for ecumenical dialogue, which presently is struggling over questions of authority and its exercise.

When the litmus paper of dissent is dunked into the cauldron of church life, then, it reveals rather quickly that communion's important beliefs and operation of authority, and reveals as well any differences within the communion between explicit and implicit accounts of these beliefs and operation. It is no surprise, then, that dissent and its treatment by our different church communions has become a focal point for ecumenical discussion and even for ecumenical tension. What a Christian communion actually believes and how it actually functions with authority to discern and teach such beliefs: these stand at the heart of what one communion wants to know about another when it enters into a common dialogue. Lukas Vischer named four conditions which must be satisfied for visible conciliar fellowship in the Church to be achieved: that we desire such unity, that we be able to celebrate the Eucharist together, that we share the apostolic faith, and that we find ways of making decisions together.[2] The last two are tested by dissent, and without some sense of commonality in these two in ecumenical discussion, the motivation for the first two is weakened.

Although dissent and the treatment it receives may look like one church's internal housekeeping and of no concern to those outside the house, the contrary is in fact the case. Such concern about each other's houses is actually a sign of ecumenical progress: as fuller communion becomes more a real possibility, Christians begin to see how much we all have at stake in each other's beliefs and exercise of authority. Let me cite just one statement by an Anglican seminary faculty which sums up the impact of dissent on ecumenical relations. A statement by General Theological Seminary called the Congregation for the Doctrine of the Faith's treatment of Charles E. Curran "a fresh and grave obstacle for Christian intellectual freedom and ecumenical credibility." It continued, "The question as we perceive it now is whether or not the Anglican Communion should envision closer ecumenical relations with a church that seems officially determined to suppress public discussion, debate,

---

2. Lukas Vischer, "Visible Unity: Realistic Goal or Mirage?" *One in Christ* 18 (1982) 20–22.

dialogue, and even disagreement on major theological issues that face the Church especially when they are raised by those who teach in its institutions of higher learning and priestly formation."[3]

DIFFICULTIES WITH DISSENT IN THE ROMAN CATHOLIC CHURCH

It is no secret that the Roman Catholic Church is having a kind of debate about the role of dissent in Church life and the treatment it should receive. The immediate context for this debate is the exercise of papal primacy during the last two decades toward certain theologians (e.g., Edward Schillebeeckx, Hans Küng, Leonardo Boff, Charles E. Curran), religious congregations (e.g., Jesuits, Discalced Carmelite nuns, orders studied by the Quinn Commission), priests and religious sisters or brothers involved in political activity (e.g., Robert Drinan, Agnes Mary Mansour), seminaries, signers of an abortion advertisement in *The New York Times,* and even bishops (e.g., Walter Sullivan in the diocese of Richmond, Virginia; Raymond Hunthausen in the diocese of Seattle, Washington; Isidore Borecky in the Ukrainian Catholic eparchy of Toronto, Ontario).[4] The larger context, however, stretches back much farther, to include the Vatican's response to Modernism, its long hesitations about historical critical methods of biblical study, its treatment of minority bishops from the First Vatican Council after that council closed, its censorship of Karl Rahner, Yves Congar, and John Courtney Murray before the Second Vatican Council opened, and, in general, what Giuseppe Alberigo has called the attempt by the magisterium to substitute itself for the work of theology.[5] What is going on here?

Well, first, what is not going on? In general, the debate about dissent in the Roman Catholic Church excludes some options from the very beginning. No one is really fighting about them; their exclusion forms one common consensus in the discussion. First, in general, Roman Catholics do not envision that dissent is possible or desirable about matters which are often labeled (I think unhelpfully) "infallible teachings" or—to put it another way—central teachings of Christian faith, what the Reformers might have called "the truths necessary for salvation," or what the medievals

3. General Theological Seminary Faculty to the Members of the Anglican-Roman Catholic International Commission, New York, 23 May 1986.

4. A summary of many of these events is in Patrick Granfield, *The Limits of the Papacy* (New York: Crossroad, 1987) 7–30, 196–97.

5. Giuseppe Alberigo, "Authority in the Documents of Vatican I and Vatican II," *Journal of Ecumenical Studies* 19 (Winter 1982) 142.

might have described as the "articles of faith," or we might call today the "Gospel." The existence of God, the full humanity and divinity of Christ, the triunity of God, the necessity of the grace of Christ for salvation: these and similar central teachings of Christian faith are not envisioned in the Roman Catholic Church as open for debate and dissent by believing Christians. While their formulation and their interpretation includes on-going discussion and revision, and while no dogmatic teaching is today understood to be their final formulation, still, their meaning is under-stood to be part of that continuity of belief through which the Church in every age and culture enters into communion with the faith delivered to the apostles.

Furthermore, Roman Catholics are not debating about whether or not the Church needs a ministry with oversight that includes teaching and decision-making, including within it a petrine ministry of oversight for the whole Church. When Edward Schillebeeckx lists a series of points on which Roman Catholic theologians agree despite their arguments with the magisterium, he does not hesitate to list agreement that "the official magisterium has a distinct and irreplaceable function" in the believing community, which includes at times the role of judging the work of an in-dividual theologian whose publications "cause profound doubts about whether he/she still stands in the line of the great Christian tradition." Schillebeeckx emphasizes that such a judgment must be made only if the community is divided by the matter, only after a period of open discus-sion and dialogue, and only in a "provisional" manner.[6] While perhaps critical of the style, procedures, presumptions, or conclusions of this pon-tificate and of earlier exercises of authority by the magisterium, Roman Catholics are not proposing the elimination of a ministry of oversight; their concern is rather with the reform of the ministry's operations.

Finally, Roman Catholic debate about dissent does not envision rela-tivism as a viable option for a theoretical base. That is, while most Roman Catholic theologians would argue for pluralism in interpretation of doc-trines, they do not wish to equate pluralism with relativism; and if some bishops accuse theologians of relativism, this remains a charge that would be resented and denied. In general, the inquiry over the historicity of human understanding (of which I will say more later) has not led Roman Catholics to embrace relativist theories; in fact, some of our most famous theologians, like Karl Rahner and Bernard Lonergan, have spent part of their effort precisely to show how the recognition of historicity is not the

---

6. Edward Schillebeeckx, "The Magisterium and Ideology," *Journal of Ecumenical Studies* 19 (1982) 17.

same as relativism, as well as to criticize relativist epistemologies. Roman Catholic discussion still envisions that true though not exhaustive understandings of the meaning of the Gospel can be achieved in a given time and place, and Roman Catholic theologians see part of their task as the assistance of such understandings.

I have listed three presumptions that are shared, among others, by participants in the Roman Catholic debate today about dissent: central dogmas are not open for dissent, the magisterium of bishops and the bishop of Rome has a distinct function in the community of faith, and no Roman Catholic theologian would wish to advocate thoroughgoing relativism. These presumptions disclose questions excluded from our debate. But what is going on within it?

Roman Catholic theology begins with a presumption in favor of the insights of the community. We could say that all Christian theology believes both that we must decide for ourselves and that we must not decide by ourselves. For a quick sense of Protestant-Catholic emphases, we might say that protestantizing strands in the Church have emphasized the first part of this insight—we must decide for ourselves—but that catholicizing strands have emphasized the second part—we must not decide by ourselves.[7] Not deciding by ourselves means that we begin with a presumption in favor of the wisdom of others, and in particular in favor of the teachings of those with the responsibility for pastoral oversight in the Church. Richard McCormick has described this presumption well: "This cast of mind and bent of will is no flabby neutralism. It is rather a strong inclination, one that would concretize itself in several ways . . . . it will mean respect and reverence for the person and his office, and continuing openness to his teaching . . . . readiness to reassess one's own position in light of this teaching . . . . great reluctance to conclude that authentic moral teaching is clearly erroneous even after one has concluded that the arguments and analyses used are less than adequate . . . . external behavior that fosters respect and support for the magisterium."[8] Nevertheless, despite this strong presumption in favor of magisterial teaching, Roman Catholic theology also has recognized for a long time

---

7. I am indebted to Jean-Marie Tillard for articulating this distinction so clearly at a meeting of the Disciples of Christ-Roman Catholic International Commission for Dialogue in Nashville, Tennessee, 8–14 December 1984; cf. the statement of that Dialogue, "The Church as Communion in Christ," *Mid-Stream* 33 (April 1994) 219–39, see #16.

8. Richard A. McCormick, "Loyalty and Dissent: The Magisterium—A New Model," *America* 122 (1970) 675.

that such magisterial teaching in areas not central to the Gospel or revelation—areas sometimes called (somewhat misleadingly[9]) "noninfallible teaching"—can be simply wrong and in need of improvement, correction, or radical reversal. Walter Principe provides a list of examples where Roman Catholic theology has changed or even reversed itself on matters less central to Christian teaching. Religious liberty, slavery, the matter and form of the sacraments of confirmation and orders, the use of historical critical methods in Scripture study: these are just a few of the many areas where teachings held by the magisterium in the Roman Catholic Church have changed.[10]

The recognition of the possibility of such error is not new. When nineteenth and early twentieth century manuals reflected on the different kinds of attitude which Roman Catholics should take toward dogmas of the faith and less central teachings by the magisterium, they distinguished between the assent of faith due to the dogmas of the faith and what they called the religious *obsequium* (translated submission, or respect, or loyalty[11]) of mind and will due to these less central teachings. Such distinctions became increasingly important in the nineteenth and twentieth centuries, Örsy remarks, when the volume of pronouncements from the popes was growing significantly, so that "a sound set of rules for the use of this source had to be worked out."[12] So, for example, Domenico Palmieri explains that assent to less central teachings is morally certain; but, he continues, "*if motives should appear which urge otherwise . . . we do not say that assent is owed,* since in these circumstances the will does not act imprudently when it suspends its assent." Such assent is morally certain, he explains, but not metaphysically certain, since, "by the very fact

9. *Pastor aeternus* did not speak of infallible teachings or noninfallible teachings, but of irreformable definitions that could be made by the bishop of Rome under certain conditions when he is "possessed of that infallibility with which the divine redeemer willed that his Church should be endowed in defining doctrine regarding faith or morals" (translation is mine in *Triumph in Defeat: Infallibility, Vatican I, and the French Minority Bishops* [Washington, D.C.: The Catholic University of America Press, 1988] 269).

10. Walter Principe, "When 'Authentic' Teachings Change," *The Ecumenist* 25 (1987) 71–73; cf. Charles E. Curran, Robert E. Hunt, *et al., Dissent In and For the Church: Theologians and "Humanae Vitae"* (New York: Sheed and Ward, 1969) chap. 3.

11. For a discussion of the translation of *obsequium* see Ladislas Örsy, "Magisterium: Assent and Dissent," *Theological Studies* 48 (1987) 487–90; "Profession of Faith and the 'Oath of Fidelity,'" *America* 160 (1989) 346.

12. Örsy, "Magisterium: Assent and Dissent," 478.

that *infallible* certitude is absent, it seems that error is not impossible and that the opposite could be true."[13] A manual by Franz Diekamp earlier in this century contains a similar recognition. "These noninfallible acts of the papal teaching ministry impose no obligation of faith, they demand no unconditional and final submission," he explains. "But decisions of this kind are, however, to be accepted with *internal religious assent* because they come from the highest teacher of the Church and possess important natural and supernatural assurances of their truth. *This obligation can cease only in the highly rare case that someone who is capable of [making] his own judgment in the question at hand, becomes convinced, after serious examination of all the reasons, that an error has been made in the decision.*"[14]

Well, though Diekamp felt that such dissent would be highly rare, others begged to differ at the publication of *Humanae vitae*, when many ordinary Roman Catholics felt they had the competence and the reasons to come to a different opinion from this teaching which was not an exercise of infallibility. Suddenly dissent became widespread and quite public. To cope with this situation, in which Patrick O'Boyle, archbishop of Washington, D.C., suspended any priest in his archdiocese from hearing confession who gave absolution to couples that admitted to using artificial contraception, and a group of more than six hundred theologians signed a statement disagreeing with the encyclical, the U.S. bishops published "Human Life in Our Day." In it, interestingly, they did not deny the possibility of theologians' dissenting from noninfallible magisterial teaching, even to the public dissenting which was rather foreign to Roman Catholic style. Rather, they set out certain conditions for public dissent: "Only if the reasons are serious and well-founded, if the manner of dissent does not question or impugn the teaching authority of the Church and is such as not to give scandal."[15] Finally, Vatican II[16] and the new code of canon law continue the distinction between the assent of faith and the religious *obsequium* of mind and will. The commentary on the latter from the Canon Law Society of America explains: "It calls for a basic attitude of

13. Domenico Palmieri, *Tractatus De Romano Pontifice* (Rome, 1877) 632, cited by Harry McSorley, "The Right of Catholics To Dissent from *Humanae Vitae*," *The Ecumenist* 8 (1969) 6.

14. Franz Diekamp, *Katholische Dogmatik nach den Gründsatzen des heiligen Thomas*, I, 3/5 (Münster: Aschendorff, 1923) 56, cited by McSorley, 6.

15. [U.S.] National Catholic Conference, "Human Life in Our Day," *Catholic Mind* 66 (Dec. 1968) 10.

16. Vatican II, *Lumen gentium*, in *The Documents of Vatican II*, ed. Walter M. Abbott (New York: America Press, 1966) #25.

religious assent based on a presumption of truth and good judgment on the part of the teaching authority. However, since teachings are included which are not infallible and can be erroneous, the principles of the pursuit of truth and the primacy of conscience still come into play. In other words, dissent is possible because the teachers mentioned in the canon can be and *de facto* have been mistaken. To search for the truth is everyone's duty and right."[17]

Now, I have cited these texts in order to make a point, and the point is the distinction between kinds of response which has been official teaching for at least a century in the Roman Catholic Church. The spirit of this teaching has been that with which I began: the presumption in favor of the community. But this presumption is given in different ways to different kinds of teachings. Perhaps Örsy sums up the point well when he explains that the assent of faith means the believer is "one with the believing Church: holding firm to a doctrine," while the religious *obsequium* of mind and will means the believer is "one with the searching Church, working for clarification."[18]

I have dwelt at some length on this tradition of teaching to show that it remains the established teaching of the Roman Catholic Church. Nevertheless, Roman Catholics and other Christians could be forgiven if they show some surprise or even incredulity at what I have been saying. While Roman Catholic theory has made the distinctions I have been noting, Roman Catholic practice rarely seems intent upon observing such niceties. Indeed, the long list of actions by this pontificate mentioned at the start of my remarks, coupled with the history of treatment of others who have dissented before them, suggests a practice in sharp contrast with the theory I have articulated. In addition, some voices today have begun to find theoretical justification for such practice. They emphasize that dissent, especially dissent by theologians who teach in a Roman Catholic institution, can cause scandal to believers. This is the concern of Joseph Ratzinger, who has drawn attention to his theoretical hesitations about dissent by a theologian. "A [dissenting] person who teaches in the name of the Church is taking what is basically a personal dissent and exaggerating its importance and its damage by propagating it," he wrote in 1984.[19]

17. James A. Coriden, Thomas J. Green, Donald K. Heintschel, eds., *The Code of Canon Law: A Text and Commentary,* commissioned by the Canon Law Society of America (New York: Paulist, 1985) 548 at canon 752.

18. Örsy, "Magisterium: Assent and Dissent," 490.

19. Joseph Ratzinger, "Dissent and Proportionalism in Moral Theology," *Origins* 13 (1984) 668.

Though in that essay he noted the distinction between teaching and research, in Toronto two years later he emphasized mainly the dangers that theologians pose to the faith of the "little ones."[20] In his letter to Curran, Ratzinger referred to the "inherent contradiction" in which "one who is to teach in the name of the Church in fact denies her teaching," a situation which he seems to think will lead to scandal.[21] Germain Grisez represents the views of some theologians and other Roman Catholics when he writes, "Even if it is uncertain whether the ordinary magisterium has infallibly taught some of the moral truths the faithful are asked to hold definitively, then still such teachings will receive the assent and practical acceptance of every faithful Catholic (*Lumen gentium*, 25). For whatever the Church teaches as certain on moral questions very probably does pertain to divine revelation more or less directly. If a particular norm—for example, one regarding some new question—is not now infallibly taught, eventually it might well be, although possibly with some development and refinement no one can foresee today."[22]

Örsy points out the problems with even the word "dissent," especially in English. It begins on a negative note and its meaning is ambivalent, suggesting to some a group wishing to secede from the community.[23] Often a theologian who has reached a different conclusion from magisterial teaching may not have a dissenting attitude at all, notes Örsy. "He may be consenting wholeheartedly to the search for a better understanding of the Christian mysteries."[24] So the word "dissent" can be misleading and can take on overtones not intended by its users. For this study, I shall use the word "dissent" to mean simply disagreement with a magisterial teaching that is not an exercise of infallibility.

Is the deeper and genuinely new situation here the emergence of dissent into the contemporary public media? Theologians with dissenting views in the past were supposed to communicate their hesitations secretly to the Vatican, not speak of them in public. But today theological debates on a variety of issues are matters of intense societal interest, and they are con-

20. Joseph Ratzinger, "The Church and the Theologian," *Origins* 15 (1986) 761–70.

21. Joseph Ratzinger to Charles E. Curran, 17 September 1985, *Origins* 15 (1986) 668.

22. Germain and Jeannette Grisez, "Divining the Moral Dilemma of Dissent," *National Catholic Reporter* 22 (6 June 1986).

23. Ladislas Örsy, *The Church: Learning and Teaching* (Wilmington, Delaware: Michael Glazier, 1987) 90–93.

24. Ibid., 93.

ducted with the eyes of the world upon them. Theologians live in a fish bowl as they argue among themselves and at times take the respectful though dissenting view. A theologian's lectures to other theologians may often be quoted immediately—sometimes in a distorted way—in major newspapers throughout the world. A theologian's articles and books may in fact be used not only for study by other theologians, but for the education of future ministers of the Church and even for the formation of conscience by catechetical instructors. When Pope John Paul II visited the United States in 1987, for example, his remarks on dissent seem to have been made in part as a response to a magazine article in which Roman Catholics were reported to feel free to dissent on a list of more and less important things all jumbled together. Was it to such a presentation that the warnings of John Paul II were directed? "It is sometimes reported that a large number of Catholics today do not adhere to the teaching of the Church on a number of questions, notably sexual and conjugal morality, divorce and remarriage," he said. "Some are reported as not accepting the Church's clear position on abortion. It has also been noted that there is a tendency on the part of some Catholics to be selective in their adherence to the Church's moral teachings. It is sometimes claimed that dissent from the magisterium is totally compatible with being a 'good Catholic' and poses no obstacle to the reception of the sacraments. This is a grave error that challenges the teaching office of the bishops of the United States and elsewhere." And he continued, "Dissent from Church doctrine remains what it is, dissent; as such it may not be proposed or received on an equal footing with the Church's authentic teaching."[25]

In 1990, the Congregation for the Doctrine of the Faith published the "Instruction on the Ecclesial Vocation of the Theologian." Addressing the bishops of the Roman Catholic Church, and "through them her theologians,"[26] the "Instruction" certainly shows serious reservations about the media as a setting for theological debate. It explains that the theologian who disagrees with the magisterium, "even if the doctrine of the faith is not in question," will "refrain from giving untimely public expression" to these divergent opinions.[27] Again, the theologian in disagreement with magisterial teaching is urged to "avoid turning to the 'mass media' but have recourse to the responsible authority, for it is not by seeking to exert the

25. John Paul II, "The Pope's Address to the Bishops: Part II," *Origins* 17 (1987) 261.

26. Congregation for the Doctrine of the Faith, "Instruction on the Ecclesial Vocation of the Theologian," *Origins* 20 (1990–91) 117, 119–26; see #1.

27. Ibid., #27.

pressure of public opinion that one contributes to the clarification of doctrinal issues and renders service to the truth."[28] Concern with media and the appeal to public opinion is so central to this "Instruction" that it even defines "dissent" in reference to this concern as "that public opposition to the magisterium of the church also called *dissent*, which must be distinguished from the situation of personal difficulties" of a theologian who, as stated earlier, "might have serious difficulties, for reasons which appear to him well-founded, in accepting a non-irreformable magisterial teaching."[29]

Listing the causes of dissent defined in this way, the "Instruction" elaborates on philosophical liberalism, misunderstandings arising from the plurality of cultures and languages, and "the weight of public opinion when manipulated and its pressure to conform."[30]

The "Instruction," then, is leery of the public media as the setting for debate among theologians about "non-irreformable" magisterial teaching. Furthermore, in its second part it explains that dissent cannot be defended by appealing to a "parallel magisterium" of theologians, to opinion polls of many Christians, or to individual freedom of conscience. Theologians with difficulties about some "non-irreformable" magisterial teaching should seek solutions in "trustful dialogue with the pastors in the spirit of truth and charity";[31] for their part, the bishops are invited "to maintain and develop relations of trust with theologians" in the same spirit.[32]

The "Instruction" does envision a relationship of reciprocity between theologians and the magisterium, since "the living magisterium of the church and theology, while having different gifts and functions, ultimately have the same goal: preserving the people of God in the truth which sets free and thereby making them 'a light to the nations.'"[33] In this atmosphere of reciprocity, a theologian should as a rule "submit loyally to the teaching of the magisterium on matters per se not irreformable"; but the "Instruction" envisions the possibility that "a theologian may, according to the case, raise questions regarding the timeliness, the form, or even the contents of magisterial interventions."[34] Some magisterial interventions of a prudential sort "might not be free from all deficiencies." The theologian's competence in history brings awareness of "the filtering which occurs

28. Ibid., #30.
29. Ibid., #32.
30. Ibid.
31. Ibid., #40.
32. Ibid., #42.
33. Ibid., #21.
34. Ibid., #24.

with the passage of time," the "Instruction" explains. "The theologian knows that some judgments of the magisterium could be justified at the time in which they were made, because while the pronouncements contained true assertions and others which were not sure, both types were inextricably mixed." It adds, "Only time has permitted discernment and, after deeper study, the attainment of true doctrinal progress."[35]

So, according to the "Instruction," what procedures should a theologian follow if the theologian has serious difficulties with such "non-irreformable" magisterial teaching? While maintaining the "fundamental openness loyally to accept the teaching of the magisterium," the theologian should strive to understand the teaching through "intense and patient reflection" and a readiness "to revise his own opinions and examine the objections" of colleagues.[36] If, despite these loyal efforts, the difficulties persist, the theologian in fact "has the duty to make known to the magisterial authorities the problems raised by the teaching itself, in the arguments proposed to justify it or even in the manner in which it is presented." This should be done in an evangelical spirit, the "Instruction" remarks, and "with a profound desire to resolve the difficulties."[37] When explained to the magisterium in this way, the theologian's difficulties "could then contribute to real progress and provide a stimulus to the magisterium to propose the teaching of the church in greater depth and with a clearer presentation of the arguments."[38]

But a theologian may still find that difficulties with the magisterial teaching remain. In such a case, the theologian should avoid turning to the mass media and should remain open to "a deeper examination of the question." Such a situation can be "a difficult trial" for "a loyal spirit," the "Instruction" comments, and then adds, "It can be a call to suffer for the truth, in silence and prayer but with the certainty that if the truth really is at stake it will ultimately prevail."[39]

This "Instruction" contains many good insights, especially on the importance of an evangelical attitude; but on the whole it remains a puzzling document in the behavior it recommends to the theologian who disagrees with some teaching that is "not irreformable." Both the Congregation for the Doctrine of the Faith and Cardinal Ratzinger, in his earlier comments, seem especially horrified that a Roman Catholic theologian, by discussing

35. Ibid.
36. Ibid., #29.
37. Ibid., #30.
38. Ibid.
39. Ibid., #31.

his or her dissenting views in public, might encourage dissent in others. Of course, it is certainly true that public dissent by a theologian can, as Örsy says, "become a feeder to a deeper attitudinal dissent in others . . . [in] concrete situations where the peace or unity of the church for some reason is seriously threatened."[40] But, as McCormick notes, whether encouraging dissent in others is morally wrong depends on what the dissenter is saying. Presumably most would today agree that encouraging dissent against the Church's support of slavery would not have been wrong. "It is simply no response to object that dissent 'encourages dissent in others,'" McCormick argues, "for if the teaching is inaccurate, that is what dissent should do."[41]

Well, it seems that the Roman Catholic Church is having a debate, and it is a debate that has serious implications for ecumenical relations and that is not likely to be immediately resolved. Beneath the arguing about the meaning of *obsequium* and the court cases and the headlines, however, I believe that deeper issues are at stake. I think three shifts in thought simmer just below the surface in Roman Catholic life; focusing on these three shifts will deepen our understanding of the debate, and I think it will also indicate the direction which a resolution of the debate should take, a resolution intimately connected with the unity of the Church.

THE SHIFT FROM A CLASSICIST WORLDVIEW TO HISTORICAL-MINDEDNESS

The Roman Catholic Church is involved today in a number of shifts in its understanding, and perhaps the most profound is well indicated in Bernard Lonergan's widely known title as the shift from a classicist worldview to historical-mindedness. Let him describe the distinction he draws for us. "One can apprehend man [*sic*] abstractly through a definition that applies *omni et soli* and through properties verifiable in every man," he writes. "In this fashion one knows man as such; and man as such, precisely because he is an abstraction, also is unchanging."[42] Or again, "The classicist is not a pluralist. He knows that circumstances alter cases but he is far more deeply convinced that circumstances are accidental and that, beyond them, there is some substance or kernel or root that fits in the classicist assumptions of stability, immutability, fixity."[43] But the recognition of the

40. Örsy, *The Church: Learning and Teaching,* 104–105.

41. Richard A. McCormick, "L'Affaire Curran," *America* 154 (1986) 267.

42. Bernard Lonergan, "The Transition from a Classicist Worldview to Historical-Mindedness," *Second Collection* (London: Darton, Longman and Todd, 1974) 5.

43. Bernard Lonergan, *Doctrinal Pluralism* (Milwaukee: Marquette University Press, 1971) 5.

historicity of human life and understandings leads to an additional insight: that "human concepts are products and expressions of human understanding, that human understanding develops over time, and that it develops differently in different places and in different times."[44] Or again, "One can apprehend mankind as a concrete aggregate developing over time, where the locus of development and, so to speak, the synthetic bond is the emergence, expansion, differentiation, dialectic of meaning and of meaningful performance. On this view intentionality, meaning, is a constitutive component of human living; moreover, this component is not fixed, static, immutable, but shifting, developing, going astray, capable of redemption; on this view there is in the historicity, which results from human nature, an exigence for changing forms, structures, methods; and it is on this level and through this medium of changing meaning that divine revelation has entered the world and that the Church's witness is given to it."[45] By historical-mindedness, Lonergan does not mean relativism, as he is at pains to point out;[46] he means rather the recognition of the historicity of human understanding that characterizes modern thought and that profoundly affects the way we think about our knowledge of the truth.

Örsy puts it more simply when he describes our time as "the age when the Church was coming to grips with the law of evolution, especially in doctrinal matters."[47] Or again, we could describe it with Rahner as the recognition that there dwell in the Church together "changeable and unchangeable factors," some part of permanent witness to the faith and some not.[48]

The Roman Catholic Church is in the process of making the shift from a classicist worldview to historical-mindedness. We can see this shift symbolized in the emphases of the two Vatican councils. Where Vatican I taught that "the meaning of the sacred dogmas is perpetually to be retained which our Holy Mother Church has once declared"[49] and spoke of

44. Ibid., 6.

45. Lonergan, "Transition from a Classicist Worldview to Historical-Mindedness," 5–6.

46. Lonergan, *Doctrinal Pluralism*, 9–12; cf. Bernard Lonergan, "Philosophy and Theology," *Second Collection*, 207–208; *Insight: A Study of Human Understanding* (New York: Philosophical Library, 1957).

47. Örsy, "Magisterium: Assent and Dissent," 473.

48. Karl Rahner, "Basic Observations on the Subject of Changeable and Unchangeable Factors in the Church," *Theological Investigations*, trans. David Bourke (New York: Seabury, 1976) 14:3–23.

49. Denzinger-Schönmetzer 3020; translation is from Josef Neuner and Heinrich Roos, trans. Latin into German, *The Teaching of the Catholic Church*, ed.

definitions that are "irreformable,"[50] Vatican II affirmed—without denying the earlier points—that "there is a growth in the understanding" in the
Church "of the realities and the words which have been handed down." It
continues, "For as the centuries succeed one another, the Church constantly moves forward toward the fullness of divine truth until the words
of God reach their complete fulfillment in her."[51] At Vatican II, the historicity of understanding is affirmed, and some practical implications of
this insight are embraced in the endorsement of historical critical tools for
the study of Scripture. This shift to historical-mindedness is confirmed
more thoroughly in the 1973 teaching *Mysterium ecclesiae* of the
Congregation for the Doctrine of the Faith when it notes that "the meaning of the pronouncements of faith depend partly upon the expressive
power of the language used at a certain point in time and in particular circumstances," that "some dogmatic truth is first expressed incompletely
(but not falsely), and at a later date . . . it receives a fuller and more per-
fect expression," and finally, that truths taught through dogmatic formulas sometimes "bear traces" of "the changeable conceptions of a given
epoch."[52] And I am just citing official documents here; the shift to
historical-mindedness has taken hold widely with Roman Catholic theologians, among whom it is the working presupposition.

Once the shift to historical-mindedness is made, we can see that the
Church is not only a teacher but also a learner. Frederick Crowe draws the
contrast between the teaching Church and the learning Church—and not
as between two groups, but as between two processes in which the whole
Church must engage. He argues that for the Church, even for the writers
of Scripture, even for the magisterium, learning comes before teaching:
"So my thesis affirms an absolute priority of learning over teaching in the
Church, even with regard to the sources, divinely created and divinely
given, of our faith. The sources are sources that have learned."[53] Learning,
he explains, means "following the ordinary cognitional processes, whether

---

Karl Rahner, trans. into English by Geoffrey Stevens (Staten Island, N.Y.: Alba
House, 1967) 38.

50. Denzinger-Schönmetzer 3074; translation is from Neuner and Roos, 229.

51. *Dei verbum,* in *The Documents of Vatican II,* ed. Walter M. Abbott (New
York: America Press, 1966) #8.

52. Congregation for the Doctrine of the Faith, *Mysterium ecclesiae, The Tablet*
227 (14 July 1973) 668.

53. Frederick E. Crowe, "The Church as Learner: Two Crises, One *Kairos,*"
Appropriating the Lonergan Idea, ed. Michael Vertin (Washington, D.C.: The
Catholic University of America Press, 1989) 371.

in the realm of nature or in the realm of grace. It means asking questions on matters of which we are ignorant; forming an idea of a possible answer, indeed forming several ideas of different possible answers; weighing the pros and cons of the several alternative ideas; finally, coming to a judgment, and being able to say 'I've learned something.'"[54] Crowe gives some examples to make his point, noting that Peter went through a process of learning to understand his Christian freedom from the Mosaic Law, and that the Church went through another process of learning before it could teach that Christ was *homoousios* with the Father.

But why should we even hesitate in making such an affirmation, asks Crowe? "It is because we have laid so much stress on the teaching Church—and this not as a function related to and integrated with a learning function, but as an office belonging to certain people—that we have not attended to the learning function, though it is primary in regard to the Church as a whole and in relation to the totality of our cognitional procedures. Thus, we are like a bird that has one wing hugely overdeveloped, while the other, through lack of exercise, has been allowed to atrophy: we can hardly take flight on wings of eagles in that condition."[55]

The recognition of the priority of learning in the Church is linked to the recognition of our historicity. Truth is grasped through a process of inquiry which takes time; the transposition of the meaning of the Gospel from one culture to another, from one epoch to another, all this takes time, time for inquiry, weighing the evidence, balancing the pros and cons, reaching a preliminary judgment, testing it, coming finally to be able to say: we've learned something.

Now how is this related to the question of dissent? Dissent is part of the process by which a community learns. "Dissent . . . is not so much a personal right," comments McCormick. It is rather "only the possible outcome of a respectful and docile personal reflection on noninfallible teaching. Such reflection is the very condition of progress in understanding in the Church. Dissent, therefore, must be viewed and respected as a part of that total approach through which we learn."[56] Part of the total approach through which we learn: dissent is the way that the Church learned earlier in its history that it needed to change its teachings about slavery, religious liberty, the matter and form of some sacraments, the use of historical critical methods in biblical study, etc. If Roman Catholics had not raised questions about the teaching they heard from the magisterium in

54. Ibid.
55. Ibid., 373–74.
56. McCormick, 676.

earlier times, the learning finally achieved would not have occurred. George Tavard explains, "Freedom of expression in the Church is not a luxury, but a requirement of the intelligibility of faith. The time needed for a serene discussion of divergences in matters of faith will allow the Spirit to manifest himself without hindrance and to create step by step the unanimity of believers."[57] Today the need for such discussion in moral matters is even more necessary, notes Örsy, because of the host of new problems which we face. He gives some examples: "May a healthy person donate one of his kidneys to his brother who needs it to survive? Are atomic weapons acceptable for legitimate self-defense? Is fertilization *in vitro* permissible? What is the right balance between the public good and the private ownership of goods?" He continues, "To find the correct solutions, it was not enough to come to an understanding of the development of doctrine; it was also necessary to see the Church anew as an evolving reality."[58]

In fact, dissent has always played an important part in the way that the Church has learned. But the recognition of this fact can only take place within a recognition of the historicity of our understanding. Right now, the Roman Catholic magisterium is often treating dissent and dissenters on the basis of its older worldview, the classicist worldview, rather than making the full shift to which Vatican II and *Mysterium ecclesiae* commit it. The magisterium is treating dissent as though it should not happen, or should not happen in public; then, quite suddenly, it rewards the dissenters and, without noting the contribution they have made, begins to endorse their views instead of the older views they were criticizing. This is a strange approach. One of my students wrote once, about some earlier thinkers, that "they tended to make it difficult to have a body at all." Somewhat like those thinkers who were uncomfortable with having bodies at all, the magisterium of the Roman Catholic Church seems rather uncomfortable about having dissent in its midst, even though such dissent has functioned often to bring about important insights that have become a part of magisterial teaching. Even though the "Instruction on the Ecclesial Vocation of the Theologian" recognizes that "time has permitted discernment" of true from false assertions made in a "non-irreformable" magisterial intervention and hence "the attainment of true doctrinal progress," it continues to envision public discussion of dissenting views

---

57. George Tavard, "Tradition in Theology: A Problematic Approach," *Perspectives on Scripture and Tradition* (Notre Dame, Ind.: Fides, 1976) 102–103.
58. Örsy, "Magisterium: Assent and Dissent," 474.

only in terms of dangers.[59] Could not such public discussion sometimes provide an opportunity for the desired discernment?

Of course, not all dissent from magisterial teaching has proved an advance in truth; but neglecting to leave space for the normal give-and-take, trial-and-error process that learning—even learning in the Church—must take means that learning will be stunted and the learners exhausted, sick, or losing heart. Furthermore, it is this situation, not dissent, which today causes genuine scandal for Roman Catholics and for our ecumenical dialogue partners. Should justice not be extended, they ask, to Charles E. Curran, Leonardo Boff, Raymond Hunthausen, Agnes Mary Mansour, and other theologians, religious, and bishops who try to learn something about how the Gospel could be proclaimed effectively in a new cultural context? The faculty of the General Theological Seminary in effect asked: Do we wish to come into closer union with a church community that acts this way?

In fact, the shift to historical-mindedness is quite important to the ecumenical movement itself. It is this shift which has assisted the many Christian communions to recognize each other's traditions as alternative and developing articulations of the one Christian Gospel, each capturing the core of the Gospel in different confessional formulations, liturgical patterns, and styles of decision-making; each with its strengths and weaknesses. The recognition of our historicity has allowed us to grow from charges of heresy to desires for unity. Was not this ecumenical movement itself first seen as dissent among our churches, though now it is understood as the work of the Holy Spirit?

The Roman Catholic Church is embroiled in a debate about dissent, then, first, because it has not fully made this first shift from a classicist worldview to historical-mindedness.

The Shift from a Pyramidal Ecclesiology to an Ecclesiology of Communion

But the debate about dissent arises as well because the Roman Catholic Church is having trouble with a second shift: the shift from a pyramidal ecclesiology[60] to an ecclesiology of communion. This shift has been widely

59. Congregation for the Doctrine of the Faith, "Instruction on the Ecclesial Vocation of the Theologian," #24.

60. Yves Congar uses the term "pyramidal ecclesiology" in "La 'réception' comme réalité ecclésiologique," *Revue des sciences philosophiques et théologiques* 56 (1972) 392–93.

discussed in ecumenical circles. A pyramidal understanding of the Roman Catholic Church emphasized the unity of the Church, but it sometimes confused unity with uniformity. Local churches were seen as pieces of a big pie which was the universal Church, and there was an increasing centralization in government and personal devotion around the person of the bishop of Rome. "The Catholic Church was in practice seen not as a communion of local Christian communities, each of them keeping its own traditions and its own ways of living faithfully the common faith, but as an *[sic]* unique and huge diocese governed by an unique and real chief and bishop, the bishop of Rome helped by the offices of his curia," writes Jean-Marie Tillard. "Membership of the Catholic community implied submission to a central government and the leaders of the local churches came to appear more as transmittors of the wishes of the Vatican than as pastors having the first responsibility in their local church. . . . It transformed the Roman Catholic community into a monolithic Church in which the most important attitude was submission to the Vatican curia rather than obedience to the Word of God."[61]

But Vatican II marks the shift from this kind of ecclesiology to an ecclesiology of communion,[62] recovered from patristic and biblical sources. Vatican II emphasized the local church in its celebration of the Eucharist as the locus of Church, and it saw the communion within God shared with those in the Church, binding them into one. The local church is given many gifts and charisms for the sake of its mission, and among them is a ministry of leadership to assist the local church to remain in the faith of the apostles and in communion with other local churches that share this faith. So Vatican II emphasized the collegiality of bishops, each from his local church, each bringing the views of his church to the college of bishops.[63] It paid special honor to those local churches in communion with Rome which maintain their own distinctive liturgical rite from the East. And it located the bishop of Rome within the college of bishops as the center and servant of communion, "a permanent and visible source and foundation of unity of faith and fellowship."[64]

Ecumenical discussions have elaborated what Jean-Marie Tillard calls this "desired ecclesiology" of communion as the model of Church most

61. Jean-Marie Tillard, "The Roman Catholic Church: Growing towards Unity," *One in Christ* 14 (1978) 221–22.

62. Jean-Marie Tillard, "The Church of God Is a Communion: The Ecclesiological Perspective of Vatican II," *One in Christ* 17 (1981) 117–31.

63. *Lumen gentium*, #22–23.

64. *Lumen gentium*, #18.

fruitful for Christian unity.[65] Especially striking as evidence of this is *The Final Report* of the Anglican-Roman Catholic International Commission, which bases itself on an ecclesiology of communion. It sees the Church as the communion that is "a sign that God's purpose in Christ is being realized in the world by grace" and "an instrument for the accomplishment of this purpose."[66] It envisions primacy and conciliarity as the two complementary elements by which oversight fosters communion; but, the *Report* adds frankly, "it has often happened that one has been emphasized at the expense of the other, even to the point of serious imbalance."[67] We get the idea that the writers have some examples in mind, and this is confirmed with their lengthy correction on what primacy ought to mean: "Primacy fulfills its purpose by helping the churches to listen to one another, to grow in love and unity, and to strive together towards the fullness of Christian life and witness; it respects and promotes Christian freedom and spontaneity; it does not seek uniformity where diversity is legitimate, or centralize administration to the detriment of local churches."[68] ARCIC interprets Vatican I and Vatican II to mean that the bishop of Rome should not stifle the distinctive features of the local churches. "Neither theory nor practice, however, has ever fully reflected these ideals," the writers continue. "Yet the primacy, rightly understood, implies that the bishop of Rome exercises his oversight in order to guard and promote the faithfulness of all the churches to Christ and one another. Communion with him is intended as a safeguard of the catholicity of each local church, and as a sign of the communion of all the churches."[69] ARCIC echoes other ecumenical dialogues in its ecclesiology of communion, such as the U.S. Lutheran-Roman Catholic dialogue on the petrine ministry, which sees the petrine function of ministry as a service of the oneness of the Church "by symbolizing unity, and by facilitating communication, mutual assistance or correction, and collaboration in the Church's mission."[70]

65. Tillard, "The Roman Catholic Church: Growing towards Unity," 220–25.

66. Anglican-Roman Catholic International Commission [ARCIC], "Introduction," *The Final Report* (London: SPCK & Catholic Truth Society, 1982) #7.

67. Anglican-Roman Catholic International Commission [ARCIC], "Authority in the Church I," *The Final Report* (London: SPCK & Catholic Truth Society, 1982) #22.

68. Ibid., #21.

69. Ibid., #12.

70. [U.S.] Lutheran-Roman Catholic Dialogue, "Differing Attitudes toward Papal Primacy: Common Statement," *Papal Primacy and the Universal Church*, eds. Paul Empie and T. Austin Murphy (Minneapolis: Augsburg Publishing House, 1974) #4.

Because of its emphasis on the local church, an ecclesiology of communion also knows the importance of reception, which it realizes is not obedience but includes evaluation and judgment.[71] So ARCIC sees the whole Church involved in "a continuous process of discernment and response" in evaluation of proposed teaching;[72] reception by the whole Church "is the ultimate indication that the Church's authoritative decision in a matter of faith has been truly preserved from error by the Holy Spirit."[73]

So Roman Catholic theology, with the help of ecumenical dialogue, has moved to an ecclesiology of communion. But Roman Catholic practice is having a harder time making this shift. While some of its practice grows out of the new ecclesiological vision, other aspects in its practice show that old habits, old styles, old patterns of authority die hard. "Neither theory nor practice, however, has ever fully reflected these ideals,"[74] comments ARCIC about the primacy of the bishop of Rome in a reflective understatement. The treatment of dissent in the Roman Catholic Church manifests more the pyramidal, centralized ecclesiology than the ecclesiology of communion recovered by Vatican II.

First of all, the exercise of universal primacy in the treatment of a Curran, a Boff, a Mansour, a Hunthausen is hardly the style which ecumenical dialogue has envisioned for this ministry. ARCIC believes that primacy does not confuse unity with uniformity, does not centralize administration to the detriment of local churches, does not stifle Christian freedom and spontaneity: but this pontificate's treatment of dissenters in fact often tends to do all of these things. ARCIC believes that "a primate exercises his ministry not in isolation but in collegial association with his brother bishops. His intervention in the affairs of a local church should not be made in such a way as to usurp the responsibility of its bishop."[75] It is sobering to read those words and then ponder some of the treatment of Hunthausen. The U.S. Lutheran-Roman Catholic Dialogue reports a "growing awareness among Lutherans of the necessity

71. Congar, 370.

72. Anglican-Roman Catholic International Commission [ARCIC], "Authority in the Church I: Elucidation (1981)," *The Final Report* (London: SPCK & Catholic Truth Society, 1982) #3.

73. Anglican-Roman Catholic International Commission [ARCIC], "Authority in the Church II," *The Final Report* (London: SPCK & Catholic Truth Society, 1982) #25.

74. ARCIC, "Authority in the Church I," #12.

75. Ibid., #21.

of a specific ministry to serve the Church's unity and universal mission," while at the same time emphasizing that renewal of the papacy is based on the principles of legitimate diversity, collegiality, and subsidiarity.[76] But these principles have often been ignored in case after case of dissent in the Roman Catholic Church.

In these recent treatments of dissent, the local church is ignored or stifled, as is the importance of reception throughout the Church. Congar contrasts an ecclesiology of the pyramid, where the power and truth come from the top down, with an ecclesiology of communion, where the gifts of the Holy Spirit are given to all, with charisms to accomplish their unique mission within the body.[77] If one thinks in terms of the pyramidal model, one will think also of a society under a visible head, and one may then attribute to the head the sole importance in reception. But if one adopts an ecclesiology of communion, one values the insights and the leadership of all of the local churches. One of the many issues raised by the recent treatment of dissent in the Roman Catholic Church is the role of the local church in the process of reception. It is interesting to listen to the reflections of Matthew Clark, bishop of Rochester, in his defense of Curran against what he suggests was an inappropriate intervention by Rome in the life of a local church. Noting that he is pastor of the church in Rochester and shares through the college of bishops in solicitude for the entire Church, Clark notes the respect in which the U.S. Church holds Curran. He praises the generosity and reverence shown by U.S. pastoral leaders in their efforts to implement Vatican II, and the vitality, creativity, and genuine goodheartedness of U.S. Roman Catholic communities. There are "faults" and "mistakes," he acknowledges, "but we are a faithful people and we will continue to serve God's kingdom in the Church with generosity." And then he adds, "My hope is that together we can find better ways to recognize and be faithful to the nature of the particular churches and the communion they form with Rome as their center, and that the Holy See will regard the bishops of our country as ones who can appropriately and ably communicate to the Holy See the shape of and challenges to pastoral life in our particular churches."[78]

His reflections show an important dimension of many issues eliciting Vatican disapproval. Many (though not all) of the positions taken by, for

---

76. [U.S.] Lutheran-Roman Catholic Dialogue, "Differing Attitudes toward Papal Primacy: Common Statement," Introduction, 10; #22–25.

77. Congar, 392–93.

78. Matthew Clark, Public Statement of Matthew Clark, Bishop of Rochester (12 March 1986), *Origins* 15 (1985–86) 694.

example, Curran illustrate insights drawn from pastoral practice within the context of North American society with its high rate of marriage breakdown, widespread Roman Catholic acceptance of artificial contraception, increased sensitivity to treatment of homosexuals, etc. The Mansour case raises the problem of Vatican neglect of due process and the issue of Christian participation in government within a pluralist society; the Boff case, the question of liberation theology as an indigenization of the Gospel in a culture of the poor; the Hunthausen case, the challenge of pastoral care in a changing society. In these and some of the other cases of Vatican treatment of dissent, there is little evidence of the solicitude which ecumenical dialogue has developed for the views of the local church as integral to reception of Christian teaching.

Congar reminds us that reception is tied to a theology of the local church, to an enlivened pneumatology, to a vision of the Church as a communion of churches, and to a theology of tradition that sees its dynamic ongoing character.[79] He could hardly have been happy about the situation some forty U.S. bishops reflect upon in a recent document about plans for the restructuring of the National Conference of Catholic Bishops and the U.S. Catholic Conference. In this document, the bishops ask why major concerns are unaddressed by the episcopal conference. They write, "If we are not, as a collegial body, dealing with the real issues or speaking honestly and openly about them, it is not because bishops are afraid to do such things. One might wonder if it has to do with the particular nature of these issues, i.e., they often involve disagreement with the approach taken by curial offices."[80] While the group of bishops emphasizes that "the Petrine ministry is essential to the church and critical to its practice," the group seeks to improve the exercise of collegiality. The bishops are concerned that teachings by the pope or by curial offices are sometimes published without first consulting the episcopal conferences. In addition, they observe, draft documents of the U.S. episcopal conference are frequently submitted to Rome before being discussed by the U.S. bishops, "and upon receiving the results, there is no dialogue. The response from Rome is treated as a directive."[81] After noting other areas of concern, they observe that "some bishops may fear to raise certain issues for open discussion lest they be considered disloyal or cause scandal." These

79. Congar, 392.

80. Rembert Weakland *et al.*, "Issues in Restructuring the Bishops' Conference," *Origins* 25 (1995) 130. The document bears the names of twelve bishops who developed the document over the period of a year and a half; a total of some forty bishops have endorsed it.

81. Ibid., 133.

bishops, the authors continue, "are aware of the great concern among some U.S. Catholics for loyalty, interpreted to mean a strict and undifferentiated application of all Roman norms, and the notion of the church as a multinational corporation with headquarters in Rome and branch offices (dioceses) around the world. One might be correct on an issue, but to speak out openly at this time is looked upon as disloyal and dangerous to the faith of the community."[82] The bishops believe that some of their concerns suggest "the need to develop a more mature, adult, collegial relationship with Rome."[83] These reflections from the pastors of some local U.S. churches manifest unfinished business as the Roman Catholic Church seeks to put into practice the ecclesiology of communion it taught at Vatican II.

In the area of ecclesiology, the Roman Catholic Church must still find the way to shift its practice into accordance with its ecclesiology of communion, the ecclesiological model most fruitful for envisioning the unity of the Church.

THE SHIFT FROM CREEPING INFALLIBILITY
TO THE HIERARCHY OF TRUTHS

The Roman Catholic Church is involved in one last shift which it is also finding difficult. This shift is less from one theoretical understanding to another; it is more from an abuse to the reform of an abuse. Like the other shifts, this one as well has large implications for dissent and ecumenical relations.

Vatican I defined the limits and conditions of infallibility when exercised by the bishop of Rome, but after the Council's close these limits and conditions were widely misunderstood. Many people, including many Roman Catholics, thought that infallibility was claimed for whatever the pope said. Little was said by popes to dissuade them from this view. Many theologians, as well, suggested in their seminary textbooks that all papal encyclicals were exercises of infallibility.[84] And so developed the phenomenon called "creeping infallibility": the aura of infallibility that has tended to surround all teachings of the pope in the last century of Roman Catholic life.

Not all theologians even at the time of Vatican I endorsed this creeping infallibility, of course. John Henry Newman is famous for his moderate

82. Ibid.
83. Ibid.
84. Walter Kasper, *Die Lehre von der Tradition in der römischen Schule* (Freiburg: Herder, 1962).

interpretation of *Pastor aeternus,* and in fact some moderate interpretations received the confirmation of Pius IX himself. But there were widespread misunderstandings, misunderstandings which minority bishops themselves had foreseen during Vatican I. Félix Dupanloup of Orléans, a spokesperson for the minority bishops, had warned: "Doubtless here theologians will be able to distinguish the nuances and the fine points and to show that this is not exactly a definition, but how will the multitude of those who are not theologians discern that the pope who is fallible even as pope in such and such an act is no longer fallible in this or that other act? How will they understand that he can be infallible and yet, by great pontifical acts [that are not *ex cathedra*], *foment heresy?* In the eyes of the public that will still be infallibility."[85] His warning sounds like prophecy today.

Now in fact I believe that infallibility, correctly understood as the assistance God gives the whole Church in every age not to lose completely the message of the Gospel, is actually a helpful idea, though its formulation at Vatican I often obscures its meaning. I think the category of infallibility helps us to distinguish central beliefs of the Christian faith from less central teachings, beliefs, and practices which embody Christian lifestyle. It is precisely this same distinction which is indicated, as I noted above, between the two kinds of responses Roman Catholic theology has discussed: the assent of faith to central matters and the religious *obsequium* of mind and will to less central teachings.

Such a distinction is very important. Not everything is of the same importance to faith. Statues of Mary, the divinity of Christ, the discipline of obligatory celibacy for clergy in the West, the existence of God, the teaching against abortion, the small vigil candles in some churches, the teaching against artificial contraception, the injunction against idolatry, the refusal to ordain women, the doctrine of the Trinity: all of these have their place in present Roman Catholic life, but they do not all carry the same weight of authority. Some of them may well be mistaken; others are at the core of Christian confession; but surely they are at least different from each other in degree of importance. Creeping infallibility tends to collapse them all together and surround them all with the aura of equal authority.

Now, I do not think that it is a coincidence that infallibility crept into such a misunderstanding. I believe that an underdeveloped theory about the primacy of the bishop of Rome in Vatican I's *Pastor aeternus* allowed the continuation of an overcentralized practice of his primacy; together

---

85. Félix Dupanloup, *Observations sur la controverse soulevée relativement à la définition de l'infaillibilité au prochain concile* (Paris: Douniol, 1869) 41.

they set the atmosphere for the misunderstanding of the Council's teaching about infallibility. The defensive stand of the Roman Catholic Church against the modern world may have been another factor in developing an all-or-nothing approach to church teachings.

But that is a topic for another discussion. For the Roman Catholic Church tried to shift away from this creeping infallibility at Vatican II. It did this by affirming the infallibility of the whole people of God,[86] but also by affirming another important idea: the hierarchy of truths. "In Catholic teaching there exists an order or 'hierarchy' of truths," teaches Vatican II, "since they vary in their relationship to the foundation of the Christian faith."[87] Congar notes the importance of this insight for ecumenical relations. Roman Catholic polemics since the Reformation have sometimes emphasized the authority of the teacher more than the content of the teacher's teaching. The hierarchy of truths directs our attention to the distinctions among teachings, and reserves the place of honor for those most central articles of the faith.[88] Furthermore, it suggests a hierarchy of errors and invites the question: which errors are serious enough for a break in communion, and which not?[89]

But the shift to the hierarchy of truths is also important for the question of dissent. Frequently dissent is attacked because it has refused to take Catholicism as a package—it has "denied the organic unity of the faith" is the way the complaint is often made. In a meeting with theologians in Toronto, Cardinal Ratzinger observed that the distinction between infallible and noninfallible teachings is a juridicization that began within the last one hundred years. Some things have been defined, he noted, but that does not mean that everything else is open to discussion. Some of the most important realities have never been defined, he continued.[90]

Örsy agrees with this conclusion, noting that "no one has ever asserted that all we have to believe has been the object of infallible pronounce-

---

86. *Lumen gentium,* #12.

87. *Unitatis redintegratio,* in *The Documents of Vatican II,* ed. Walter M. Abbott (America Press, 1966) #11.

88. Yves Congar, "On the '*Hierarchia Veritatum,*'" trans. Uta Kriefall, in *The Heritage of the Early Church: Essays in Honor of the Very Reverend Georges Vasilievich Florovsky,* eds. David Neiman and Margaret Schatkin, *Orientalia Christiana Analecta* 195 (Rome: Pontifical Institute of Oriental Studies, 1973) 411–18.

89. Ibid., 419.

90. Joseph Ratzinger in discussion with theology professors of the Toronto School of Theology, Alumni Hall, University of St. Michael's College, Toronto, 15 April 1986.

ments."[91] If a teaching remained undebated, "no council or pope ever thought of infallibly defining it."[92] So, he explains, "some of the noninfallibly stated doctrines may well be integral parts of the deposit of revelation."[93] But, he adds, "it follows also, with no less force, that a good portion of the noninfallible propositions is no more than respectable school opinion, and as such not part of the universally held Catholic doctrine. Theologians should not be easily castigated for criticizing or rejecting such teachings; to say that *all* noninfallible teaching forms an organic unity with infallible magisterium is nonsense."[94]

For that matter, who would suggest that only infallible teachings should be taught by Roman Catholic theologians? "Authoritative, noninfallible teaching, after all, could be reasonably construed to cover a great deal that one might want to insist a Catholic theologian hew to if he or she is teaching in the name of the Church—the condemnation of racism, for instance, or slavery, or judicial torture," points out *Commonweal*. But it adds, "The fact is that if Charles Curran's moderate, scholarly, nuanced manner of dissenting cannot be recognized as responsible, then virtually no one's can."[95]

Distinguo was a word constantly used by Thomas Aquinas. "The alternative to distinguishing is confusion," warns Lonergan.[96] The ability to distinguish between central and less central aspects of the Gospel remains an important skill for the Church.

Sometimes people have a rather juridical notion of infallibility that equates "infallibility" with "formally defined"; this leads them to argue for the necessity of holding more than "infallible teachings," but leaves them without sufficient criteria to distinguish between central and less central matters. A nonjuridical grasp of infallibility would help reach such criteria, and ecumenical dialogue has assisted Roman Catholic thought in its movement toward recovering such a grasp.[97] But the shift to the idea of the hierarchy of truths reminds us in another way of a reason for such terms as "infallibility," "articles of faith," and "truths necessary for salva-

91. Örsy, "Magisterium: Assent and Dissent," 480.

92. Ibid., 481.

93. Ibid., 486.

94. Ibid.

95. The Editors, "Doctrine and Dissent: The Curran Case," *Commonweal* 113 (1986) 165.

96. Bernard Lonergan, "Cognitional Structure," *Collection*, eds. Frederick Crowe and Robert Doran, *Collected Works of Bernard Lonergan* (Toronto: University of Toronto Press, 1988) 4:214.

97. See, for example, Edward Schillebeeckx, "The Problem of the Infallibility of the Church's Office: A Theological Reflection," in *Truth and Certainty*, eds.

tion." Some things are more central to God's revelation than others. Dissent from such central matters is a threat to communion in faith and should be a concern for all of our churches. But dissent in less central matters is a less serious matter and should be treated more under the rubric of an unfinished process of reception. The shift from an aura of creeping infallibility to the implications of the hierarchy of truths may help the Roman Catholic Church take this attitude toward dissent on less central matters.

CONCLUSION

In this article, I have argued that dissent functions as a litmus test for a church's views, and that the Roman Catholic Church has opened a debate about dissent that has serious ramifications for ecumenical relations. While its official teaching implies the possibility of dissenting from teachings that are not central, its recent practice suggests otherwise. Beneath the surface of the debate, I found three shifts that the Roman Catholic Church is committed to making, but has not yet fully made: the shift from a classicist worldview to historical-mindedness; the shift from a pyramidal ecclesiology to an ecclesiology of communion; and the shift from creeping infallibility to the hierarchy of truths. These are shifts, then, in our epistemology, our ecclesiology, and our setting of priorities. When the Roman Catholic Church takes steps to deepen our grasp of the theoretical meaning of these shifts and to implement them in our practice, we also serve the search for the unity of the Church.

I said at the start of this article that the Roman Catholic Church excludes certain things from its debate on dissent, and let me now add that I believe these exclusions are strengths that we bring to the ecumenical dialogue with other communions. Our firm sense that the core of Christian confession is not open for debate, that a relativist worldview of truth is not really a Christian alternative, and that a ministry of oversight to the universal Church can serve Christian communion and proclamation: these convictions we bring as gifts to offer in discussion with others.

Schillebeeckx and Bas van Iersel, *Concilium*, vol. 83 (New York: Herder and Herder, 1973) 77–94; Heinrich Fries and Johann Finsterhölzl, "Infallibility," *Sacramentum Mundi;* ARCIC, "Authority in the Church I," #15, #19; "Authority in the Church II," #23–33; [U.S.] Lutheran-Roman Catholic Dialogue, "Teaching Authority and Infallibility in the Church," *Teaching Authority and Infallibility in the Church*, eds. Paul Empie, T. Austin Murphy, and Joseph Burgess (Minneapolis: Augsburg Publishing House, 1980) 11–68.

But we also bring weaknesses, and I have mentioned the three insufficiently completed shifts as the weaknesses we are experiencing in the debate today about dissent. I am exhorted to this task by *Unitatis redintegratio* itself when it teaches that "the primary duty" of Roman Catholics doing ecumenical work "is to make an honest and careful appraisal of whatever needs to be renewed and achieved in the Catholic household itself, in order that its life may bear witness more loyally and luminously to the teachings and ordinances which have been handed down from Christ through the apostles."[98]

But all of our church communions bring strengths and weaknesses with them into the ecumenical discussion. It is through dialogue with each other that the Holy Spirit is acting to enable us to correct each other's faults and to learn from each other's witness. This is why I am so hopeful about ecumenical dialogue: I believe that it is a means of reform of the many communions so that they can be brought again into the full unity for which Christ prayed. You can see why I find it easy to agree with Vatican II in concluding that the ecumenical movement is a work of the Holy Spirit in our day.[99]

98. *Unitatis redintegratio,* #4.
99. Ibid., #4.

8

ECUMENISM AND FEMINISM
IN DIALOGUE ON AUTHORITY[1]

What can the ecumenical movement and the Christian feminist movement contribute to the discussion on authority in the Church? What do they have to say to each other?

At first glance, ecumenists or feminists might answer: "Little or nothing." Some ecumenists see in the feminist movement only new obstacles in the path toward Church unity with its search for mutual recognition of ordained ministries and common structures of decision-making. And some feminists see the movement for Church unity as simply a confirmation of a patriarchal status quo, with new agreements reinforcing an old boys' network of episcopal and other ordained authorities. To hear and take seriously the voices of both movements today is a demanding task.

But, as a participant in each movement, I want to suggest that both ecumenism and feminism offer useful suggestions for the reform of the theology and practice of authority. Each movement offers important criticisms of the other as well. By entering into dialogue with these movements, and setting them in dialogue with each other, the churches that seek greater solidarity with women by the year 2000 will find themselves enriched.

1. This article in a slightly different form was published in a collection of women's essays sponsored by the Commission on Faith and Order of the National Council of Churches of Christ in the U.S.A. to mark the Ecumenical Decade: Churches in Solidarity with Women, as "Ecumenism and Feminism in Dialogue on Authority," in *Women and Church*, ed. Melanie May (Grand Rapids, Mich.: William B. Eerdmans Publishing Co. & New York: Friendship Press, 1991) 118–37.

COMMON CONCERNS OF ECUMENISM AND FEMINISM ON AUTHORITY

The two movements have a number of common concerns about authority. Each movement is very interested in authority, actually, and very critical of the way authority is often understood and practiced. This common concern about authority in its practice within the life of the Church, as well as in its theoretical understanding, helps make each a movement for reform and renewal of the Church, rather than simply a school of thought.

Feminism seeks to liberate the Church from false interpretations of the Scriptures, interpretations supporting men's superiority or domination over women. "The Women's Movement errs when it dismisses the Bible as inconsequential or condemns it as enslaving," argues Phyllis Trible. "In rejecting Scripture women ironically accept male chauvinistic interpretations and thereby capitulate to the very view they are protesting." But, she continues, "the hermeneutical challenge is to translate biblical faith without sexism."[2] To this end, Trible rereads the story of Adam and Eve to reveal their equality in creation; it is sin which leads to a distortion of this good creation, when a pattern of domination and subjugation begins. To this end as well Elisabeth Schüssler Fiorenza criticizes the preachers and writers who maintain "that the submission of women and their subordinate place in family, society and church were ordained and revealed in the Bible."[3] To counter this perspective, she points to the non-sexist traditions that lie behind the New Testament, traditions of egalitarian and interpersonal styles of authority in early Christian communities where women and men exercised ministries of leadership.[4] Other writers emphasize the positive images of women in the Gospels,[5] or the favorable attitude of Jesus toward women.[6]

2. Phyllis Trible, "Depatriarchalizing in Biblical Interpretation," *Journal of the American Academy of Religion* 41 (1973) 31.

3. Elisabeth Schüssler Fiorenza, "The Study of Women in Early Christianity: Some Methodological Considerations," *Critical History and Biblical Faith: New Testament Perspectives*, ed. Thomas J. Ryan (Villanova: College Theology Society, 1979) 35.

4. Ibid., 41–45; cf. Elisabeth Schüssler Fiorenza, *In Memory of Her* (New York: Crossroad Publishing Co., 1984) 97–241.

5. Raymond Brown, "Roles of Women in the Fourth Gospel," *Theological Studies* 36 (1975) 688–99; cf. Constance Parvey, "The Theology and Leadership of Women in the New Testament," in *Religion and Sexism*, ed. Rosemary Radford Ruether (New York: Simon and Schuster, 1974) 117–49; Elisabeth Moltmann-Wendel, *The Women around Jesus* (New York: Crossroads, 1982).

6. Mary Rose d'Angelo, "Women and the Earliest Church: Reflecting on the Problematique of Christ and Culture," in *Women Priests*, eds. Leonard Swidler and Arlene Swidler (New York: Paulist Press, 1977) 195.

At the same time, Schüssler Fiorenza echoes other writers when she warns that the Bible itself contains an "androcentric interpretation and selection of early Christian traditions."[7] "*All* early Christian writings are culturally conditioned and formulated in a patriarchal milieu," she warns. "Biblical revelation and truth are not found in an a-cultural essence distilled from patriarchal texts, but are given in those texts and interpretative models which transcend and criticize their patriarchal culture and religion."[8] Hence the authority of the Bible itself is rightly discerned only when it is read as living tradition, with a critical hermeneutic that seeks the liberating word of God's revelation in the midst of history.[9]

In addition to their commitment to the elimination of false understandings of the authority of men over women in the Bible, or even of a false understanding of the authority of the Bible itself, feminists also wish to reread the Christian tradition in order to correct theology or practice that condones a pattern of men's domination over women in the Church or the world. Margaret Farley looks for the sources of sexual inequality in the history of theology, and finds them in "the identification of women with evil" and "the identification of the fullness of the *imago Dei* with male persons."[10] This identification was furthered by the probably unreflective appropriation of the cultural viewpoint during the patristic period, exemplified in Philo, that linked men with spirit and women with matter.[11] Such a faulty theological anthropology in a variety of forms was used for centuries by theologians to argue in favor of the subordinate character of women and against the ordination of women.[12] Feminist

---

7. Schüssler Fiorenza, "The Study of Women in Early Christianity: Some Methodological Considerations," 37.

8. Ibid., 39.

9. See Elisabeth Schüssler Fiorenza, "Feminist Spirituality, Christian Identity, and Catholic Vision," in *Womanspirit Rising*, eds. Carol Christ and Judith Plaskow (San Francisco: Harper and Row, 1979) 146; Elisabeth Schüssler Fiorenza, "Feminist Theology as a Critical Theology of Liberation," *Theological Studies* 36 (1975) 611–12, 616.

10. Margaret A. Farley, "Sources of Sexual Inequality in the History of Christian Thought," *Journal of Religion* 56 (1976) 164.

11. Rosemary Radford Ruether, "Misogynism and Virginal Feminism in the Fathers of the Church," in *Religion and Sexism: Images of Woman in the Jewish and Christian Traditions*, ed. Rosemary Radford Ruether, 150–83; cf. George Tavard, *Woman in Christian Tradition* (Notre Dame: University of Notre Dame Press, 1973) especially 97–121.

12. Francine Cardman, "The Medieval Question of Women and Orders," *The Thomist* 42 (1978) 582–99.

theologians are critical of arguments based on such an unchristian anthropology, and they are ready to criticize contemporary uses of these traditions that would rest on such arguments as well—even the more subtle arguments of today that claim the natural complementarity of men and women.[13] Similarly, they criticize presentations from Christian tradition that consistently portray God in male images, or that use Christ's maleness as an argument against women's ordination. For them, such arguments and practices approach idolatry. Mary Daly pointed out long ago, "If God is male, then the male is God."[14] This is a lesson about authority that feminists have learned well.

Because of women's experience of male domination and of marginalization in some decision-making roles, feminists argue, women have an important sensitivity to the misuse of authority. Such sensitivity alerts them to a host of abuses, ranging from the distorted use of authoritative sources through the dynamics of subjugating interpersonal relationships and the structures of power that can continue a patriarchal worldview or atmosphere. Hence feminists urge the radical reform of the ordained ministry, not just its inclusion of women. Hence also they urge a model of consultation and consensus in decision-making, with an emphasis on the participation of all and the equality among members of the Church. Many feminists seem wary of any authoritative traditions or leaders; they are quick to recognize the role of prophecy in the Church, and they even describe the women's movement as a prophetic movement calling for repentance and reform of the Church. For them, this is essential to being in Christ.

Ecumenism has a set of sensitivities and proposed reforms strikingly similar to those of feminism.

Ecumenists, too, know the dangers of a distorted use of the Scriptures as proof texts to illustrate the correctness of the views of the speaker or the speaker's tradition. The history of church divisions can be charted as a history of disagreements about the correct reading of the Scriptures. In order to be faithful to the authority of the Scriptures in their true meaning, ecumenical dialogue groups consistently seek fresh readings of controversial scriptural texts,[15] sometimes appointing a special exegetical

---

13. Margaret Farley, "Discrimination or Equality? The Old Order or the New?" *Women Priests*, eds. Swidler and Swidler, 310–15; cf. Tavard, especially 211–19.

14. Mary Daly, "After the Death of God the Father," in *Beyond God the Father*, 2d ed. (Boston: Beacon Press, 1973) 19.

15. See, for example, Anglican-Roman Catholic International Commission [ARCIC], "Ministry and Ordination," #8, 13; "Authority in the Church II," #2–9 in

commission to study the scriptural questions before they begin their own work in the dialogue.[16]

At the same time, the ecumenical movement also stresses the importance of reading the Scriptures within a living tradition. It is by Tradition, with its many traditions, that the Gospel is carried through the centuries, stated the 1963 Faith and Order Commission meeting in Montreal.[17] The Anglican-Roman Catholic International Commission [ARCIC] understands the role of authoritative teaching within this context. "All generations and cultures must be helped to understand that the good news of salvation is also for them," it argues. "It is not enough for the Church simply to repeat the original apostolic words. It has also prophetically to translate them in order that the hearers in their situation may understand and respond to them. All such restatement must be consonant with the apostolic witness recorded in the Scriptures. . . ."[18] Prophetic translation, says ARCIC, means defending the Gospel against error and formulating it in fresh ways for every culture and age. Sometimes formulations of the living tradition of the Church become authoritative, "part of its permanent witness."[19] But this occurs only with reception by the whole Church. "The assent of the faithful is the ultimate indication that the Church's authoritative decision in a matter of faith has been truly preserved from error by the Holy Spirit," explains ARCIC.[20] Concern with consensus-models of decision-making, the conciliar nature of the Church,

---

The Final Report (London: SPCK & Catholic Truth Society, 1982); [U.S.] Lutheran-Roman Catholic Dialogue, "Differing Attitudes Toward Papal Primacy," #9–13; "Teaching Authority and Infallibility in the Church," #5–16, and "Justification by Faith," #122–49, in *Building Unity*, eds. Joseph A. Burgess and Jeffrey Gros (New York: Paulist Press, 1989).

16. See, for example, Raymond Brown *et al.*, eds., *Peter in the New Testament: A Collaborative Assessment by Protestant and Roman Catholic Scholars* (Minneapolis: Augsburg Publishing House, 1973); Raymond Brown *et al.*, eds., *Mary in the New Testament: A Collaborative Assessment by Protestant and Roman Catholic Scholars* (Philadelphia: Fortress Press, 1978).

17. Faith and Order Commission, "Scripture, Tradition and Traditions," in *Fourth World Conference on Faith and Order*, eds. P.C. Rodger and Lukas Vischer (New York: Association Press, 1964) 50–61.

18. ARCIC, "Authority in the Church I," *The Final Report*, #15.

19. Anglican-Roman Catholic International Commission [ARCIC], "Authority in the Church II," *The Final Report* (London: SPCK & Catholic Truth Society, 1982) #24.

20. Ibid., #25.

and the prophetic promptings of the Spirit receive a lot of attention in ecumenical proposals about authoritative sources.

Like the feminist movement, the ecumenical movement also knows about abuse of authority, and it resolutely argues against any ecclesiology that furthers such abuse. It begins discussions of authority with the authority of Christ. "The confession of Christ as Lord is the heart of the Christian faith," ARCIC begins when it turns to the question of authority. "To him God has given all authority in heaven and on earth. As Lord of the Church he bestows the Holy Spirit to create a communion of men [*sic*] with God and with one another. . . . The Church is a community which consciously seeks to submit to Jesus Christ."[21] But all of the members of the Church, through common life in the body of Christ, are enabled "so to live that the authority of Christ will be mediated through them."[22] While recognizing the variety of gifts, the ecumenical movement starts its discussion about gifts and ministries with the authority of Christ and the granting of the Holy Spirit to all of the baptized. "God bestows upon all baptized persons the anointing and the promise of the Holy Spirit, marks them with a seal and implants in their hearts the first installment of their inheritance as sons and daughters of God," says *Baptism, Eucharist, and Ministry* [BEM].[23] At the same time "the Holy Spirit also gives to some individuals and communities special gifts for the benefit of the Church, which entitle them to speak and be heeded. . . ."[24] It is in this context that ecumenical statements locate ordained ministry; and in general the ecumenical movement is more positive about ordained ministry than feminism has been. The ordained ministers are not only representatives of the community, they also are "representatives of Jesus Christ to the community."[25] The Church needs such persons publicly and continually responsible for pointing to the Church's dependence on Christ and thus providing, "within a multiplicity of gifts, a focus of its unity."[26] Such ministry, for ARCIC, "is not an extension of the common Christian priesthood but belongs to another realm of the gifts of the Spirit."[27]

---

21. ARCIC, "Authority in the Church I," #1, 4.

22. Ibid., #3.

23. World Council of Churches, "Baptism," *Baptism, Eucharist and Ministry* (Geneva: World Council of Churches, 1982) #5.

24. ARCIC, "Authority in the Church I," #5.

25. World Council of Churches, "Ministry," *Baptism, Eucharist and Ministry* (Geneva: World Council of Churches, 1982) #11.

26. Ibid., #8.

27. ARCIC, "Ministry and Ordination," #13.

At the same time, ecumenical statements are not naive about ministry by the ordained. "The authorities in the Church cannot adequately reflect Christ's authority because they are still subject to the limitations and sinfulness of human nature," comments ARCIC. "Awareness of this inadequacy is a continual summons to reform."[28] Churches that wish to overcome their differences regarding ordained ministry "need to work from the perspective of the calling of the whole people of God," comments BEM.[29] "The authority of the ordained ministry is not to be understood as the possession of the ordained person but as a gift for the continuing edification of the body in and for which the minister has been ordained," it continues.[30] And while recommending the recovery of the threefold ministry, including an episcopal ministry of oversight, BEM states clearly, "The threefold pattern stands evidently in need of reform . . . [it] raises questions for all the churches."[31]

The ecumenical movement shows its sensitivity to abuse of authority particularly when it discusses the possibility that all churches might come into full communion with the bishop of Rome, whose oversight could provide a petrine ministry or universal primacy for the sake of the unity of the whole Church in the Gospel. The Lutherans in the U.S. Lutheran-Roman Catholic Dialogue are ready to acknowledge the possibility "that God may show again in the future that the papacy is his gracious gift to his people."[32] But full communion with the papacy was broken in the sixteenth century, the Lutherans say frankly, because the papal teaching and practice were in such need of reform that they seemed a contradiction of the Gospel. If the papacy were reformed sufficiently to serve the Gospel, "papal primacy will no longer be open to many traditional Lutheran objections."[33] The principles of legitimate diversity, collegiality, and subsidiarity are a quick checklist that signers suggest as means to the "renewal of papal structures."[34] The "one thing necessary," explain the Lutheran partners, "is that papal primacy be so structured and interpreted that it clearly serve the gospel and the unity of the church of Christ, and that its exercise of power not subvert Christian freedom."[35]

---

28. ARCIC, "Authority in the Church I," #7.

29. World Council of Churches, "Ministry," #6.

30. Ibid., #15.

31. Ibid., #24–25.

32. [U.S.] Lutheran-Roman Catholic Dialogue, "Differing Attitudes Toward Papal Primacy: Common Statement," #28.

33. Ibid.

34. Ibid., #22–25.

35. Ibid., #28.

ARCIC shows a similar attention to the abuse of authority by those with the ministry of oversight in the Church. "Although primacy and conciliarity are complementary elements of *episcope* [oversight] it has often happened that one has been emphasized at the expense of the other, even to the point of serious imbalance," ARCIC comments, adding, "When churches have been separated from one another, this danger has been increased."[36] More bluntly, when writing about the authority of the bishop of Rome among the churches, ARCIC explains that it "does not imply submission to an authority which would stifle the distinctive features of the local churches. The purpose of this episcopal function of the bishop of Rome is to promote Christian fellowship in faithfulness to the teaching of the apostles." But ARCIC members add, "Neither theory nor practice, however, has ever fully reflected these ideals."[37]

Nevertheless, they believe that a universal primacy is "part of God's design" for the Church.[38] A universal primate could make a decisive judgment that becomes part of the Church's permanent witness, though its reliability is ultimately indicated by its reception in the Church. A ministry by the universal primate can serve the Gospel by "helping the churches to listen to one another, to grow in love and unity, and to strive together towards the fullness of Christian life and witness. . . ."[39] When it acts this way, ARCIC points out, it will serve the local churches and their communion. A universal primate should not stifle freedom, legitimate diversity, or local traditions, ARCIC continues in its frank understated manner. And "Anglicans are entitled to assurance," members agree, "that acknowledgement of the universal primacy of the bishop of Rome would not involve the suppression of theological, liturgical and other traditions which they value or the imposition of wholly alien traditions."[40]

So the ecumenical discussions are both enthusiastic about ordered ministries in the Church and realistically critical about the actual ways that ministers have abused and can abuse their authority. At the core of this enthusiastic and critical perspective stands an ecclesiology of communion.[41] The ecumenical movement recovers this ecclesiology of com-

36. ARCIC, "Authority in the Church I," #22.
37. Ibid., #12.
38. ARCIC, "Authority in the Church II," #15.
39. ARCIC, "Authority in the Church I," #21.
40. ARCIC, "Authority in the Church II," #22.
41. Anglican-Roman Catholic International Commission [ARCIC], "Introduction," *The Final Report* (London: SPCK & Catholic Truth Society, 1982) #1–9; Joint Commission for Theological Dialogue between the Roman Catholic Church

munion from the New Testament and the patristic writings, with their emphasis on the local churches that are in communion with each other while retaining appropriate diversity. Ecumenical dialogues consistently reject a pyramidal ecclesiology, which has a top-down understanding of authority and tends to treat the local churches as parts of a big, undifferentiated monolith directed from the top. Such pyramidal pictures of the Church are a recent innovation in theology, ecumenists point out, that developed after the Church became divided. By recovering the scriptural and patristic vision of the Church as a communion of local churches, ecumenists hope to find the usable traditions that once allowed Christians to remain in full communion.

I have been arguing that feminism and ecumenism have much more in common than might be recognized on first inspection. Let me summarize. Both movements seek the reform of the Church in its theology and its practice. Both are concerned to correct misreadings of the Scriptures. Both read the history of the Church with a critical recognition of abuses, and with a positive eye for the recovery of more authentic traditions, a usable past. Both believe that the Church must act as a living tradition, subject to Christ and leery of idolatrous theories or practices. Both emphasize decision-making by consensus and conciliar consultation. Both are suspicious of traditions that do not listen to all of the voices in the discussion.

Let me give an example of the mutual misunderstanding between feminists and ecumenists. A few years ago, one of my students in a theology course was a woman from the United Church of Canada seeking commissioning as a diaconal minister. In her paper on the issue of episcopal oversight, she commented, "The power base of the episcopate begins with the pope, rather than the people; it is a top-down theory of power and authority, not a bottom-up theory of empowerment that I am used to. . . . For me, it epitomizes patriarchy." In the same month that I read this paper, Barbara Harris was elected by her diocese to be consecrated a bishop in the Episcopal Church in the United States. Some of my Roman Catholic colleagues, as well as some vocal Anglican leaders, saw her episcopal consecration as the close of serious work for the unity of the Anglican and Roman Catholic communions.

But both my student and my colleagues seemed to be overlooking the possibilities. My student had failed to hear from ecumenists that they too opposed a "top-down" ecclesiology, and that the ecclesiology of communion

---

and the Orthodox Church, "The Mystery of the Church and of the Eucharist in the Light of the Mystery of the Holy Trinity," *One in Christ* 19 (1983) 188–97.

offered an understanding of *episcope* [oversight] that would respect the distinctive traditions of her own communion. My colleagues had failed to hear from feminists that feminists too sought to defend and translate the Gospel in new ways, and that they saw the consecration of a woman bishop as a public stand against a faulty anthropology but within the historic structures of a threefold ministry so praised by ecumenists. An appreciation of the common elements that ecumenism and feminism share might make them powerful partners in the work of reform of the Church.

What Feminism and Ecumenism Can Teach Each Other about Authority

But their partnership would be strengthened if these two movements would also start learning from each other. I have dwelt at length on what they have in common, but let me say something more briefly about what they ought to be teaching each other.

Ecumenism could reap benefits from the feminist movement, which crosses denominational lines in a startling way and brings thousands of Christians together with a passionate intensity of purpose. While talks on ecumenism may draw only a handful of listeners and books on ecumenism may have trouble finding an audience, talks and books on women in the Church are best sellers. My women students from their many church traditions feel a deep kinship with each other as they ponder the reality of their position within different church communities. The commonality of women's experience of the Church can be a deeper bond among Christian women than its later divisions. The ecumenical movement, which knows well the phenomenon of defining a tradition as "the other, not us," should welcome this recognition of commonality. Furthermore, it should examine the ways that the Church's theory or practice treats women as "other."

But more fundamentally, the ecumenical movement needs to ask itself why feminism creates a bond of such passionate intensity among women, a bond that crosses denominational lines so effectively. I believe it is because, for feminists, the truth of the Gospel itself seems threatened by any theology or practice that legitimates a domination of men over women. An Anglican bishop, himself a feminist, put it this way: "Would I really want to be in full communion with a Church that did not ordain women?" For him, this question is hard to answer. Theological anthropologies that identify women with subordinate roles; understandings of ordination that demand maleness of the ordained because Christ was a male; doctrines of God that present God continually in male imagery: all of these seem to feminists to distort the Gospel message in a fundamental way. When they hear ecumenical statements repeat such views, or urge patience in the face of them, feminists wonder about the price of unity. Many of them see the relationship between ecumenism and feminism as a choice between unity and truth. Conceiving it this way, they choose truth. Shouldn't the ecumenical movement welcome the spirit of commitment to the fresh translation of the truth of the Gospel that such a choice represents?

In addition, the feminist movement might succeed in teaching ecumenists to reconceive the ordained ministry more thoroughly. An ecclesiology of communion should allow ecumenism to renew and reinterpret ordained threefold ministry so as not to confuse it with hierarchy. But too often ecumenical discussions can slip into hierarchical-business-as-usual in their consideration and implementation of mutual recognition of ordained ministries and of a petrine ministry in the Church. Feminism holds the promise of a fresh interpretation of ordination and other ministries that would free them from cultural forms apt to communicate domination rather than service.

Finally, feminist theology has raised a very important question in its criticism of some theological anthropologies used as arguments against the ordination of women. Rather than simply explaining or defending their church practice, ecumenists from churches that do not ordain women should also show willingness to reexamine the arguments their churches use against this practice, and to criticize these arguments when they are faulty. "Openness to each other holds the possibility that the Spirit may well speak to one church through the insights of another," BEM stated,[42] and the ecumenical movement should not miss this opportunity for a serious discussion about the substantive issues involved. Furthermore, as the Canadian Roman Catholic bishops recognized in their response to ARCIC, to use the disagreement about the ordination of women as an excuse to stop ecumenical work would be to miss the Gospel mandate of the work for unity. "To allow the question of the ordination of women to delay the efforts to achieve full communion would be to disregard the urgency of Christ's mandate for unity," they observed.[43]

At the same time, the ecumenical movement has a good deal it can teach the feminist movement. While both movements in their contemporary form emerged at the beginning of this century, the ecumenical movement

42. World Council of Churches, "Ministry," #54.

43. Canadian Conference of Catholic Bishops, "Response of the Canadian Conference of Catholic Bishops to the ARCIC-I *Final Report*," *Ecumenism* 88 (December 1987) 15.

shows more skill at self-criticism than its counterpart. We might consider the reasons for this self-critical skill. I suggest that the ecumenical movement has a better sense of the pervasiveness of sin and the Fall.

Now what do I mean by that? I mean that feminism often tends to project evil onto others: men, patriarchy, the institutional church, the ordained ministry. It is not adequately reflective about its own failings and sins. Women also are complicit in the structures of sin as well as solidary in the inheritance of grace, but some romantic feminists easily overlook this. Feminists who argue that women's different, special nature will overcome authoritarianism, abstract rationalism, militarism, and the rape of the earth seem a bit naive about their own potential for evil. Such views are not limited to feminists; Mother Teresa is reported to have said that women would make better priests than men. "No man can even come close to the love and compassion a woman is capable of giving," she is reported to have said, though she later explained that she supported the Vatican's teaching against women's ordination.[44]

Some feminists, of course, have recognized this failure among their colleagues. In commenting on romantic goddess and Wicca forms of feminism, Rosemary Radford Ruether warned in 1980 against stereotypical identification of men or male systems with evil, so that women "can be the great innocents or victims of history."[45] But, she suggested, such stereotypes are not really conducive to valid self-knowledge and development for women, since they are rooted in a false anthropology. "Women need to acknowledge that they have the same drives and temptations to sin as males have—not just sins of dependency but also the sins of dominance, of which they have been less guilty (not for want of capacity, but for want of opportunity). . . . If we are really to effect change, we must take responsibility for the capacities for both good and evil in all people," she observes.[46] The creation of a feminist spirituality calls for "greater modesty and greater maturity than those still deeply wounded by patriarchal religion have generally been able to muster," she concludes.[47] More recently, black women remind their white sisters that feminist theology is complicit with evil when it is used to the advantage of the privileged speakers, rather

44. "Women Would Be Better Priests: Mother Teresa," Associated Press Report in *Toronto Star*, 1 April 1984.
45. Rosemary Radford Ruether, "Goddesses and Witches: Liberation and Countercultural Feminism," *Christian Century* 97 (1980) 844; cf. Rosemary Radford Ruether, *Sexism and God-Talk* (Boston: Beacon Press, 1983) 104–109.
46. Ibid., 845.
47. Ibid., 847.

than as a means for overcoming oppression throughout the whole com-munity.[48] But why are such warnings necessary among feminists, and why are they not heeded more widely?

The ecumenical movement is founded on the insight that the division of the Church contradicts the will of Christ; the fault for this situation was shared by all parties to the division. To overcome the division of the Church, a conversion is necessary; "there can be no ecumenism worthy of the name without a change of heart," taught Vatican II in its Decree on Ecumenism, *Unitatis redintegratio*.[49] With conversion comes a confession of guilt in the pasts of all of the churches who are speaking, along with a spirit of repentance. The Church continually needs to be reformed: ecu-menists are clear on this. While such recognition does not seem to dampen their zeal for mutual criticism, perhaps it does make them more alert to the deep faults of their own tradition as well, and more ready to hear good from those with whom they disagree. Even the incredibly painstaking process of consensus-writing demanded by agreed statements of ecumenical dialogue groups—when every participant must agree to every word—calls for a high degree of listening and repentance. Feminists warn often against idolatrous ideas, and correctly; but ecumenists know perhaps more deeply how easily we can make our own communities and convictions into idols. By giving a central place to repentance and conver-sion from the evil with which all of the participants are complicit, the ecu-menical movement is more prepared to be self-critical and to grow.

The sense of sin is especially useful in the attitude toward tradition and its reform, an important and delicate matter for both feminists and ecu-menists. The proper response to tradition, Georges De Schrijver suggests, demands both an appreciative understanding of a tradition, and a stand

---

48. Jacquelyn Grant, "Introduction to Womanist Theology," a course at New York Theological Seminary, New York, January 1989; cf. Jacquelyn Grant, "Womanist Theology: Black Women's Experience as a Source for Doing Theology with Special Reference to Christology," *Journal of the Interdenominational Theological Center* 13 (Fall 1985–Spring 1986) 195–212; P. Murray, "Black Theology and Feminist Theology: A Comparative View," in *Black Theology: A Documentary History*, eds. J. H. Cone and G. S. Wilmore (Maryknoll, N.Y.: Orbis Books, 1979) 398–417; Cherrie Moraga and Gloria Anzaldua, eds., *This Bridge Called My Back: Writings by Radical Women of Color* (Watertown, Mass.: Persephone Press, 1981); Rosemary Radford Ruether, "Third World Women's Double Oppression," *National Catholic Reporter* 19 (11 Feb. 1983) 20.

49. Vatican II, *Unitatis redintegratio*, in *The Documents of Vatican II*, ed. Walter M. Abbott (New York: America Press, 1966) #7.

of suspicion or critical distance that asks: Why should I listen to this tradition? Who was excluded from its formulation? etc.[50] But we could add: if both appreciative understanding and critical distance are necessary, the first must precede the second. Criticisms based on a misunderstanding of a tradition are not ultimately very helpful, even when they seek to serve a good aim.

Ecumenists have learned well the need to understand traditions sympathetically before criticizing them. In fact, one could understand the whole of the ecumenical movement as a commitment to the first moment of response to tradition—the appreciative understanding of a tradition, especially a tradition not one's own. Ecumenism is fueled by the conviction that Christians are in real if not full communion, and the suspicion that many ideas once thought contradictory may turn out to be compatible if more deeply explored. Training in the ecumenical dialogue schools participants to give the benefit of the doubt to the partner first, and only then to ask, in the spirit of the Gospel, about understandings or practices that seem wrong or unfaithful.

Feminists might benefit from such training. Two areas especially come to mind.

Feminists should be more discriminating in their criticisms of the past if they have not really grasped what earlier thinkers were saying. The elimination of the doctrine of the Trinity without a hearing would seem a serious mistake for Christian feminists to risk, but I don't hear much concern expressed among them about this. For example, at last the churches have begun to recognize each other's baptism, after working towards this goal for decades. Blithely to eliminate the baptismal formula used for centuries of the Church's history and replace it with formulations made up in the last fifteen years, as some feminists propose, seems to overlook the complexity of the issues involved. The role of repetition in worship, the significance of biblical language, the value of a shared formulation, the language of mutuality and egalitarian relationship implied in trinitarian "person" talk: all of this can be overlooked in some feminist proposals of the Creator-Redeemer-Sanctifier type. Such forgetfulness would be unfortunate.

Now I am not equating a change of baptismal formula with the elimination of the doctrine of the Trinity. But helpful proposals have been made for the recovery of earlier baptismal formulations or even for the introduction of new trinitarian language, proposals that are neither patriarchal nor naively innovative, and that show more understanding of the

---

50. Georges De Schrijver, "Hermeneutics and Tradition," *Journal of Ecumenical Studies* 19 (1982) 32–47.

depth of the trinitarian issues involved.[51] Feminists would draw more authentically on their own respect for consensus if they attended more carefully to such a widespread foundational tradition about God as a communion of mutual love.

Another area of tradition and its reform is the issue of ordained ministry and other structures of authority in the Church. As I said above, feminist theology gives the Church a good opportunity to rethink the nature of the ordained ministers and their relationship to the whole community. On the other hand, feminists might show a more realistic appreciation for structures, however flawed, that have served the proclamation of the Gospel and the unity of the Church. This caveat might be extended to our discussion of ministries of oversight in the Church. The Canadian Roman Catholic bishops warned against a utopian attitude, commenting, "Reconciliation of our communions ought not to be delayed by false hopes for a utopian ideal."[52] While we should not use such an insight as an excuse to avoid the difficult work of reforming the Church, should it not at least be a part of our dialogue?

CONCLUSION

I have been arguing that the ecumenical movement and the feminist movement have a great deal in common. In addition, I have urged them to learn something from each other.

It is not hard for the churches to be in solidarity with women over the next decade. What is hard is the reform of the exercise of authority in the Church for the sake of the mission of the Gospel. But both ecumenism and feminism are movements for reform in the Church. Both ecumenism and feminism each have something to teach and something to learn if their contributions are to be used to best advantage. That may take us more than a decade, but we could begin.

51. David R. Holeton, "Changing the Baptismal Formula: Feminist Proposals and Liturgical Implications," *Ecumenical Trends* 17 (1988) 69–72; cf. Catherine Mowry LaCugna, "Baptism, Feminists, and Trinitarian Theology," ibid., 65–68. For insightful discussions showing the positive value of new proposed formulations or images, see Mary Rose D'Angelo, "Beyond Father and Son," in *Justice as Mission: An Agenda for the Church*, eds. Terry Brown and Christopher Lind (Burlington, Ont.: Trinity Press, 1985) 107–118; Elizabeth A. Johnson, "The Incomprehensibility of God and the Image of God Male and Female," *Theological Studies* 45 (1984) 462–63.

52. Canadian Conference of Catholic Bishops, "Response of the Canadian Conference of Catholic Bishops to the ARCIC-I *Final Report*," 16–17.

9

FORMATION FOR TRANSFORMATION: THE ECUMENICAL DIRECTORY SETS A BIG AGENDA[1]

Some of the most innovative material in the new ecumenical Directory falls within its understated category called "ecumenical formation." If the guidelines on ecumenical formation are carried out as they are proposed in this "Directory for the Application of Principles and Norms on Ecumenism," the Roman Catholic Church will be significantly different in twenty years. My twenty-two years of teaching divinity students has convinced me of the power that teaching can have when it is carried out in the context of a total personal formation. Done in the right way, formation plus information yield something new: transformation.

Such transformation is really what the ecumenical movement is seeking. As Vatican II's Decree on Ecumenism, *Unitatis redintegratio,* taught, ecumenism means a change of heart toward other Christians, a conversion in attitude toward their traditions and emphases. Vatican II believed that this change of heart must be accompanied by a change of mind, a new understanding of other Christians; and so it recommended common study, common prayer, common witness, and dialogue in order to grow toward this new understanding. The new Directory shares this vision of Vatican II, and it provides concrete suggestions and an overall attitude to implement the vision. "Bearing in mind the nature of the Catholic Church," it explains, "Catholics will find, if they follow faithfully the indications of the Second Vatican Council, the means of contributing to the

1. This essay was first presented at a seminar of the National Workshop on Christian Unity in Providence, R.I. in April 1994. It was published in a very slightly different form in *Ecumenism* (#117, March 1995) 23–26; *Ecumenism* is also published in French.

ecumenical formation both of individuals and of the whole community to which they belong."[2]

To understand the approach of the Directory to ecumenical formation, one should do more than simply read chapter three of the Directory, though it is in this third chapter that the bulk of information on ecumenical formation is available. But it can be found in other chapters of the Directory as well, especially in chapter one. There the Directory lays out in a concise but clear manner the theological foundations for the ecumenical movement, emphasizing the unity of the Church in God's plan and the nature of the Church as communion. While noting that other churches and ecclesial communities retain in reality a certain though not full communion with the Catholic Church, the Directory adds, "No Christian, however, should be satisfied with these forms of communion. They do not correspond to the will of Christ, and weaken his church in the exercise of its mission."[3] The rest of the Directory then unfolds as a practical guide to remedying this situation.

At the Heart of Roman Catholicism

The Directory understands the search for the restoration of unity among Christians to be the specific focus of the ecumenical movement. But it believes that this search is intrinsic to Christian faith. "Those who are baptized in the name of Christ are, by that very fact, called to commit themselves to the search for unity,"[4] it explains. In other words, the Directory does not envision ecumenism as a form of external relations Roman Catholics have with other churches. On the contrary, the Directory sees ecumenism as internal to what it means to be a Roman Catholic today. To me, the Directory is at its most exciting on this point, which recurs throughout its guidelines. The Directory repeats the conviction of Vatican II that "'concern for restoring unity pertains to the whole church.'" Therefore, it explains, "all the faithful are called upon to make a personal commitment toward promoting increasing communion with other Christians."[5]

---

2. Pontifical Council for Promoting Christian Unity, "Directory for the Application of Principles and Norms on Ecumenism" [title printed as "1993 Directory for Ecumenism"] *Origins* 23 (1993–94) 129, 131–60; see #55.

3. Ibid., #19.

4. Ibid., #22.

5. Ibid., #55.

The Directory then believes that "the objective of ecumenical formation is that all Christians be animated by the ecumenical spirit, whatever their particular mission and task in the world and in society."[6] In other words, the Directory sees ecumenical formation to be a component of the Christian formation of Roman Catholic Christians, just as moral growth and a spirit of prayer should be included in every Roman Catholic's formation.

ECUMENICAL FORMATION FOR ALL

To ensure the formation of all the faithful, the Directory urges that preaching, catechesis, liturgy, spirituality, and social action be informed by knowledge about the Scriptures, the history of church divisions, the positions of other churches, and the results of contemporary ecumenical dialogues. At times the Directory is quite specific in its advice. For example, Roman Catholics are to be taught "the whole doctrine of the Catholic Church, respecting in a particular way the order of the hierarchy of truths and avoiding expressions and ways of presenting doctrine which would be an obstacle to dialogue." In addition, catechists are told that when they are "speaking of other churches and ecclesial communities, it is important to present their teaching correctly and honestly."[7] Catechesis should make clear "that dialogue has created new relationships which, if they are well understood, can lead to collaboration and peace."[8] If Roman Catholic catechesis begins actually to implement the directives given here, some exciting new viewpoints will begin to take root.

Where should this ecumenical formation for all Roman Catholics be occurring? The Directory again casts a wide net in its vision of responsibility for formation, naming parishes, schools, church associations or movements, and families as places where ecumenical formation should occur. So, for example, parishes are told that one of their great tasks is "to educate" parishioners "in the ecumenical spirit," which "calls for care with the content and form of preaching, especially of the homily, and with catechesis."[9] While many Roman Catholic parishes all but ignore ecumenism today, the Directory sees it as a central parish responsibility; to help implement this vision in the parish, it also calls for a parish pastoral program in ecumenical activity and a parish member charged with promoting this program. In schools, even young children should be

6. Ibid., #58.
7. Ibid., #61.
8. Ibid.
9. Ibid., #67.

"taught genuine ecumenism";[10] in groups or movements, members should be imbued with a "solid ecumenical spirit."[11] Such work should continue through university education, where Roman Catholic universities have a special role to play through research, teaching, conferences, journals, and opportunities for common witness, residence, and worship among students.[12] Finally, families should take care "not to entertain prejudices, but on the contrary to search for the truth in all things";[13] I can think of a lot of dinner conversations that might sound different if this viewpoint were implemented! The Directory especially singles out "mixed-marriage families" and explains that they have "the delicate task of making themselves builders of unity."[14]

ADDITIONAL ECUMENICAL FORMATION FOR PASTORAL MINISTERS

What about the ecumenical formation of pastoral workers? The Directory believes that one preparing for ordination should be a person "checking regularly his own language and capacity for dialogue so as to acquire an authentically ecumenical disposition."[15] Quite insistent on this viewpoint, the Directory explains again, "Ecumenical openness is a constitutive dimension of the formation of future priests and deacons."[16] Episcopal conferences are charged with ensuring that programs of theological study for ordination candidates "give an ecumenical dimension to each subject and provide specifically for the study of ecumenism."[17] The Directory is interesting in its specificity about theological course work. On the one hand, it wants "an ecumenical approach" to "every theological discipline,"[18] but it also calls for a course focused specifically on ecumenism, taught early in the program of theological studies, which it feels should be "compulsory."[19] The Directory even provides a content outline of such a course. It explains that nonordained pastoral workers also need an ecumenical for-

10. Ibid., #68.
11. Ibid., #69.
12. Ibid., #89.
13. Ibid., #66.
14. Ibid.
15. Ibid., #70.
16. Ibid., #76.
17. Ibid., #72.
18. Ibid., #77.
19. Ibid., #79.

mation parallel to that of ordination candidates, adapted to their level of studies if it is a different level.

My own experience in teaching ministry students for twenty-two years confirms the value of the Directory's advice. Theology students need a general sensitivity to ecumenism in all of their courses but they also need a course where they can probe in depth the particular issues that have divided Christians. In such a course on ecumenism, they focus specifically on the new theological work overcoming divisions so that they themselves can be agents of reconciliation, not division, after their entry into pastoral ministry.

The Directory demands a great deal of ordained and nonordained pastoral ministers, even after their theological studies. It calls for their "continuous aggiornamento" in a "permanent formation" because of the "continual evolution within the ecumenical movement."[20] The resources of Roman Catholic universities, theological faculties, seminaries, and specialized ecumenical institutes are all urged to play a role in this permanent formation.

EXPERIENCES WITH OTHER CHRISTIANS

Ecumenical attitudes are often gained when Christians from different traditions meet regularly in dialogue, prayer, or common witness; studies then allow such experiences to be probed and their implications examined. The Directory recognizes the importance of ecumenical experiences for formation, and it wants future pastoral ministers themselves to share in such experiences. I have seen how actual collaborative meetings or projects on ecumenism are often the crucible in which ecumenical attitudes are first nurtured.

But sometimes the experience of a single ecumenical meeting or project can actually engender defensiveness on the part of participants unfamiliar with Christians from other church traditions. Threatened by another church's viewpoint, alienated initially by its different forms of expressing the Gospel, perhaps unclear or insecure about their own tradition: participants can sometimes leave a single meeting or project more negative toward other Christians than they were when entering. On the other hand, sometimes a single meeting or project of ecumenical dialogue can engender an anti-intellectualism threatening to dialogue: participants are filled with good will for each other but they recognize the enormity of the history of Christian division. Unable to settle all of this in a one-night

20. Ibid., #91.

session, they often are tempted to the conclusion that doctrinal viewpoints are insignificant.

To overcome these twin dangers of single meetings or projects on ecumenism, I often ask participants to name, or at least think of, one strength of their own church tradition and one strength of another church tradition. This allows the session to begin on a positive note, and suggests the vision of a gift exchange where all of the churches have something to give to each other and something to receive. A more mature group can be asked to think of or name a strength from their own church tradition and then a weakness. This helps ease people into a self-critical style in the company of others. Of course, everyone must answer both questions. This requirement helps guide them past that polemical atmosphere so familiar in our past in which we name the strengths of our own church tradition and then the weaknesses of the others!

The theme of ecumenical experiences moves us out of chapter three, focused strictly on ecumenical formation, and into the other chapters of the Directory that touch on common prayer, cooperation, dialogue, common witness, and the structures serving ecumenism. There, too, however, the reality of ecumenical formation continues to shape the directives given, since actual experiences of Christians together are often the deepest source of ecumenical formation.

THE DIRECTORY'S "SLEEPER"

On the whole, the discussion of ecumenical formation may be the "sleeper" in the Directory. When receiving the Directory, many people will turn first to the chapter on common prayer to see what possibilities for intercommunion are given. Others will focus on the importance of cooperation in social issues or common witness. But when they turn to the chapter on ecumenical formation, they will discover a huge and exciting agenda laid out for the whole Roman Catholic Church. According to this agenda, formation in ecumenism for all Roman Catholics should begin in the parish, school, and family settings of their youth, and it should continue throughout their lives as Roman Catholics. In addition, to enable the pastoral ministers to carry out this project, an intensive, deeper formation in ecumenism throughout their theological studies is planned, and this deeper formation should mature so that it becomes a permanent part of readiness for ministry. Behind the innocuous term of "ecumenical formation" stands the reality of conversion and the change that conversion demands. The effects of such ecumenical formation would be a profound transformation of the Roman Catholic Church.

10

ROMAN CATHOLIC THEOLOGY TODAY: A GUIDE FOR THE PERPLEXED IN A TIME OF RENEWAL[1]

I was asked to describe and discuss the state of Roman Catholic theology today in a way recognizable to my Roman Catholic colleagues but intended largely for the illumination of Protestant, Anglican, and Orthodox colleagues and especially for the guidance of the Pew Charitable Trusts, which has historically been familiar mainly with the evangelical movements within Protestantism in North America.

The activity of self-description to others feels quite familiar to me. I have been involved in ecumenical bilateral and multilateral dialogue for many years, and I think that self-description—a kind of collective autobiography—is a first and important step in the process of dialogue. Like autobiography, the activity of self-description presumes—not that others (Protestant, Anglican, and Orthodox) do not know the language of Roman Catholic theology—but rather that they approach it like a second or third language: well known, perhaps, but not the way they first learned to speak. In Canada, we know the great fruitfulness that ensues when people can speak their own language well and also are involved in learning another. Self-description, then, like autobiography, is the process of speaking and describing my own Roman Catholic language in this context of multilingual discussion. It prepares for a second step, a dialogue that goes beyond self-description to mutual criticism and convergence of understandings of the apostolic faith.

1. This paper was presented in a slightly different form to Protestant, Orthodox, Anglican, and Roman Catholic theology professors attending a consultation on the renewal of contemporary theology in service of the apostolic faith, sponsored by the Pew Charitable Trusts in Pasadena, California at Fuller Theological Seminary in March 1992.

I have also been thinking about both theology and self-description for a long time. I decided to be a theologian when I was ten years old, because it seemed like the most exciting and important thing that anyone could do: that alone gives you a hint of the heady atmosphere of Roman Catholic theology over the last forty years, when movements of renewal in biblical and liturgical studies and social justice were affecting active lay Roman Catholics like my parents and even touching the life of an earnest ten-year-old little girl in Roman Catholic grammar school, who was already a fervent member of the Boy Savior Club and later of the Young Christian Student movement for the formation of lay Christian leaders. My task of self-description in the ecumenical context began somewhat later, at twenty-two, when in the fall of 1969 I was the only Roman Catholic in the course on the Reformation at Yale Divinity School and was politely asked if I would like to say a word in favor of the sale of indulgences.

I take it that the self-description called for here is not that of the diary—a sometimes tedious recounting of events as they come up, day by day, issue by issue. Nor is it that of the *apologia*—an uncritical defense of Roman Catholic theology in all of its forms and concerns. It is rather the collective autobiographical sketch, an overview of the major moves and characteristic preoccupations of Roman Catholic theology, done for the purpose first of understanding.

I take it for granted, too, that at the heart of Roman Catholic theology and of any Christian theology is the search for understanding and proclamation of the faith handed down by the apostles, the faith about the tri-une God and the goodness of the creation God made, about the Fall and its continuing effects in human history, about the redemption won once-for-all through the life, death, resurrection, and ascension of Jesus Christ, fully God and fully human, about the continuing power of Christ's gracious work offered to all humankind through the power of the Holy Spirit in the community of the new creation that is the Church, about the hope of glory when the kingdom of God will come in fullness. This one apostolic faith, proclaimed in the Scriptures, celebrated in the liturgy and in the ecumenical councils, this is the faith of the Church. What I wish to do here is speak about a theology which serves that faith.

Before I begin, let me make two further points about Roman Catholic theology that can lead to misunderstanding if overlooked. First, it is a very collective, communal enterprise. Like Orthodox theology, Roman Catholic theology is done collectively, rather as a corporate person thinking through an issue. I realized this one summer, about both Orthodox and Roman Catholics, when attending the Institute for Ecumenical and Cultural Research in Collegeville, Minnesota. In a group discussion, we had been asked to speak in the first person about our understanding of creation. Where many were giving personal witness or testimony about experiences from their lives, the Orthodox theologian kept saying, "The Creed says. . . ." Some people felt that he was not speaking in the first person: but I finally realized that he was speaking in the first person plural—as a corporate person, really. He was saying, "We believe." This style is very characteristic of Roman Catholic theology as well, and affects Roman Catholic theologians constantly. In official ecumenical meetings I often find myself turning to my Roman Catholic colleagues and saying, "What do we think about this?" There is the constant sense that an individual's theological opinion, while it may be correct, must always be tested in the Church and is ultimately for the sake of the Church.

In saying this, I do not mean that the Church always has the wisdom to recognize the truth a theologian might be stating—the Church's authority may be wrongly used to stifle prophecy or wisdom (and I will return to that later). I mean rather that Roman Catholic theologians never work alone, never feel themselves unrelated to the collective enterprise of the Church, even if that relationship includes opposition to some particular church teaching in a certain period. I remember some Protestant colleagues saying once that the North American Academy of Ecumenists, in which I have been active, gave members a chance to express their views without being concerned to represent the views that others in their communion or church would feel. I finally realized that I simply had no idea of what they were talking about because Roman Catholic theologians form such a collectivity. To put it one way: just because my colleagues are not present at a meeting does not mean that they are not with me, because I carry them around in my head. I carry around in my head—as interpretations of the teachings of the Bible—the sometimes conflicting opinions of Karl Rahner, Edward Schillebeeckx, Thomas Aquinas, Augustine of Hippo, Rosemary Ruether, John Chrysostom, Gustavo Gutierrez, Monika Hellwig, Athanasius, Bernard Lonergan, Elisabeth Schüssler Fiorenza, Joseph Ratzinger, Yves Congar, Jean-Marie Tillard, etc., not to mention the teachings of the councils, of various pontificates, and of the repeated celebration of the liturgy. If you think this might make for a fairly crowded mind, you are right, but this crowded mind of jostling colleagues whom I carry always with me is part of the gift and the burden of Roman Catholic theology. Put it this way: as a Roman Catholic theologian, I may be tired, confused, or misunderstood—but I am never alone.

As a final preliminary point, let me underline the difficulty of translation of terms or scenarios from one tradition to another. The issues and the terms of Roman Catholics may sound similar to Protestant concerns, for instance, but there are some significant differences. Take the term, "liberal," for example: in the Roman Catholic Church in the last twenty-five years, a "liberal" Catholic was someone who believed in the centrality of the Scriptures, thought that liturgy should be celebrated in the language of the people, disagreed perhaps with magisterial teaching against artificial contraception but wished that the pope and bishops would take even stronger stands against war and the imbalance of global resources, believed that the restriction of ordination to celibate men in the Latin rite Catholic Church should probably be ended, and sought methods of evangelization that addressed modern concerns. This description would probably not fit what Protestants or Orthodox mean when they talk about a "liberal." As with any work of translation, good self-description of our churches knows that the same words or labels in two different conceptual frameworks can have very different meanings.

I want to make four points about Roman Catholic theology today that give a kind of overview of its major characteristics. I am less concerned to take up individual topics, but want instead to talk about the kind of general developments I see as a grid on which to locate individual topics. I will not be talking about Roman Catholic biblical exegesis, which I take to be somewhat more familiar and in a somewhat different field from my own. The theology I want to discuss would understand itself to be handing on the biblical faith; many Roman Catholic theologians would even speak, as Karl Rahner does, of the Scriptures as the "unnormed norm" of all later theology and dogmatic formulations.[2]

A Time of Renewal

Well, first of all and most obviously, Roman Catholic theology is now and has been for most of the century in a time of very creative renewal. The communal event at the heart of this renewal was Vatican II, which received and taught a vision of Revelation, Church, liturgy, ecumenism, evangelization, social justice, and interreligious dialogue that was markedly different from the more defensive picture which had been standard Roman Catholic thought and style before the Council's surprising decisions. But we should not imagine that the renewal of theology in this century began with Vatican II. In fact, it was the renewal of theology that made possible the shifts in thought of Vatican II and opened the door to further renewal. The work of new approaches to biblical scholarship, along with the renewal of widespread study of the Bible in the Roman

---

2. Karl Rahner, "Scripture and Tradition," *Sacramentum Mundi* 6:56.

Catholic Church, preceded the Council and helped shape its atmosphere. Similarly, the exacting and usually hidden work of liturgical scholars— often little-known Benedictine monks working quietly in monasteries to recover the history of liturgical texts—this hidden work prepared the ground that led eventually to the flowering of the liturgical reforms authorized at Vatican II. The Council, then, stands at the heart of the renewal of Roman Catholic theology in this century, the renewal that brought about the Council and the renewal that flowed from it afterwards.

What kind of experience was Vatican II? Perhaps it is hard for other traditions to catch the meaning of this Council; perhaps even for Roman Catholics living now, thirty-six years after its start, its excitement has faded or was never known. I think that Antonio Acerbi is correct when he says that the Council was primarily "a great spiritual experience."[3] It was not first an adaptation to the times, he believes, nor a rationalization based on the social sciences, nor an accommodation to the demands of the contemporary world, although something of all of these was involved. It was first, he argues, the experience of "the reform of the Church for its own mission, under the sign of fidelity to the Word of God."[4] He writes:

> We witnessed in the Council a unique and wonderful event: a vast social grouping, an ancient and highly stabilised institution, embarking with extraordinary sincerity on a programme of research, in order to be more faithful to its own mission. . . . The Church who was questioning herself about her mission and the conditions in which she carried it out, intended to set aside the human securities that were hers as a result of her past, in order to place herself in an attitude of listening and obedience before the Word of God, and to acquire once again the freedom and strength that come from fidelity to the gospel.[5]

Note that this spiritual experience of renewal in the Gospel was closely linked to the renewal of theology. That is both a strength and a weakness about the Council. It is a strength because it shows the strong foundation in theory on which the Council rests—this was no passing enthusiasm of a few weeks, but a Council of three years that had been prepared for by decades of preliminary theological work and would be followed by more. At the same time, it shows the problems of this renewal. I believe that the

3. Antonio Acerbi, "Where Does the Church Stand?" *Concilium*, Vol. 146, eds. Giuseppe Alberigo and Gustavo Gutierrez (New York: Seabury Press, 1981) 79.
4. Ibid., 80.
5. Ibid.

meaning of this renewal was carried first and mainly in theology—not so much in popular practice, nor in the implementation by bishops, nor in the communication in public discourse, all of which tended to follow later and not always in accord with the Council's shift in theory. A simple way to put this, as Jean-Marie Tillard has done, is to say that the Roman Catholic Church has just begun to receive Vatican II, and that some of its teachings have been more fully received by communions other than the Roman Catholic communion itself.[6]

On the one hand, then, it has been the renewal of theology that is at the heart of the spiritual experience of renewal that was the Council. Theology hence accomplished a major work here. On the other hand, I was startled a few years ago to meet a neighbor's wife, six years younger than I and a graduate of Roman Catholic schools, who had never heard of Vatican II and had no idea of anything it might have meant or continue to mean. The spiritual experience of the Council was the product of good theology and the spur of more good theology, but that theology was not always communicated well in church, academic, and public settings. Perhaps this is a concern of the Pew Charitable Trusts program on the renewal of theology: it asks why theology has not had more impact, or at least received more attention, in public discourse.

The renewal of Roman Catholic theology, with Vatican II at its heart, has led to two activities, each of which is important for those who would fund projects that continue the apostolic tradition.

RECOVERY

The first activity is one of recovery. I put under this rubric the vast amount of historical and exegetical scholarship that floods Roman Catholic journals and publishing houses. More obvious is the major involvement of Roman Catholic exegetes in historical critical and other contemporary methods of biblical study, which is not my focus here. Less obvious but also significant is the effort to recover the whole history of theology and receive it in new ways for the sake of contemporary projects.

An important example of such recovery is the retrieval of biblical and patristic ecclesiology. By such studies, Roman Catholics have rediscovered the ecclesiology of communion that emerges from these early texts, and have made this ecclesiology of communion a major building block in ecumenical discussions on overcoming the divisions in the Church that keep

6. Jean-Marie Tillard, "Did We Receive Vatican II?" *One in Christ* 21 (1985) 276–283.

us from a common mission. Or think of the Reformation studies, now shared so easily among Protestants, Anglicans and Roman Catholics in the West. Historical studies of late medieval Catholicism and the Reformation have allowed new evaluations of the meaning of that period of divisions for the apostolic faith today. They have led to developments of ecumenical significance such as agreed statements on justification between Lutherans and Roman Catholics in the U.S. and between Anglicans and Roman Catholics at the international level.

But Roman Catholics have also been busy studying those traditions unique or characteristic to themselves. A growing body of studies on Vatican I, for example, emerged in the 1960s, when new materials on that Council became more accessible to scholars. Instead of accepting the rather triumphalist historiographical accounts of Vatican I with its definition of papal infallibility, scholars (and I am among them) have returned to that Council's records to ask new questions. What were the views of minority bishops at Vatican I? How did they see the question of infallibility and of papacy? In general, what was at stake in this nineteenth-century debate about God's assistance to the Church in its faithful transmission of the apostolic faith in every age? How much were these debates influenced by fears about political revolutions, atheism, materialism, rationalism, abuse of papal power? What in fact did this Council teach about God's assistance to the Church, and what in this teaching might be of lasting significance for the apostolic faith?

This kind of critical retrieval or recovery of our history among Roman Catholic scholars is a hallmark of our scholarship in this century. I have given just a few examples, and I could give more. What is the significance of Thomas Aquinas' understanding of natural law and its relationship to God's grace for Christian discussion of ethics in the public forum? What did St. Augustine teach about women's nature and why did he teach this? How did medieval theologians handle diversity on doctrinal matters, and what were the limits of such diversity? What was at stake at the Council of Nicea, and how did the *homoousion* serve to carry the apostolic faith? How exactly was Matteo Ricci proposing to adapt Christianity to Chinese culture in the sixteenth century, and was the pope right in opposing him? Is it possible yet to sort out the tangled web of the controversies over Modernism, and to discern where in all of this the apostolic faith was threatened and where it was not? All of these scholarly retrievals are efforts to discern how the Christian Gospel was carried and made alive in the history of the Church.

Of course there is nothing unique in critical historical retrieval of the past: every Christian tradition does this in certain ways. In Roman

Catholic theology it plays an especially significant role because of our high valuing of tradition, our faith that Christ and the Holy Spirit have been with the Church in every age and that therefore we can expect to find traces of their presence in every age. Because theology is such a collective enterprise, Roman Catholics feel bound to take into account the views not just of other living theologians but also of all the dead ones. Karl Rahner reminds us that theology is the history of forgetting as well as remembering, of neglecting as well as attending to the concerns of the cloud of witnesses who went before us.[7] Roman Catholic theology does not want to forget the past.

But all remembering includes selection and interpretation. George Tavard writes that "the real problem of tradition concerns two aspects. First, how do we read the testimonies of the past, whether these are theological, doctrinal, canonical, or liturgical? Second, how do we reconstruct for the present and the future a living synthesis of what the authors of the past constructed for their time?"[8] Tavard here sees a similarity in the reading of Scripture or of tradition. In both cases, interpretation is needed to discern the apostolic faith, and such discernment always emerges in the living consciousness of believers. "But if such is the case," he comments, "the problem of tradition amounts to the question of discerning the Spirit. . . . Tradition emerges when the faithful interpret the memory of the past as normative for the faith of the future. But this can be done only through the discernment of the Spirit after a sustained and graceful *metanoia.*"[9] In the process of discernment, of selecting and interpreting, historical theology can function either as a fortress or a launching pad, Walter Principe reminded Roman Catholic scholars.[10] In this century, such studies have served as a launching pad for renewal, a shared tool for growth through which Roman Catholic scholarship has frequently succeeded in remembering the best of the past and in criticizing the worst. This is a necessary component for renewal.

But recently historical study has been waning in Roman Catholic theology in North America. In the Catholic Theological Society of America,

---

7. Karl Rahner, "Current Problems in Christology," *Theological Investigations,* trans. Cornelius Ernst (Baltimore: Helicon Press, 1961) 1:51.

8. George Tavard, "Tradition in Theology: A Problematic Approach," *Perspectives on Scripture and Tradition* (Notre Dame, Ind.: Fides Publications, 1976) 98.

9. Ibid., 103–104.

10. Walter H. Principe, "The History of Theology: Fortress or Launching Pad?" *Catholic Theological Society of America Proceedings* 43 (1988) 19–40.

some dozen continuing seminars in contemporary questions surge on from year to year, while the one historical theology seminar struggles along with dwindling membership. More alarming is a pattern among doctoral candidates at Roman Catholic theological faculties which Principe drew to the Society's attention. In an informal study of doctoral dissertations at Roman Catholic graduate schools of theology in North America from 1979–1990, he found a significantly low percentage of historical dissertations. For example, at one Roman Catholic theology school, of ninety-two dissertations, fourteen were on biblical topics, fourteen on historical themes or authors, and sixty-four on twentieth-century themes and authors. In another graduate school made up of church schools from several traditions including Roman Catholic, he found, among ninety-five dissertations, fifteen were on biblical subjects, sixteen on historical material, and sixty-four on twentieth-century themes or authors. Although this survey was not extensive, it indicates an alarming problem of concern to professors at Roman Catholic schools.[11]

Let me give you two examples to illustrate the dangers of taking a short-cut past historical study. There are some approaches that are so eager to be launched that they do not even pause to find a launching pad. Roman Catholic faculties of theology have a number of Roman Catholic doctoral candidates interested in feminist issues, and some of them focus on Rosemary Ruether's theology. They study her discussions of Christian anthropology with their lengthy and serious criticisms of patristic, medieval, and Reformation thinkers. But sometimes these candidates do not study the patristic, medieval, and Reformation thinkers that Ruether has read, and so they are in no position at all to evaluate whether Ruether is correct or incorrect in her criticism of these authors and therefore in the anthropology that flows from these criticisms. Here is another example. Scholars are concerned with process theology, which is based on criticism of what it calls "classical" doctrines of God as elaborated by Augustine, Aquinas, Calvin, etc. But, again, some scholars have not read the writings of Augustine, Aquinas, or Calvin, and so they cannot possibly judge the correctness of process theological criticisms. Now, for the record, I think that Ruether's criticisms of the anthropology of patristic writers are generally correct and that process criticisms of Augustine, Aquinas, and Calvin are generally incorrect; but I am sure that no good judgments of the work of these contemporaries can be made without knowing the work of those they oppose.

11. Walter H. Principe, "Catholic Theology and the Retrieval of Its Intellectual Tradition: Problems and Possibilities," *Catholic Theological Society of America Proceedings* 46 (1991) 78.

If I were to make a recommendation to the Pew Foundation in this first area of recovery or retrieval of the history of theology, then, I would say: seek out and actively support it. Seek opportunities to nurture the study of Christian tradition used as a source of renewal, as a launching pad into the present and future proclamations of apostolic faith.

TRANSPOSITION

But that brings me to the second activity in Roman Catholic theology, which is transposition. I take this word from Frederick Crowe among others; Crowe takes it from the field of music, where a piece is transposed into another key just as Christian doctrines must be transposed into another century.[12] But transposition, of music and of doctrines, is a tricky business. A piece may be transposed, but adjustments must be made for it to remain the same song in another key. What are the adjustments, and what is the heart of the song? How can we sing the song of Christ in our time and place? This is the question of transposition.

Can Christian theology transpose doctrines from one century to another without changing their meaning? Roman Catholic theology has had a lot of trouble with that question. After a nervous hesitation in its response to so-called "modernists" who began to ask this question, it has relaxed into a "yes" among both its theologians and even, in *Mysterium ecclesiae* in 1973, a careful "yes" by the magisterium as well. Recognizing the historicity of our formulations and of our conceptual frameworks, theologians and the magisterium at last concluded that while the meaning intended in dogmatic formulations cannot change, the formulations themselves might need changing precisely in order to clarify, illumine, and deepen the same meanings, to transpose the song of Christ into a new key rather than lose the tune.[13] The Second Vatican Council recognizes the historicity of our understanding with the image of growth: "There is a growth in the understanding of the realities and the words which have been handed down," the Council taught, since "God who spoke of old, uninterruptedly converses with the Bride of His beloved Son; and the Holy Spirit, through whom the living voice of the gospel resounds in the

12. Frederick Crowe, "The Church as Learner: Two Crises, One *Kairos*," *Appropriating the Lonergan Idea*, ed. Michael Vertin (Washington, D.C.: The Catholic University of America Press, 1988) 382.

13. See Congregation for the Doctrine of the Faith, *Mysterium ecclesiae, The Tablet* 227 (14 July 1973) 667–670.

Church, and through her, in the world, leads unto all truth those who believe and makes the word of Christ dwell abundantly in them. . . ."[14]

With the recognition of the historicity of formulations and conceptual frameworks, Roman Catholic theology acknowledged what had been clear to mainline Protestants for some time, clear more recently and guardedly to evangelical Protestants, and not a preoccupation among Orthodox theologians. But this recognition by Roman Catholics puts them in a unique position. On the one hand, Roman Catholics know fairly clearly that historicity does not mean relativism. On the other hand, they know also the shrinking of church life and of thought that comes from the refusal to notice our historicity: they had to live with those for some decades in this century. Bernard Lonergan and Karl Rahner here are typical of the best of Roman Catholic theology in this century: a major purpose of their writings is to show how theology can avoid both "classicism" (Lonergan's term for the denial of historicity) and also relativism.[15] Their work provides a solid foundation for a faithful transposition of the Gospel into our time, I believe, because it shows the way forward for Christians of our day who share the modern recognition of historicity but who fear denials of the possibility of truth claims that have sometimes accompanied this recognition.

Like the work of recovery or retrieval, the work of transposition floods Roman Catholic theology faculties and theology journals. In fact, of the two tasks, recovery and transposition, it is transposition that dominates the theological mood. Much of the work of transposition seems like complex translation work: How can we speak of the presence of Christ in the Eucharist in a way that avoids Aristotelian categories and benefits from biblical work on remembering and the liturgical studies of symbol? How can we speak of the Trinity in a way that communicates today what was taught about consubstantiality in the fourth century at the Council of Constantinople? What is the theological significance of ordination now that we realize the complex and developmental character of the emergence of the threefold ministry within the Church of the second century? How can the apostolic faith about Jesus Christ, truly God and truly

14. Vatican II, *Dei verbum,* in *The Documents of Vatican II,* ed. Walter M. Abbott (New York: America Press, 1966) #8.

15. Bernard J. F. Lonergan, "The Transition from a Classicist Worldview to Historical-Mindedness," *A Second Collection* (Philadelphia: Westminster Press, 1974) 5–6; cf. Karl Rahner, "Basic Observations on the Subject of Changeable and Unchangeable Factors in the Church," *Theological Investigations,* trans. David Bourke (New York: Seabury, 1976) 14:3–23.

human, be proclaimed to avoid both a mythological monophysitism and a flattening contemporary Arianism? How can we present the truth about God's grace in a way that serves a contemporary spirituality and a commitment to social transformation? All of these are doctrinal teachings that call for transposition into a modern key.

Let me return to an area I know well, the field of Vatican I studies, to illustrate some further points about transposition. Transposition goes badly if recovery, retrieval work has not been done first. For Vatican I, we need to know the preliminary proposed texts, the discussions, the viewpoints of the minority as well as the majority, the pressure of the times, the meaning of the final resolution in the text of *Pastor aeternus* and its aftermath. But all of that is just recovery. Today, Roman Catholic theology has a further task to accomplish. It must ask: How can we speak today about the concrete assistance God gives the Church in teaching, and especially in teaching when the faith is challenged or denied? Because I think this was the question at the heart of the debate on papal infallibility at Vatican I. In the nineteenth century, the majority of Roman Catholic bishops who assembled for Vatican I were preoccupied with strengthening the authority of the pope, were unable to think about the historicity of formulations or conceptual frameworks, and were unprepared explicitly to recognize other Christians as part of the one Church of Christ. Now in the twentieth century, when all of these factors have changed, which part of these bishops' thought on what they labeled "infallibility" is of value for Christian witness to the apostolic faith, and what must be discarded? Theology will be unable to answer these questions if it fails to do its recovery homework, but more than recovery is needed for Roman Catholics to say something faithful today about God's assistance to the Church in its teaching that will be important for all Christians. That is the further step of transposition, and on this topic of infallibility it is unfinished business in theology.

Perhaps the area of Roman Catholic transposition that is best known and most widely appreciated in the public forum is teaching of the last hundred years on social justice. Here I think that Roman Catholic theology and ethics have made a lasting contribution to the contemporary proclamation of the apostolic faith. As we celebrate the centenary of *Rerum novarum* and look back at the teachings by popes and by episcopal conferences on contemporary social and ethical questions, we can surely take the sweep of these involvements as a kind of achievement in transposition. Brian Hehir sees this social teaching rooted in the biblical teachings on the sacredness of the human person, our stewardship for the earth, the prophetic vocation to denounce injustice, and the Incarnation of God in Jesus Christ.[16] But how could the Church proclaim the meaning of these teachings for the common good in a world shrinking in size, torn by conflict, troubled by a persistent imbalance in sharing material resources? Based on its biblical foundation, contemporary Roman Catholic social teaching developed the idea that the Church has as part of its mission to stand as a sign and safeguard for the dignity, the transcendence of the human person and for the common good. As Hehir explains, the Constitution on the Church in the Modern World, *Gaudium et spes,* then confirms what papal and episcopal statements had been teaching for decades before it: that Christian faith and hence the mission of the Church inherently involves a social dimension.[17] The 1991 Synod of Roman Catholic bishops taught that the social dimension is a constitutive element of the preaching of the Gospel. I take liberation theology to be a kind of local reception of some of the meaning of this social teaching in the context of a desperately poor culture. And in our own culture, the pastoral statements of both the Canadian and U.S. bishops on the economy and on peace are examples of reception of social teaching in North America. Catholic social teaching of the last hundred years is a transposition that is succeeding, although its radical implications for Christian practice have barely been put into effect.

But if recovery work has been correctly done, then transposition also must include a lot of criticism and disposal work as well. Not every song sung about Christ in our past is a song we should keep on singing. Feminist theology is a good example of transposition that involves a correction of earlier errors in our teaching. Having recovered the thought of biblical, patristic, medieval, and Reformation thinkers, feminist theologians have moved on to note the problems with this thought when it presents women not fully in the image of God and God so frequently imaged and described only in male terms. To transpose the doctrine of the image of God to our day in a faithful way, feminist theology notes, some earlier mistakes must be avoided. Work in ecclesiology among Roman Catholics also includes a large-scale disposal operation: disposal of triumphalist self-understandings of the Roman Catholic Church that were crafted in apologetic opposition to Reformation developments, and are understandable but should not be continued. And many new tasks flow from this disposal work in transposing the doctrine of the Church into a modern key:

16. Brian Hehir, "The Cry for Justice and the Worshipping Church: *Rerum novarum* and the Development of Catholic Social Teaching," a lecture given at St. John's University, Collegeville, Minn., 11 July 1991.

17. Ibid.

when Vatican II recognized that the one Church of Christ extends "beyond the visible limits" of the Roman Catholic Church,[18] it also opened the door to a process of reception of all teachings faithful to the Gospel held by other communions as well. So Roman Catholics are rethinking and revising their teachings on the Church, grace, the sacraments, the *filioque*, and the saints as part of their new reception of Protestant, Anglican, and Orthodox traditions.

My discussion of transposition up until now has focused on the task of bringing forward the proclamation of the Gospel so that it addresses those who live in our time, with its recognition of historicity. But part of this recognition involves the renewed awareness of cultural diversity as part of the human historical condition and of true catholicity as a genuine aspect of the Church. So another part of the work of transposition involves what we can call inculturation or contextualization. My missionary friend tells of saying to his African congregation, "Jesus Christ is the Messiah, the Son of David," and then of being asked by them: "What's a Messiah? And who's David?" To communicate to them, he had to find new terms and a new conceptual framework to get across the truth of the Gospel. His effort marks part of the work of transposition.

In one sense, there is nothing new about inculturation. The mission to proclaim Christ to the Gentiles is the start of this process. The *homoousion* of Nicea is another step, a step which paradoxically inculturated the Gospel in the Graeco-Roman world by taking a countercultural stand against neoplatonic Arianism. What is new about inculturation is the awareness of its necessity and its complexity; what is new also for Roman Catholics is the reality of emerging—for the first time at Vatican II, Karl Rahner says—as "World Church," no longer just an exporter of European theology to Second and Third World cultures.[19] Inculturation raises a host of new questions. Is the practice of Levirate marriage in Africa, when a man marries as a second wife the widow of his dead brother, is this practice against the Gospel of Christ? What is the significance of local worship traditions when Christian liturgy seeks to become truly indigenous? What role will Second and Third World churches have in the reevangelization of the First World? What is true evangelization in cultures where Christians find themselves a tiny minority of the population? And what is to be said about the uniqueness of Christ that remains true to the apostolic faith as

---

18. Johannes Willebrands, "Vatican II's Ecclesiology of Communion," *Origins* 17 (1987–88) 32.

19. Karl Rahner, "Basic Theological Interpretation of the Second Vatican Council," *Theological Investigations,* trans. Edward Quinn (New York: Crossroad, 1981) 20:78.

Christianity moves into a new phase of encounter with the religions of the world in these cultures? I take liberation theology to be an example of a fairly successful answer to questions about the Gospel arising in a culture of poverty, but there will be many new inculturations in the future of theology in the Roman Catholic Church.

Transposition of the Gospel is the contemporary mood of Roman Catholic theology; this transposition is being done in a spirit of renewal, and in a spirit of exuberant creativity; and it is an essential aspect of theology. But transposition is fraught with challenges as well as opportunities, because transposition demands criteria and their skillful use, a sense of the meaning of the apostolic faith and of how it is to be preserved but restated creatively. I have given my opinion that such criteria will surely be missing if scholars have skipped their recovery homework. But they will be missing as well if scholars today ignore the thought of Christians from other traditions, if they fail to combine prayer and witness with their scholarly exploration, or if they work at the service only of the academy and not the believing community. Attention to the presence of these realities as necessary conditions for finding the correct criteria for faithful transposition would be important for the Pew Charitable Trusts to consider. I'm not sure, for example, that all of the Christology emerging from the crucible of interreligious dialogue is really faithful to the apostolic tradition; in fact, some of it seems based on a modern Arianism or a kind of relativism about the possibility of truth claims. The search for criteria by which to distinguish true from false or reductionist transpositions of the apostolic faith is one of the major tasks of Roman Catholic theology today.

I have been summarizing reflections on the two sides of theology—recovery and transposition—and trying to give you some flavor of these aspects in Roman Catholic theology. Let me repeat that they are being carried out in a spirit of renewal, even exuberance, after an experience of many decades when they were less widely nurtured. At the same time, there is a wide debate about one topic that is going on throughout the Roman Catholic Church, within theology and also within Church life itself, that affects everything else being done in theology. It is a debate that trickles through the study of the early Church, that pokes its way into Reformation scholarship, that shows up as theologians discuss Christology, or ecclesiology, ordination, the history of councils, New Testament texts, the nature of women, the understanding of sin. Some would say it is the question of method, but I think that it is the question of authority. Roman Catholics are having a long, complex, widely-flung debate about authority.

A DEBATE ABOUT AUTHORITY

It is the debate about authority that frequently gets into the secular news-papers and that is perhaps the most perplexing or strange to those from Protestant, Anglican, or Orthodox communions, so I want to say a few things about it. The sources that caused the debate about authority could be traced to Vatican I where, Guiseppe Alberigo comments, authority was substituted for theology.[20] Or it could be traced back to the seventeenth century where Lonergan finds the pedagogy of the dogmatic thesis re-placing the inquiry of the disputed question.[21] Or perhaps it should be traced back to the sixteenth century and the defensive responses to the Protestant Reformation that led the Roman Catholic Church's ecclesiol-ogy to proceed, as Congar says, under the rubric of authority.[22] But what-ever its cause, a debate about authority is part of the mood of Roman Catholic theology today. Several factors shape this debate: one is the re-newal of Roman Catholic theology itself, another is the fairly recent pres-ence of many lay persons, women, and Third World persons in the Roman Catholic Church as theologians, another is the ecumenical dialogue with other church traditions, another is the way the papacy is exercising its authority.

Let me emphasize that this debate is a theological debate, it is not just a discussion of strategy or ecclesiastical organization. It focuses on impor-tant questions about the Church and an authoritative teaching of the ap-ostolic faith.

Part of this debate focuses on the renewal or reform of the papacy and the episcopacy in their ministerial exercise of oversight in teaching and leadership in the Church. The question for Roman Catholics is not whether to continue to have popes and bishops who exercise authority; the question is rather how their authority should be exercised: in a pyra-midal way or a collegial, conciliar way? Vatican II said that bishops should relate in a collegial or conciliar way in exercising authority, each hearing from the others and contributing the perspective of his own local church. The role of the bishop of Rome in the midst of this college of oversight is

20. Giuseppe Alberigo, "Authority in the Documents of Vatican I and Vatican II," *Journal of Ecumenical Studies* 19:1 (1982) 142.

21. Bernard J. F. Lonergan, "Theology in Its New Context," *A Second Collection* (Philadelphia: Westminster Press, 1974) 57.

22. Yves Congar, "*L'ecclésiologie de la Révolution française au Concile du Vatican sous le signe de l'affirmation de l'autorité,*" in *L'ecclésiologie au XIX siècle,* Unam Sanctam, vol. 34 (Paris: Éditions du Cerf, 1961) 77–114.

to be a minister of the unity of the bishops with each other and through them of all in communion with them. But while this was the vision affirmed by Vatican II in an ecclesiology of communion, this vision has proved much harder to put into practice. Debating the practice, not the theory, of this vision is one area of Roman Catholic discussion today. The Vatican's treatment of Raymond Hunthausen, bishop of Seattle, exemplifies a recent case of what many Roman Catholic theologians saw as a failure of collegial behavior by the bishop of Rome. Vatican treatment of Cardinal Jozef Glemp, former archbishop of Krakow, would be seen as a more successful intervention by Rome in the work of a bishop in his diocese.

A second part of this debate on authority focuses on the relationship between the teaching authority of theologians and the teaching authority of bishops, including the bishop of Rome. Again, the question is not whether or not to teach the basic truths of the apostolic faith like the Trinity, the divinity and humanity of Christ, the need for grace: all such articles of faith are seen as essential to the assent of faith made by every Roman Catholic theologian. The question falls into the area of secondary or related teachings: Is *in vitro* fertilization acceptable? Should ordination in the Latin rite be restricted to celibate men? Is the use of artificial contraception wrong? Is the possession of nuclear weapons for the purpose of deterrence wrong? To present magisterial teaching in such areas, Roman Catholics are not expected to give the assent of faith. In these areas, the teaching of the Roman Catholic magisterium has changed many times in the past; it could change again in some areas. Theologians must be able to do the groundwork to consider and prepare such changes, even if it means an occasional disagreement with magisterial teaching in these areas. But should such disagreements be carried out in scholarly journals, in seminary classrooms, or even in public popular parish lectures? The Vatican does not mind some disagreements in scholarly journals, but it is clearly very nervous about extending the disagreements into classrooms or more popular settings. Also, when is a question really a secondary matter such that it could become a disputed question? This, too, is in itself debated lately. The treatment of Charles Curran by the Vatican is a recent example where many theologians would be critical of the Vatican's action toward a theologian whose moderate views mirrored those of many other Roman Catholic theologians on certain disputed questions in human sexuality. On the other hand, Vatican censure of Paul Pohier a few years ago for his views on the resurrection did not seem as inappropriate to theologians, since the resurrection is central to Christian faith and certainly not a disputed question.

A final area of the authority debate focuses on the contribution that a local church or region makes to all the other local churches or regions. What should Third World churches be teaching us all about the Gospel meaning of justice? What should Second World churches teach us about evangelization and accommodation to culture? What should First World churches contribute about a Gospel vision of the equality of women and men? These are just a few examples about the interchange that should be taking place within the whole Church. Eventually such interchange must include a judgment about the truth or appropriateness of new insights. Many theologians would be critical of the negative response that the Vatican initially gave to the liberation theology movement in Latin America. They would be happier with the Vatican's second response to this movement.[23]

Each of these three areas of debate on authority has generated large amounts of discussion. Let me repeat, I think this is a theological discussion, not simply one of strategy or church politics. And it is important for all Christian churches, not just for the Roman Catholic Church. The question of authority in teaching and in leadership is a central question facing every church today. Support for theological scholarship in this debate on authority seems well merited.

I was asked to speak about Roman Catholic theology, and I have done my best to give an overview of what is happening in this field. Let me emphasize my conviction, however, that no Christian communion today should do its theology in isolation from the theology and life of all of the other communions. The increasing commitment to a common discernment of the apostolic faith, and the conviction that such discernment is possible only in common, are among the most significant contributions of our age to true evangelization. I honor the Pew Charitable Trusts for sharing in this commitment and this conviction.

As I come to the end of my overview on Roman Catholic theology, I remember the story about the farmer who was taken to the zoo to see a giraffe. He looked at the giraffe for a while; then he shook his head firmly and said, "I don't believe it." I hope that Roman Catholic theology does not draw that reaction from you. Roman Catholic theology may not quite fit into the pastures with which you are familiar. At times, like the giraffe, it seems gawky, and it does not fit into some theological landscapes. But I believe that it makes its own graceful contribution.

---

23. Roger Haight, "Liberation Theology," *The New Dictionary of Theology,* 570–76.

INDEX